Walt Disney World for Military Families 2018

By Steve Bell

Copyrights and Trademarks

Published by Magic Shell Media
P.O. Box 33823, Dayton, OH 45433
© 2017-2018 Stephen Bell
ISBN: 978-0-9996374-0-1

All rights reserved. No part of this book may be reproduced in any form or by any means, electronic or mechanical, including photocopying, recording, or by an information storage and retrieval system, without written permission from the publisher or author, except in the case of a reviewer, who may quote brief passages embodied in critical articles or in a review provided to the general public free of charge and for non-commercial purposes. This book may not be reproduced or copied except for the use of the original purchaser.

Limit of Liability and Disclaimer of Warranty: The author and publisher have used their best efforts in preparing this book, and the information provided herein is provided "as is." Stephen Bell and Magic Shell Media make no representation or warranties with respect to the accuracy or completeness of the contents of this book and specifically disclaim any implied warranties of merchantability or fitness for any particular purpose and shall in no event be liable for any loss or profit or any other commercial damage, including but not limited to special, incidental, consequential, or other damages. Although every precaution has been taken to verify the accuracy of the information contained herein, no responsibility is assumed for any errors or omissions, and no liability is assumed for damages that may result from the use of this information.

Trademarks: This book identifies product names and services known to be trademarks, registered trademarks, or service marks of their respective holders. They are used throughout this book in an editorial fashion only. In addition, terms suspected of being trademarks, registered trademarks, or service marks have been appropriately capitalized. Use of a term in this book should not be regarded as affecting the validity of any trademark, registered trademarks, or service mark. Neither the author nor publisher makes any commercial claim to their use. Stephen Bell and Magic Shell Media are not associated with the Walt

Disney Company, Shades of Green, or any other company, product, governmental agency, or vendor mentioned in this book.

This book is unauthorized and unofficial. It has not been reviewed by The Walt Disney Company and is in no way authorized, endorsed, or approved by the company, its sponsors, partners, or affiliates.

This book is dedicated to my Bride, Tracy. Tracy, my love, my friend, my partner, without you none of this would have been possible!

Through the many ups and downs in this experience that we call life you have been there for me. I couldn't imagine doing any of this without you.

I Love You, Steve

Contents

COPYRIGHTS AND TRADEMARKS	3
CONTENTS	6
Overview	3
How This Book Is Organized	4
The 2018 Spring Edition	5
1. DISNEY MILITARY DISCOUNTS, A BRIEF HISTORY AND OVERVIEW	7
What's This Chapter About?	7
Other Military Discounts	12
The Future	12
Wrap Up	13
Ready for More?	13
2. DISNEY'S ARMED FORCES SALUTE	15
What's This Chapter About?	15
Ticket Discounts and Resort Discounts	18
Memory Maker Discount	24
Rules, Rules, Rules…	25
Why are there all these rules?	29
Wrap Up	30

| Ready for More? | 30 |

3. SHADES OF GREEN RESORT — 31

What's This Chapter About?	31
Shades of Green Overview	31
Shades of Green, the Resort	38
Disney Benefits at Shades of Green	49
Shades of Green's History	49
Wrap Up	52
Ready for More?	52

4. WALT DISNEY WORLD TICKETS — 53

What's This Chapter About?	53
Shades of Green's Stars and Stripes Passes	56
Florida Residents	57
One Ticket Per Person	58
Where can I buy my Military Discounted Tickets?	59
Using Your Tickets	62
Ticket Safety	63
What's the right ticket?	66
Wrap-up	68
Ready for More?	68

5. WHEN TO GO TO WALT DISNEY WORLD   69

What's This Chapter About?   69

Military Considerations   69

My Suggestions   73

Planning Your Disney Vacation Timeframe   74

General Public Considerations   76

Wrap Up   87

Ready for More?   87

6. WHERE TO STAY AT WALT DISNEY WORLD?   89

What's This Chapter About?   89

Staying On Walt Disney World Property   90

Walt Disney World Owned Resorts   91

The Resorts   103

The Disney Vacation Club Resorts   170

Disney Resort Wrap Up   171

On Property, Non-Disney Resorts   172

Staying Off Walt Disney World Property   189

Wrap Up   191

Ready for More?   192

7. WALT DISNEY WORLD'S THEME PARKS   193

What's This Chapter About?   193

Attractions	193
FastPass Plus	194
Single Rider Lines	195
Disney Characters	196
Dining	196
Shopping	198
Package Delivery	198
Bag Check… Bag Check…… Bag Check!	199
Free Wi-Fi	199
Strollers, Wheel Chairs, and Scooters	199
Lockers	200
Theme Park Hours	201
Extra Magic Hours	201
Theme Park Capacity Closures	202
Magic Kingdom	204
Epcot	226
Disney's Hollywood Studios	250
Disney's Animal Kingdom	264
Touring Disney World's Parks	276
Wrap Up	277
Ready for More?	277

8. WALT DISNEY WORLD'S NEW TECHNOLOGY 279

What's This Chapter About?	279
What Makes up My Magic Plus?	280
Steps For Using My Disney Experience	291
Disney's PhotoPass and Memory Maker	292
Wrap up	295
Ready for More?	295

9. WALT DISNEY WORLD DINING 297

What's This Chapter About?	297
Dining Terms at Disney World	297
Disney Dining Overview	299
Walt Disney World Dining Discounts	303
The Disney Dining Plan	305
Free Dining	307
Other Ways to Save	308
More Tips	309
Wrap Up	311
Ready for More?	311

10. OTHER THINGS TO DO AT WALT DISNEY WORLD 313

What's This Chapter About?	313
The Electrical Water Pageant	313

Disney World's Water Parks	314
Disney Springs	315
Disney's BoardWalk	325
Walt Disney World Golf	327
Miniature Golf	329
Backstage Tours	329
Water Craft Rentals and Cruises	332
Sports Related Activities	333
Horse-Drawn Carriage Rides and Excursions	335
ESPN Wide World of Sports	336
Walt Disney World's Special Ticketed Holiday Parties	337
Other Non-Disney Theme Parks and Activities	340
Wrap Up	342
Ready for More?	342

11. TRANSPORTATION FOR YOUR WALT DISNEY WORLD VACATION   343

What's This Chapter About?	343
Getting to Walt Disney World	343
Getting Around Walt Disney World	349
How can I get to Universal Studios or Sea World?	360
Stroller Rentals	361

Scooter Rentals	362
Wrap Up	363
Ready for More?	363

12. WALT DISNEY WORLD DISABILITY INFORMATION — 365

What's This Chapter About?	365
Before you arrive	365
Parking for Guests with Disabilities	365
At the Theme Parks	366
Wrap Up	372
Resources	373
Ready for More?	374

13. TIPS FOR YOUR WALT DISNEY WORLD VACATION — 375

What's This Chapter About?	375
The Basics	375
Personal Security, Safety, Severe Weather, Shelter in Place	382
Theme Park Etiquette	383
Ready for More?	386

14. WRAPPING IT ALL UP — 387

Welcome to Walt Disney World for Military Families!

Planning a Walt Disney World vacation can be a complex endeavor for any family. During your planning you'll make many decisions that will affect all aspects of your vacation. Throw in the complexities of a military deployment schedule or the many varied military deals and discounts which are available from multiple sources and it can become a daunting task.

Relax and take a deep calming breath. This book is here to help you navigate all of those complexities. This is the only Walt Disney World book ever written specifically for the military community. I will present to you all of the information required to make informed decisions on how to plan for and save as much as possible on your Walt Disney World vacation as a military family.

A Disney vacation has never been more affordable for military members and their families, whether you are Active Duty, Reserve, Guard, or Retired, there is a discount for you. Disney's Armed Forces Salute beats any general public discount and we've got a whole chapter dedicated entirely to the Salute!

This book has literally been 47 years in the making. The research and experience that has gone into this book started with my family's first visit to Walt Disney World in 1971, the year it first opened. That first trip was then followed by well over 60 visits (both single and multiday trips), three years of working for Disney World in the Magic Kingdom theme park, 28 years of using military discounts to save as much as possible on my family's Disney World vacations, and over 17 years helping other military members plan for and save on their Disney vacations both at my military units and via my website MilitaryDisneyTips.com.

Disney Relaxation

A Disney vacation is a unique experience; in that it is so immersive that it is very easy to leave behind the everyday cares, worries, and stress of the outside world.

It's the perfect place for a military family to spend time together and think of nothing else. It's the ideal location for a pre-deployment getaway, for reconnecting after a deployment, or for a special treat for the kids while mom or dad is away.

I'm so excited to be able to present to you the 2018 Spring Update version of this popular book. It was so much fun to write and especially to research!

I hope this book will be a very useful resource for you in your planning and decision making process.

Steve Bell

Overview

The chapters in this book are organized in a totally different order than any other book which covers the Disney parks.

This is because there is a large amount of military specific information to cover first which will affect all of the normal basics where all other books start. We focus first on things such as military discount availability and military schedules.

My intent is to give you the background information, which is important to our community first, followed by more general information, and then flow smoothly into the planning process while keeping the military info in mind.

This book is specifically targeted at military visitors especially the discounts available to them and provides a comprehensive explanation of all of the options available for military families. Ticket discounts, room discounts, dining discounts, merchandise, and other discounts are all covered.

There are many rules that go along with these discounts; you'll find them all here. Many are not published by Disney or anywhere else for that matter, but have been gathered from both official Disney sources and human intelligence sources within the Disney cast.

This book will also give you an overview of everything that Disney World has to offer. You'll get a brief overview of all of WDW's theme parks, resorts, restaurants, and entertainment options. As we talk about these, any military specific information or discounts will be mentioned.

We'll be talking about the history of Disney's military discounts, how they've evolved over the years and what to expect in the future.

We will thoroughly cover **Shades of Green, a US Military Armed Forces Recreation Center** located right on Walt Disney World property.

We'll also talk about how Walt Disney World's new My Magic Plus technology works with military tickets and discounts.

How This Book Is Organized

The four chapters following this one cover material applicable only to the military. Here we'll discuss the various discounts and options that are only available to our community.

Then we will discuss deciding when to go which has several special considerations that military families need to think about before getting to the point where the general public starts their planning.

We will then talk about your options to consider when deciding where to stay: Disney, non-Disney, DoD, on property and off property as well as what discounts are available at each.

Next we'll cover things to do at Walt Disney World, from the theme and water parks to golf, mini-golf and shopping.

We'll also get to things like dining and transportation. In these chapters we'll cover military specific information as well as everything else.

A very important chapter is the one about Disney's new technology, like FastPass Plus and Magic Bands and how they work with military tickets.

We'll cover information on disability access for the wounded warriors or retirees who might need to know what is available for them.

And then we'll wrap it all up with some Disney vacation tips and advice.

The 2018 Spring Edition

This update to the third edition of Walt Disney World for Military Families. It was written to cover the 2018 calendar year Disney Armed Forces Salute.

Prices quoted in the book will be 2018 prices unless noted otherwise. We've done our best to be as accurate as possible, but you should verify prices yourself as they are subject to change by those who set them.

Every effort has been made at the time of publication to make the information presented in this book as accurate and comprehensive as possible. Both the Walt Disney World Company and Shades of Green are constantly making changes and trying new things, so inevitably there will be some differences in details when you take your vacation.

Ready to jump in? Let's go…

First we are going to take a look at the history of Disney Military discounts and we'll see just how good we have it now!

1. Disney Military Discounts, a Brief History and Overview

What's This Chapter About?

In this chapter we will talk about the long-term history of Disney Military Discounts, what it was like in the past and how good we have it now.

We'll go over how the military discounts available to the military community for their Disney vacations have changed over the years.

Military discounts, whether from Disney or other sources, are usually a very fluid situation that could change at any time, so we'll also touch on how things look for the future.

Tickets

I started my military career back in the early 80s (I retired just a few years ago) and as far back as I can remember in my career my Base Ticket Office sold slightly discounted tickets for Walt Disney World.

For the majority of my career these were all that was available for the military community and they really didn't save you very much. These tickets are still available today and depending on the length and options purchased, you will save between four and eight percent off of the regular general public gate ticket price.

Several times over the years Disney has offered specially priced or sometimes even free, tickets for the military member. A couple of examples of this are:

- After the first Gulf War, Disney World offered a free one-day ticket for military members.

- During the first half of 2002 due to the post 9/11 travel industry slowdown, they offered a free seven-day ticket for the member and 50% off tickets for up to five of their guests. As the travel industry recovered, Disney discontinued this special military offer.

After the 2002 offer once again all that was available were the regular military discounted tickets. Then in 2009 Disney started what is called the Disney Armed Forces Salute. This new offer came after the economic downturn and travel industry slowdown that began in the fall of 2008. These Salutes are individual offers for a set timeframe.

Here is a brief history of the Salute Discounts since then:

- The first Salute began in January 2009 and was initially a partial year offer, which was then extended 3 times, eventually through the end of the year.
- January 2010 saw another 7-month long offer, which was then extended twice through the end of the 2010 Disney fiscal year (September 2010).
- In October 2010, after a 22-day break, Disney offered the first full yearlong offer (25 October 2010 – 28 September 2011).
- In April 2011 Disney made a surprise announcement that the ongoing offer would be extended through 28 September 2012, making it a 2-year long offer.
- September 2012, 2013, and 2014 each saw one year long renewals
- In June 2015 the 28 September 2014 – October 2015 offer was extended through just prior to Christmas 2015. This was in preparation to switching to a calendar year offer period.
- On 24 September 2015 Disney switched to offering a Calendar Year Salute Offer for 2016. It ran from 3 January through 19 December.
- On 28 September 2016 Disney announced the second calendar year offer for 2017.

- On 28 September 2017 Disney announced the new 2018 Disney Armed Forces Salute.

This Military Salute offers highly discounted theme park tickets for military members and their guests. These tickets have very detailed rules and restrictions because of the huge savings they offer. These tickets are about half off of the regular gate price!

Military Salute Ticket Discount History:

- 2009 – A free 5-day base ticket for the member. Up to five 5-day base tickets for family and friends for $99 plus tax, Park Hopper, Water Park Fun and More could be added to the tickets for $25 plus tax each.
- 2010 – The member and up to 5 family and friends could purchase 4-day base tickets for $99 plus tax. Park Hopper, Water Park Fun and More could be added to the companion tickets for $26 plus tax each.
- 2010-2012 - The member and up to 5 family and friends could purchase 4-day Park Hopper or Water Park Fun and More tickets for $138 or both options for $165.
- 2012-2013 - The member and up to 5 family and friends could purchase 4-day Park Hopper or Water Park Fun and More tickets for $156 or both options for $184.
- 2013-2014 - The member and up to 5 family and friends could purchase 4-day Park Hopper or Water Park Fun and More tickets for $169 or both options for $198.
- 2014-2015 - The member and up to 5 family and friends could purchase 4-day Park Hopper or Water Park Fun and More tickets for $177 or both options for $207.
- 2016 - The member and up to 5 family and friends can purchase 4-day Park Hopper or Water Park Fun and More tickets for $196 or both options for $230.

- 2017 - The member and up to 5 family and friends can purchase 4-day ($209) or 5-day ($224) Park Hopper or Park Hopper plus Water Park Fun and More tickets for $246 4-day/$261 5-day.
- 2018 - The member and up to 5 family and friends can purchase 4-day ($226) or 5-day ($246) Park Hopper tickets or Park Hopper plus tickets for $266 4-day/$286 5-day.

Each Salute offer normally runs for only a one yearlong period. Each year the Salute requires a renewal in order to continue for another year.

For much more information about the Disney Armed Forces Salute you should check out the Disney Armed Forces Salute chapter as well as the Walt Disney World Tickets Chapter.

Rooms

Shades of Green

Shades of Green is an Armed Forces Recreation Center, which opened its doors on Walt Disney World property in 1994. Shades of Green offers resort rooms for military members, their families, and other supporters of the military at a much lower cost than the surrounding Disney lodging.

Shades of Green has three price categories which are based upon the sponsor's pay grade, with junior members paying the least. Shades of Green's prices remain the same all year round, except during occasional special promotions. Prices are increased on a fiscal year basis.

Shades of Green has two main room types, standard and poolside, as well as a few suites which sleep between six and twelve people.

You will find much more about Shades of Green in the chapter devoted to the military resort.

Disney Resorts

Since 2009, Disney has offered highly discounted resort rooms as part of the Disney Armed Forces Salute. Through 2017 the amount of the discount was based upon the Disney resort price category and varied from 30 to 40 percent off of the full regular room rates (30% off Value Resorts, 35% off Moderate Resorts & 40% off Deluxe Resorts). Starting in 2018 Disney is not offering a set percentage off of each resort category, discount amounts vary but are "up to" the previously stated percentages, though at times lower based upon available inventory.

Disney has many different "price seasons" throughout the year, as well as three different prices during most weeks no matter the price season. Friday and Saturday nights are often priced at a higher rate, Thursday and Sunday at a mid rate, Monday to Wednesday are the cheapest. Because of this there can be more than 45 different prices for each room based on the date and day of the week. The price for your room even with the military discount can vary greatly based upon the time of year that you go.

Disney World has numerous different room types differentiated by resort type and view. The type of resort i.e. value, moderate, or deluxe, affects the size of the rooms and the amenities offered by the resort. The room view also affects your price within that resort as rooms with parking lot views are cheaper than the one's looking out on greenery, water (pool, lake, or river), or those that are closer to the lobby.

You will find much more information about the Salute room discounts in the Disney Armed Forces Salute Chapter and more about Disney's Resorts in the Where to Stay at WDW chapter.

Other Military Discounts

There are other establishments (resorts, restaurants, and entertainment venues) both on and off Disney property as well as other theme parks in Central Florida, which offer military discounts on a full time or occasional basis.

Read all about these in the Other Things to Do at Walt Disney World Chapter.

The Future

As I said above Disney's Armed Forces Salute is a temporary offer. By this I mean that it is renewed on an annual basis and that Disney has not committed to making it a permanent discount.

The Salute has been running almost continuously since January 2009. There was a 3-day break in resort room discounts and a 22-day break in ticket discounts during October 2010.

You might have also noted a trend as you read earlier, that being that Disney has instituted military salutes during downturns in the economy that affect the travel industry. When the travel industry improves there is always the possibility that Disney will discontinue offering the Salutes as they have in the past.

In recent years the travel industry has seemed to rebound sufficiently for Disney to stop offering the Salutes, but the summer of 2016 saw a downturn in attendance, which surely helped in the decision to continue for 2017; and then spring 2017 saw projected attendance so low that Disney World cancelled their ticket blockout dates (dates the tickets could not be used) for the Disney Armed Forces Salute tickets during Spring Break. The new 2018 Offer has no blockout dates for tickets (though it does for rooms).

While Disney has repeatedly stated in recent years their commitment to the military community, I'm beginning to be less hopeful that the outstanding Armed Forces Salute will continue to run for many more years to come.

Recently experts in the civil Disney fan community have begun to express worry about general public discounts for 2019 plus Disney World just instituted unheard of parking fees at their Resort Hotels. The Star Wars expansion of Disney Hollywood Studios is expected to draw unprecedented volumes of people to WDW! Disney has had to make huge capital investments in new Resorts and infrastructure.

The new parking fees, lower military room discounts, anticipated seasonal ticket pricing, and postulated lack of general pubic room discounts all add up to an environment where I can anticipate Disney deciding not to renew the Disney Armed Forces Salute.

Wrap Up

The take away from this chapter is that now is (always) the time to start planning your Disney vacation. The 2018 Disney Armed Forces Salute currently runs through 19 December 2018. There is no way at this time to know if there will be a 2019 Disney Armed Forces Salute, so if you are on the fence about when to go, just do it!

Ready for More?

The biggest expenses while enjoying a Disney World vacation are your theme park tickets, resort room, and food. In the next few chapters we'll go over in depth all of the military discounts that are available in these areas. We'll also sneak in a chapter on Disney World's new tech, as that goes along with tickets and rooms.

2. Disney's Armed Forces Salute

What's This Chapter About?

In this chapter we'll cover all the specifics of Disney's fantastic offer for military members as well as all of the published and unpublished rules.

The Disney Armed Forces Salute allows qualified individuals to purchase steeply discounted Disney theme park tickets and stay in Disney resort rooms at fabulous discount prices. The offer is for both Walt Disney World near Orlando, Florida and Disneyland in Anaheim, California.

Overview

The Disney Armed Forces Salute is a special temporary offer, which runs for a specified time period. I say it is temporary, because it is still a "relatively" new discount (now in its 10th year) and each self-contained Salute offer runs for a specific timeframe. A new and totally separate Salute must be offered by Disney in order for the Salute to "continue" into the next year.

Each year Disney evaluates many factors (most of which have nothing to do with the military offer) prior to deciding if they will renew the discount or not. The timing of this decision is driven by the timing of these other factors throughout the company, such as annual revenue projections.

Each individual Salute offer runs for approximately one year (give or take a few days). In the early years the dates of the offer coincided with Disney's fiscal year (not the federal fiscal year) starting at the beginning of the first work week of the year and ending on the last workday of the year on dates in either September or October each year.

In 2016 Disney decided to switch to offering the Salute on a calendar year basis. In order to do this they extended the FY 2014-2015 Salute that was due to end on 3 October 2015 through just before Christmas. Then in 2016 they offered calendar year based offer. This was followed by the 2017 and 2018 calendar year offers.

It is very important to note that at press time there are two totally separate and different Disney Armed Forces Salute offers that have been announced.

The 2018 Salute started on 1 January 2018 and runs through 19 December.

Eligibility

The Armed Forces Salute is offered to the following individuals:

-Current military members:

- Active
- Reserve
- National Guard
- Coast Guard
- USPHS/NOAA Officers

-Retired military members:

- Active
- Reserve
- National Guard
- Coast Guard
- USPHS/NOAA Officers

-100% Service Connected Disabled with the DAVPRM code on their military issued ID.

-Spouses of the above, in place of the member.

Note the Disney Armed Forces Salute benefit is for the member only. While spouses may use their member's benefit, they are not entitled to a benefit of their own. They only use the discounts in place of the member, not in addition to.

Non-spouse dependents are not eligible.

-Un-remarried Widows of eligible members are entitled to their departed spouse's discounts.

-Foreign partners/Coalition partners who are stationed at a US base are eligible. They must have a permanent US Military issued ID (CAC card with blue stripe).

In all cases a current, valid military issued ID is required for this discount. VA cards, State driver's licenses indicating Veteran Status, and DD-214s are not acceptable.

Blockout Dates

There are dates during which the Armed Forces Salute ticket and room offers cannot be used. Disney refers to these as "blockout dates," not blackout dates as some mistakenly refer to them, they are dates when the discount is blocked from use. These blockout dates coincide with the very busiest times of the year, such as Christmas week, the peak of Spring Break, and sometimes Thanksgiving weekend.

With the new calendar year offers the Christmas blockout is handled by ending the offer prior to the Christmas rush and not starting a potential new offer until after the rush in the beginning of January.

An important note is that in the spring of 2017, with only about a month's notice Disney cancelled the Spring Break blockout dates for Walt Disney World. While there was no announcement as to why, it was because projected attendance was lower than desired. And with the 2018 Salute announcement Disney did not publish any ticket blockout dates (though there are room blockouts for spring).

Ticket Discounts and Resort Discounts

The Disney Armed Forces Salute is actually a combination of two different discounts. There is a resort room discount, which is offered and controlled totally by Disney. Then there is the ticket discount, which Disney offers, but is controlled by terms negotiated with the military Morale, Welfare, and Recreation (MWR) establishment.

Another very important point is that the Walt Disney World and Disneyland Salute offers are totally separate and any discount limits are not cumulative between the two. You may use your full ticket limit at both Disneyland and Walt Disney World.

Tickets

The Disney Armed Forces Salute offers special military tickets. These tickets are for a specified number of days and come in several varieties.

Qualified individuals may purchase up to a maximum number of theme park tickets per offer.

Currently you may buy a total of 6 tickets per eligible military member during the 2018 Armed Forces Salute Offer.

Tickets from one year's offer are not valid during another year's offer!

These tickets are non-refundable once purchased! The tickets are valid for the entire length of the offer. There is no 14-day expiration like the general public Disney tickets. You may use some days on one trip and the rest on another, or take days off during a single vacation. Any days left on the tickets will expire at the end of the offer period.

There are no adult or children's versions of these tickets, as there are for all other Disney tickets.

The Salute tickets are for ages 3 and up. But, no matter what your age, it is a huge savings. Under age 3 is free.

Ticket Specifics

For 2018 there are two ticket option choices for your ticket, both come in a 4 or 5-day ticket length:

- The Theme Park Hopper Option, which allows you to visit multiple parks on the same day.
- The Theme Park Hopper Plus Option, which allows you to visit multiple parks on the same day plus entrances to a variety of non-theme Park Disney venues. *For more on the Park Hopper Plus Option see the Walt Disney World Tickets chapter.*

2018 Disney World Armed Forces Salute Prices (1 January 2018 through 19 December 2018)

4-day tickets:

- Four-Day Theme Park Hopper Ticket for $226.00
- Four-Day Theme Park Non-Hopper plus Water Park and More Ticket for $266.00

5-day tickets:

- Five-Day Theme Park Hopper Ticket for $246.00
- Five-Day Theme Park Non-Hopper plus Water Park and More Ticket for $286.00

The Ticket Blockout dates for the 2018 Salute are:

- As stated above none at WDW for 2018!

These tickets can be purchased at your local Base Ticket Office, Shades of Green, or Disney Theme Park ticket booths (Tax will be added at Walt Disney World ticket booths). Shades of Green and some ticket offices will ship.

Upgrades

The Park Hopper Plus option may be added at any time until all days on the ticket are used, by paying the price difference of the ticket with both options ($40 plus tax).

4-Day tickets may be upgraded to 5-Day tickets after arrival for the price difference.

All Armed Forces Salute tickets may be upgraded to any type of annual pass, again for the price difference between the Salute ticket and the full price pass plus tax.

Where to upgrade – Tickets purchased at Shades of Green may be upgraded there at their prices with no tax. Tickets purchased elsewhere (on base or from Disney) must be upgraded at Disney World Ticket or Guest Relations windows.

Ticket Activation

If you buy your Disney's Armed Forces Salute tickets anywhere else than directly from a Disney ticket booth or Shades of Green, you will need to activate your tickets before they can be used for park entry. This must be done in person at a Disney location by the military member or by the spouse in place of the member with all of those you are activating tickets for present. Adults must have a photo ID (drivers license etc. for non-military).

The tickets may be activated at all theme park ticket and Guest Relations windows as well as the two Disney Springs Guest Relations locations.

Once your tickets are activated there is no need for the party to stay together. You may visit the park at different times, visit entirely different parks, and even use the tickets on entirely different days.

Resort Rooms

The Disney Armed Forces Salute offers Disney resort rooms at both Disney World and Disneyland at a great discount.

Qualified individuals may book up to a maximum of three rooms at a time at Disney World (two at a time at Disneyland) during the Disney Armed Forces Salute offer period. This discount may be used as many times as you'd like during the entire Salute offer period, unlike the Salute ticket discount, there is no limit to the number of times the discount may be used. The only limit is the number used at one time.

There are Blockout dates during which Disney does not offer the Salute discounts. These are "peak attendance" dates.

The Resorts offering the discount, room types, and number of rooms at these rates are limited at each individual resort. It is not a wide open offer; rather, when the limit is reached on a specific room type at a particular resort on a specific date, no more rooms of that type at that resort on that date will be offered unless someone cancels. For 2018 the discount is on a sliding scale. When Disney has the most need to fill rooms the discount will be the highest, as rooms fill the discount will be reduced until at some point it will not be offered (by resort, room type, and date). To indicate the uncertainty as to what discount you will receive; I've added the words "up to" for 2018. You or your travel agent will have to call to check discounts for your dates.

There are very few discounts allowed on the more expensive rooms, while many more are available on the lower priced rooms. You should reserve as far in advance as possible. You must pay a one-night deposit at the time you reserve your room.

For 2018 the discount rates are:

- Up to 40% off Deluxe Resorts
- Up to 35% off Moderates and Fort Wilderness Cabins

- Up to 30% off Value Resorts

The Resort Room Blockout dates for the 2018 Salute are:

- 25 March - 5 April 2018

The Disney Resorts Offering the Discount

- Boulder Ridge Villas at Disney's Wilderness Lodge
- Disney's All-Star Movies Resort
- Disney's All-Star Music Resort
- Disney's All-Star Sports Resort
- Disney's Animal Kingdom Lodge
- Disney's Animal Kingdom Villas – Jambo House
- Disney's Animal Kingdom Villas – Kidani Village
- Disney's Art of Animation Resort – Family Suites only
- Disney's Beach Club Resort
- Disney's Beach Club Villas
- Disney's BoardWalk Inn
- Disney's BoardWalk Villas
- Disney's Caribbean Beach Resort
- Disney's Contemporary Resort
- Disney's Coronado Springs Resort
- Disney's Grand Floridian Resort & Spa
- Disney's Old Key West Resort
- Disney's Polynesian Village Resort
- Disney's Polynesian Villas & Bungalows – Studios only
- Disney's Pop Century Resort
- Disney's Port Orleans – French Quarter
- Disney's Port Orleans Resort – Riverside
- Disney's Saratoga Springs Resort & Spa
- Disney's Wilderness Lodge
- Disney's Yacht Club Resort
- Disney's Fort Wilderness Resort and Campground

WDW Offer excludes the following room types:

- Boulder 3-bedroom villas
- Campsites
- Copper Creek Villas at Disney's Wilderness Lodge
- The Little Mermaid Standard Rooms at Disney's Art of Animation
- Bungalows at Disney's Polynesian Villas & Bungalows

Why are there Blockout Dates?

"Why can't I use my Disney Armed Forces Salute tickets or room discounts at Disney World or Disneyland during Spring Break?"

This is a common response that I hear when military families first learn that the Disney Salute is not valid on certain days.

Since January 2009 the Disney Armed Forces Salute has always had days that the special military discount tickets could not be used for admission to Disney's theme parks or for resort discounts.

They are typically the weeklong period, which includes Christmas and New Year's a week or two during Spring Break, and occasionally rooms are blocked for Thanksgiving weekend. In the past, Fourth of July was also blocked out for the Magic Kingdom.

During each individual Salute offer the blockout dates are slightly different, depending on nationwide school schedules.

Disney's main purpose behind the blockout dates is to dissuade you from visiting during those times, as there will already be way too many people in the Disney theme parks!

Disney's military salute blockout dates are during peak attendance periods. During these timeframes Disney often closes their theme parks individually to arriving guests during the day due to reaching maximum attendance. Only those staying on property are allowed in, others are turned away.

These high attendance days, for lack of better words are simply miserable in the theme parks. There are just way too many people, lines are unbearable, and you'll be unable to accomplish all that you'd like to do.

I think it's really a blessing in disguise that you can't use your Armed Forces Salute tickets during Spring Break or other peak times. It forces you to re-evaluate your vacation schedule and plan to go at another (much more pleasant) time if possible.

Yes, this may involve taking the kids out of school, but you can take along class/homework and make opportunities to turn the vacation into a learning experience.

Memory Maker Discount

Starting in 2017 Disney World began offering a military discount on Memory Maker in conjunction with the Armed Forces Salute, this continues for 2018.

What is Memory Maker? Almost everywhere you go in the Disney theme parks, you'll see Disney PhotoPass Photographers. They are stationed at all of the best, most scenic locations at which you can have your picture taken, for example in front of Cinderella Castle or with France and the Eifel Tower in the background at Epcot's World Showcase.

They are also at some of the character meals (Chef Mickey's, Hoop-Dee-Doo Revue, Tusker House breakfast, 'Ohana breakfast, 1900 Park Fare, and Spirit of Aloha dinner show), and at Character Meet and Greets.

Many thrill rides also have automatic cameras to capture your reactions to the most thrilling part of the ride in photo or video form.

Memory Maker is a package deal for purchasing these photos.

Taking the photos is a free service, you can decide later if you want to purchase the photos. Just have your Magic Band or park ticket scanned to identify who you are and get your picture taken.

You can then review your photos online using your My Disney Experience account or the PhotoPass/Memory Maker sites.

You can purchase the Memory Maker product for the discounted price of $98.00 from January 1, 2018 through December 19, 2018

The discounted Memory Maker product can only be purchased at Walt Disney World theme park ticket windows by Eligible Service Members or their spouses

Reports from on scene indicate that you need to purchase at a Guest Relations window!

See the Disney Technology chapter for more on Memory Maker.

Rules, Rules, Rules…

Disney Armed Forces Salute Ticket Rules

What follows is a long list of rules for the Disney Armed Forces Salute some of these are published online by Disney and some are not. Even though Disney does not publish them online, they are how this discount is administered.

Armed Forces Salute tickets may not be used after the end date of the Salute offer. The tickets become invalid and will not work for park entrance at midnight on the last day of the offer period. 2018 tickets may not be used in 2019 if a Salute is offered.

Armed Forces Salute Tickets lose any dollar value of any unused days or water park visits when they expire at the end of the offer.

Armed Forces Salute tickets are non-transferable and must be used by the same person at all times. Disney has procedures in place to ensure this.

The member or spouse may purchase additional Armed Forces Salute tickets for whomever they'd like, family or friends.

One of the tickets must be activated for the use of the member or spouse.

Armed Forces Salute tickets are non-refundable. If you buy them on base and later find that you can't use them you will not be allowed to get a refund.

2018 Armed Forces Salute Hopper tickets may be upgraded to add the Park Hopper Plus Option. This may be added any time prior to the end of the offer as long as the ticket has not been used up for the difference in price.

Armed Forces Salute tickets may not have additional days added on. However a 4-day Salute ticket may be upgraded to a 5-day.

Armed Forces Salute tickets may however be upgraded to all Disney World Annual Passes.

Armed Forces Salute tickets are limited to a total of 6 tickets during the 2018 Salute offer period.

The spouse may buy and use the Armed Forces Salute tickets in place of the member (not in addition to).

Disney has always had an exception to the ticket limit for large families. By "Large Family" Disney means a mom, dad, and their dependent children. This does not include the member's adult children (without military IDs), parents, in-laws, siblings, cousins, friends, friend's kids, etc.

The exception works like this: For immediate families larger than 6, Disney will make an exception to the 6-ticket rule. For example, if a family has six dependent children, Disney will allow all members of the family to purchase Armed Forces Salute tickets; that is for Mom, Dad, and their six kids. This exception is ONLY in-person direct from Disney NOT from Base Ticket Offices or Shades of Green.

Salute tickets may be used back to back by the same individuals, up to the offer limit. This is good for smaller parties that want more than 4 or 5 park days per person.

The member or spouse must activate tickets purchased at military resellers (Base Ticket Offices) in person with all members of their party present at the Disney parks. What this means is that you cannot activate a ticket for someone who isn't with you. If some members of your party will not join you until sometime later in your trip, you may activate tickets for those with you initially, and then when the stragglers arrive you may then activate their tickets, as long as you have not fully used up your ticket.

A picture ID of any type is required for all adults during the activation process. The member or spouse doing the activation must present a current, valid military ID.

Those on terminal leave must have a current military ID; DEERS and VA Cards do not qualify.

Tickets purchased directly from Disney and Shades of Green are activated during the purchase process.

One ticket must be activated for the use of the member or spouse unless they are a Disney pass holder.

Members or spouses who have a Disney Annual Pass may purchase Armed Forces Salute tickets for those accompanying them without obtaining one for themselves. One Salute ticket must remain unpurchased in reserve for the member though.

Once the tickets are activated the party can split up. For example some go to one park and some to another, or even use the tickets on entirely different days through the end of the offer period. The Military ID is checked only upon ticket activation.

Disney Armed Forces Salute Room Discount Rules

The number of rooms allocated for this offer is limited. Minimum length of stay requirements may apply for Friday or Saturday arrivals.

Members or their spouses may book up to a maximum of three rooms at a time using the discount. The member or spouse must occupy one of the rooms. All rooms must be at the same resort and check in on the same day.

Valid Military ID will be required upon check-in.

No other group rates or other discounts may be applied.

Advance reservations are required.

Additional per-adult charges apply if there are more than two adults per room.

Members or their spouses may use the Armed Forces Salute room discount as many times as they'd like during the offer period at both Walt Disney World and Disneyland.

There are blockout dates when the discount is not valid. Stays on those nights would be at the full price or another discount rate if available.

Disney charges each night individually at the rate for that day e.g. Sun-Thurs, Fri-Sat, AFS blockout dates, etc. The rate at check in does not carry through the entire stay.

Walt Disney World for Military Families 29

The number of rooms and room types at these rates are limited. Once the set number (not published) of each room type at a specific resort is sold out for a specific date the discount becomes unavailable for that room type at that specific resort on that specific date.

Most room types from the basic standard view, to 2-bedroom Disney Vacation Club suites are eligible for the room discount, based upon availability.

The Little Mermaid rooms at the Art of Animation Resort have never been eligible for this discount.

The more expensive rooms are offered in much smaller quantities.

The Armed Forces Salute Room Discount is what Disney calls a "room only" reservation. The tickets that you will use on your trip are up to you to provide. You may use any ticket that you are able/eligible to purchase with your room reservation.

The Armed Forces Salute room discount cannot be stacked or combined with any other Disney room discount or special offer, for instance other general public discounts, packages, the occasional periods of "Free Dining," Pass holder, Florida Resident, etc.

You may add any paid Disney Dining Plan to your Disney Armed Forces Salute room only reservation.

Why are there all these rules?

There are so many rules associated with the Disney Armed Forces Salute because of what a fantastic deal it is. The rules are there to keep people from abusing the offer.

Disney makes this generous offer to help military families. The intent of the discounts is for the military member to spend time with family and friends at Disney's Resorts and in the parks, or for the spouse to be able to do so when the member can't go.

Disney does not intend for members to buy these half off tickets (with their funds or other's) and give them away to people who are not eligible and will be going without the member or worse yet for the member to sell them for a profit.

Disney – "Armed Forces Salute tickets may be purchased at participating U.S. military sales outlets ONLY by Eligible Service Members or their spouses (but not both), for use by themselves and other family members and friends, as provided herein. **These Tickets may not be otherwise transferred, distributed or resold.** "

Wrap Up

Well, that was a lot to take in. But the Disney Armed Forces Salute is the best thing to come along in recent history for military families to save on their Disney vacations! If you can work within the guidelines, you will save significantly!

Ready for More?

In this chapter we learned about the Disney Armed Forces Salute, a wonderful combination of ticket and room discounts offered to the military community by the Walt Disney Company. In the next chapter we'll cover Shades of Green, a special benefit at Disney World, for the military, offered by the military.

3. Shades of Green Resort

What's This Chapter About?

This chapter is all about the Shades of Green Resort, which is an Armed Forces Recreation Center Resort located right on Walt Disney World property.

Military families can stay right in the middle of the magic at a fantastic resort for very reasonable rates!

In this chapter we'll cover in detail all that Shades of Green has to offer for your Walt Disney World vacation.

Shades of Green Overview

At Shades of Green you will find all of the amenities that you'd expect at any very nice resort destination: a selection of restaurants, recreational options, valet parking, bellhop service, spa, fitness room, two pools, free Wi-Fi, and self-service laundry facilities, plus a military discounted ticket sales office and mini Exchange.

I'm often asked by people whether staying at Shades of Green will be like staying at billeting on base and nothing could be further from the truth! Shades of Green is a well maintained first class resort.

The resort was originally built, owned, and operated by the Walt Disney World Company under various names. But since 1994 it has been an Armed Forces Recreation Center.

Shades of Green is a wonderfully spacious hotel. It was remodeled and expanded in 2004 and has 586 of the largest standard resort rooms on

Walt Disney World property, as well as eleven family suites which sleep from six to twelve.

You do not have to be a guest at Shades of Green to visit. Those wishing to buy tickets for Disney or other Orlando venues with a military discount, or those who would like to use the Exchange or restaurants are welcome to do so. All transactions at Shades of Green are tax free.

Be aware that Shades of Green is a Department of Defense facility and there is a military ID check at the entry gate and on buses returning to the resort from Destinations around Walt Disney World. Buses also require a valid Shades of Green Resort ID as their use is exclusively for those staying there

Shades of Green Eligibility

Shades of Green is not open to the general public and it has an extensive list of just who is eligible to be a guest of the resort. The various statuses are:

Armed Forces and their Families: Members on US Military Active Duty, Reserve, and National Guard, Cadets and Midshipmen of the Army, Navy, Air Force, Coast Guard, and Merchant Marine Academies. The required ID is a Common Access Card. (Members of the Reserve and Guard do not need to be on active duty orders in order to be eligible).

Other Uniformed Services: Public Health Service, and National Oceanic and Atmospheric Administration Commissioned Corps. The required ID is DD Form 2, PHS 1866-1 or 1866-3.

Armed Forces Retirees and their Family Members: Retired from Active Duty, Reserves, and National Guard with or without pay (gray area) the required ID is DD Form 2, 1173 or 1173-1.

Others separated from the Armed Forces and their Family Members:

- Honorably discharged veterans with 100 percent Service-connected disability the required ID is a DD Form 1173 or DD Form 2765.
-Involuntarily separated service members under the Transition Assistance Management Program the required ID is a DD Form 2.
-Personnel separated under the Voluntary Separation Incentive (VSI) and Special Separation Benefit (SSB) programs: for two years after separation the required ID is a DD Form 2.

Former and/or Surviving Spouses and Family Members:

-Un-remarried surviving spouses of personnel who died while on active duty or while in retired status the required ID is a DD Form 1173 or 1173-1.
-Un-remarried former spouses who were married to military members for at least 20 years while the military member was on active duty the required a ID is DD Form 1173.

Other Supporters of the Department of Defense:

-Military personnel of foreign nations and their family members when assigned or attached to a U.S. military unit or installation or on U.S. Travel Orders the required ID is a US issued CAC with blue strip, DD Form 1173 or 2765.
-U.S. employees of firms under contract to Department of Defense working in the Pacific Region outside the U.S. on Department of Defense Government orders the required ID is a US issued CAC with blue strip, DD Form 1173 or 2765.
-Other personnel on official business with Department of Defense as may be specifically authorized by the General Manager or his designee the required ID is a DD Form 1173 or 2765.

U.S. Department of Defense Civilians and Family Members:
Current and retired (APF and NAF) Department of Defense (DoD) and Coast Guard (CG) civilian employees. DOD or CG ID card, Retired ID card, or current Leave and Earnings Statement with photo ID required for check-in.

Separated, Non-Retired Members of the Armed Forces: In the months of January and September, Shades of Green allows Veterans who did not retire to be guests at the resort. These are months in which the resort is not filled to capacity, so rather than have the rooms unfilled, they are opened up to all who served. The required ID is a DD Form 214. Note this program has been running since January 2010 and could be discontinued at any time. Call to check.

Shades of Green Room Rates

You'll find Shades of Green has very reasonable room rates when compared to many of the Disney World Resorts and other hotels in the local area. Rates are based upon your pay grade or status, with junior members paying much less to help them afford a Disney vacation.

Shades of Green's rates are constant all year long, except for various specials, which they run from time to time.

The Disney resorts on the other hand have numerous price seasons throughout the year as well as having their prices fluctuate based on the day of the week (Friday and Saturday nights are often more expensive). The price for a specific Disney resort room can vary anywhere from 1.4 to over 2 times the cheapest price for that room depending on the time of year.

Shades of Green room rates:

Fiscal Year 2018 - 1 October 2017 – 30 September 2018

	Category #1	Category #2	Category #3
Standard Room	$115.00	$145.00	$155.00
Poolside Room	$125.00	$155.00	$165.00
Junior Family Suite	$295.00		

Magnolia Suite	$280.00
Family Suite	$325.00
Garden Suite	$325.00
Palm Suite	$445.00

Fiscal Year 2019 - 1 October 2018 – 30 September 2019

	Category #1	Category #2	Category #3
Standard Room	$119.00	$149.00	$159.00
Poolside Room	$129.00	$159.00	$169.00
Junior Family Suite	$299.00		
Magnolia Suite	$284.00		
Family Suite	$329.00		
Garden Suite	$329.00		
Palm Suite	$449.00		

The above rates are based upon two adults occupying a standard/poolside room and four adults occupying suites. These rates have changed very little, with just slight increases since 2009. FY 2016 & 2017 saw the biggest increases in recent years particularly with the suites, but FY 2018 rates only increased a modest four dollars per night for all rooms.

For additional adults 18 years or older add $15 each. For single occupancy, subtract $2. There is a $7 per night parking fee if you park your vehicle. There is no State or local tax added to these rates.

Deposit - One night's lodging rate deposit is charged at the time of the reservation to secure your room. If you need to cancel more that 30 days prior to check in you will receive a refund. If you cancel within 30 days or make your reservation within 30 days of arrival and then cancel you will lose your deposit.

The maximum occupancy for standard and poolside rooms is five, The Garden Suite sleeps four, the Magnolia suite sleeps five, junior suites sleep six, suites sleep eight and the Palm Suite sleeps up to 12!

Those eligible to stay at Shades of Green may sponsor rooms for those who are not eligible. This is great if you'd like to have a group vacation with non-military family or friends. The maximum number of rooms that an eligible sponsor may reserve including their own is three. Spouses of eligible members may also sponsor 3 additional rooms, bringing the total to six. Over the Christmas-New Year's period the total allowed is limited to three rooms only. Sponsored guests must check in on the same day as their sponsor and check out the same day or earlier. Sponsored guests must be accompanied by the Military/DoD sponsor at check-in and throughout the stay.

Shades of Green Guest Categories

The category that you fall into for your pricing depends on your pay grade or status. Party size and identification verification is required upon check in.

Category #1 - E-1 to E-6 and Cadets (E-1 thru E-6 and Cadet sponsored rooms will receive the rate that applies to Category #2.)

Category #2 - E-7 to E-9, O-1 to O-3, WO-1 to CW-3, Widows, Medal of Honor Recipients, 100% Disabled Veterans and Category #1 sponsored rooms.

Category #3 - O-4 to O-10, CW-4, CW-5, Active and Retired DoD Civilians, Foreign Military assigned to US installations, DoD Contractors assigned to US installations, Category #2 & #3 sponsored rooms.

Shades of Green Discounts

Since the advent of the Disney Armed Forces Salute in 2009, Shades of Green has begun offering discounts off of their already low rates.

Shades offers two kinds of discounts, short term and long term.

The short-term discounts are offered as numerous different named discounts throughout the year. Some discounts are a month or so long, some are just for a few specific days during a month. These discounts are offered during lean booking times to try to fill rooms. As the rooms fill, the discount amount, amenities included, and/or available dates will be reduced.

Short-term discounts are good to very good deals, typically knocking 10% to 25% off of your room rate. Sometimes the discount is for the room only, but at other times two free adult breakfasts per night will be included and even more rarely two free adult breakfasts and dinners will be included.

Short-term discounts are typically offered in the months of January through May and August through early December. These are not continuous discount periods, rather the months in which there are dates with discounts. These discounts are announced on no particular schedule. Short-term discount may include all days in a month or just a few days through the month.

The long-term discounts are nowhere as good a deal as the short term ones. Both of the long-term discounts include room and breakfast for very slightly discounted rates of 5 dollars or less off per night.

In late 2017 Shades of Green began an 18 – 24 month long renovation (in stages) of the Magnolia Wing, reducing room inventory. Due to this both discount percentages and dates have been negatively effected. Discounts have settled out to be 15% off during 2018.

Shades of Green, the Resort

Shades of Green is a Magic Kingdom Area Resort located across the street from Disney's Polynesian Village Resort. It is not however located on the Magic Kingdom Monorail line.

Shades is located between and shares a parking lot with two of Disney's championship golf courses, the Palm and Magnolia Courses.

It is a very tranquil resort; during the day the pools and grounds are used lightly. With 586 rooms it is a comparatively small resort, Disney's Value and Moderate Resorts have up to almost 3000 rooms and can be very hectic all day!

On average I've found over the years that Shades of Green's guests are much more friendly to, and considerate of each other. After all, we are all part of the same big family! Guests more often than not, greet each other in passing or strike up conversations, where at a Disney resort guests will just pass each other without even looking at each other, much less saying "Hi" or "Good Morning."

Although Shades of Green has among the most spacious rooms on Walt Disney World property they are not themed in Disney fashion as are the Disney resorts. You could pick the entire resort up and place it anywhere else in the US and it would fit right in.

The resort is composed of three areas, the central main area and the two guestroom wings off of each side of the main area.

The central main area is where you will find the lobby and front desk, most of the restaurants, the ticket sales office, fitness center, conference rooms, and bus transportation.

The Magnolia Wing has guest rooms on three floors, both of the resort's pools, and the Magnolia Spa. This wing along with the main area comprises the original extent of Shades of Green before its 2002 expansion. All poolside rooms are in this wing; all other views in this wing are either of the golf course or Shades' grounds.

If being near the pools is important to you, this is your wing!

The Palm Wing contains guest rooms on five floors, and the parking garage. Views here are of the golf course and Shades grounds. Shades has no parking lot or dumpster views, while the Disney resorts do.

All but one of the suites (the Magnolia Suite) are located in this wing.

If having a room much closer to where you park your car at the end of a long day is more important to you, or you need a suite this is your wing!

Both wings have their own guest laundry facility.

With the bus stop located near the lobby, both guest wings have rooms that are closer to the bus stop and some that are much further.

Guests arriving at Shades of Green by car should follow the signs to the Magic Kingdom theme park.

Please note that this area has been under heavy construction for all of 2018 for a new flyover and reroutes of roadways have happened several times.

In general as you approach the Magic Kingdom parking lot tollbooth follow the signs to the Polynesian Village Resort and Shades of Green.

A little over three quarters of a mile from where you passed the tollbooth you'll turn left at a traffic light onto Seven Seas Drive. After turning left stay on this road till it ends (just over half a mile) you'll pass the Polynesian entrance on the way. You'll then have the option to go left or right, you'll turn right. Shades of Green will then be just ahead on your left.

Guests arriving at the Orlando International Airport are responsible for finding their own way to Shades as well as paying for that transportation.

Shades of Green Rooms

Shades of Green's Guest Rooms are fairly comparable to the Disney Deluxe Resorts such as the Polynesian. The views from most every room are spectacular. Views throughout the resort are unique and interesting. The lush tropical landscaping provides an incredible backdrop.

Standard Guest Rooms

At 480 Square feet Shades of Green's rooms are among the roomiest to be found on Walt Disney World Resort property. Guest amenities in Shades of Green's oversized, standard guest rooms include two queen size beds and a single sleeper sofa. Each standard guest room features either a private balcony or patio, with two chairs and a table.

All rooms include: a refrigerator, in-room safe, free Wi-Fi, in-room movies/video games, coffee maker, hair dryer, and an iron and ironing board.

Poolside Rooms

Poolside rooms are identical to the standard rooms in size and amenities. The only difference is that their rear sliding door opens towards a view of one of the two pools. You can walk directly from your room's patio to the pool.

Family Suites

Shades of Green also offers twelve Family Suite combinations. The Garden Suite sleeps 4 guests, The Magnolia Suite sleeps 5, Junior Suites sleep up to 6 guests, Family Suites sleep up to 8 guests and the Palm Suite sleeps up to 10. Because the number of suites, availability is very limited these rooms reserve quickly. If you are interested in making a reservation for a suite, I suggest you do so as soon as you confirm your vacation dates.

Guest amenities in the Junior and Family Suites include a separate bedroom with King size bed and full-size bath, living area with two queen size fold out sofa beds, an additional full bath, and dining table with chairs.

The Family Suites feature a fold down Murphy Bed for the 7th and 8th guests.

The Magnolia Suite features two bedrooms with two queen beds each plus a fold down couch for one.

The Garden Suite is a 2 rooms suite that sleeps 4 the master room has 1 king bed and the living area has a queen pull out sofa.

Pets are not permitted. Shades of Green is a smoke-free resort.

Shades of Green Dining

You will find several different dining options at Shades of Green. They run the full spectrum of service, from the Java Café counter in the lobby to Mangino's table service Steak House.

In this chapter look for these keys to the rough cost of restaurants and meals they offer:

- $ = Less than $15 per adult
- $$ = $15 - $30 per adult
- $$$ = $30 - $60 per adult
- $$$$ = $60 plus
- B = Breakfast
- L = Lunch
- D = Dinner
- S = Snack

Here is the restaurant run down:

Mangino's Steakhouse – D$$ Table service – "Steakhouse classics infused with old-world charm." Open 5-10 pm.

Note: Manginos Steakhouse has recently transitioned from an Italian Bistro, which it had been since its opening in 2014. MDT has not yet had the chance to visit for a review.

Mangino's also offers a Bistro To Go Menu for carry out 6 – midnight.

Room Service is available 7:00 to 10:30 am and 6 pm to midnight.

The Garden Gallery – BD$ Buffet meal - Rotating themed buffets include a great selection of international cuisine and a fresh fruit, soup and salad bar. Themes include Mexican, Italian, Oriental, and American menus depending on the night. It is also located on the lower lobby level. Open 7 – 11 am & 5 – 9:30 pm.

The breakfast buffet includes: Pastries, breads, eggs, omelets, waffles & Mickey pancakes, quesadilla, biscuits and gravy, bacon, sausage, and fresh fruit. A la Carte is also available.

This restaurant is the primary location for a hot breakfast and can become very busy in the mornings. I recommend grabbing a quick coffee and breakfast sandwich or pastry from the Java Café or Express Café on the way to the parks instead.

Evergreens Sports Bar & Grill – LD$ Table service – Evergreens is located next to the Mill Pond Pool. Evergreens serves sandwiches, wraps and burgers, salads, pizza, wings, and nachos. A full bar and beer is on tap. Open 11 am – midnight.

Watch the game on one of the many TVs, while the kids enjoy the extensive attached game room or just grab a drink to enjoy by the pool!

Express Cafe – BLS$ Quick Service – The Express Café features breakfast sandwiches, pastries, snacks, fresh coffee, tea and more. After breakfast they offer a selection of great sandwiches. Open 7 am – 2 pm.

The Express Café is located next to the bus loading area.

Java Cafe - BS$ Quick Service - The Java Café is located in the lobby. They serve fresh Starbucks coffee and assorted pastry items, a variety of flavors of handmade ice cream cones and Sundaes, and adult beverages (beer, wine, and spirits). Get your morning Joe and a pastry here before you head out to the parks! Open all day. Open 6 am – 10 pm.

On the Greens Grill – LS$ Quick Service - On the Greens is a Disney owned Quick Service Location located very near the Magnolia Pool. It is a drive-up location for golfers at the Palm and Magnolia Courses. They serve quick and delicious grilled hot dogs, Italian sausage, steak burgers, sandwiches, quick snacks and cold drinks. Open mid-morning until prior to dinner.

Special Events

Shades of Green often puts on special events for various holidays like Christmas, New Years, the Fourth of July, Oktoberfest, etc. They also offer special meals on certain nights of the week (often Fridays), such as Prime Rib, New England Clam Bake, and Surf and Turf.

Shades of Green Pools

There are two very beautiful outdoor pools at Shades of Green. Both are located in the original Magnolia Wing. Both pools are heated and handicap accessible, the Magnolia Pool features zero entry walk in and both pools have assistive lift devices.

The Mill Pond Pool is formed roughly in the shape of the Mickey Mouse head icon. It is located at the rear of the Magnolia Wing.

Evergreen's is conveniently located next to the pool for snacks and drinks.

This pool will be the kid's favorite with its water slide and kid's splash/play area. The kid's playground is close by as well.

The Magnolia Pool is located on the side and near the front of the Magnolia Wing. The On the Greens Snack Bar is located nearby for snacks and drinks. The hot tub is also located alongside the pool.

The Magnolia Pool is a "U" shaped pool with zero entry walk-ins at both of the tops of the U, while the bottom of the U is the deeper end. The hot tub is attached along this bottom of the U. A volleyball net is strung across one of the sides for some in-pool fun. Flotation devices are available.

This being a military installation, there are safety procedures in effect for both pools.

The pools will be closed in the event of thunder and lightning for 30 minutes. The 30-minute period will be reset for each subsequent lightning strike. The pool deck area must be evacuated completely.

Also when rainfall is so hard that the bottom of the pool becomes invisible, the pool will be closed until visibility improves. The pool deck area doesn't need to be evacuated when this occurs.

Both pools are fenced with childproof entrances.

Shades of Green Military Ticket Sales

At Shades of Green's Ticket Sales Office you may purchase Disney Armed Forces Salute Tickets as well as all other varieties of Disney World tickets, plus tickets for other local attractions like: Universal Studios Orlando, Sea World, and many other Orlando/Central Florida area attractions.

Prices at the Shades of Green Ticket Sales Office are comparable to those that you'd find at your local Base MWR Ticket Office and no sales tax is charged.

The Ticket Office will link your Disney tickets to your Magic Bands (purchased elsewhere or from previous trips) for you at the time of purchase.

Shades of Green's Guests are able to pre-purchase their tickets before ever leaving home. This is a very important benefit as Disney World's new FastPass Plus system allows you to make attraction reservations from home ahead of time, but a valid ticket is required to do so.

Simply email advancedtickets@shadesofgreen.org for forms and instructions.

How it works: You'll select the tickets you'd like to purchase (Disney or other), submit eligibility verification, and payment. Then Shades of Green will FedEx your tickets for aa additional $10 fee.

Shades of Green's Exchange

Shades of Green has an Armed Forces Exchange Service General Store on property. It's a small convenience store that has a selection of Disney items as well as Orlando and Florida souvenirs.

They also carry typical sundry items such as: soda, water, milk, and juice, liquor, beer and wine, snack foods, breakfast items, over the counter medicines, and many more items. They are open 7am till 9pm.

Shades of Green's Magnolia Spa

The Magnolia Spa offers a wide range of services to help you relax. Everything from massages and facials to mani-pedis and salon/barber services are available as well as Princess and Pirate makeovers for the little ones.

Shades of Green Fitness

Shades of Green offers a small fitness center for your use 24/7 that features an assortment of weight machines, steppers, and treadmills.

The following equipment is available:

Cardio Equipment:

- Three (3) Treadmills
- Two (2) Adaptive Motion Trainers (AMT)
- Two (2) Upright Bikes
- One (1) Recumbent Bike

Strength Machines:

- Abdominal Crunch
- Lat. Pull-down
- Chest Press
- Lateral Shoulder Raise
- Bicep Curl
- Leg Extension
- Prone Leg Curl

Other Equipment:

- Free weights (up to 50lbs)
- Medicine Balls
- Exercise mats
- Adjustable bench

Yoga classes are offered Monday through Thursday at various times and at different skill levels.

The current schedule which is subject to change is:

Monday – 3:15-4:15 Vinyasa Flow Yoga
Monday – 4:30-5:30 Walk, Weights, and Stretch

Tuesday – 8:30-9:30 Energy Flow Yoga
Wednesday – 3:15-4:15 Vinyasa Flow Yoga
Thursday – 7:00-8:00 Cardio Yoga

Two lighted tennis courts are also available.

Shades of Green Arcade

There is a good-sized arcade located along side Evergreens Sports Bar & Grill and the Mill Pond Pool. You can enjoy video games and games of skill using purchased tokens.

Shades of Green Family Technology Center

The Family Technology Center was donated to Shades of Green by Raytheon, serves as the military guests' "home away from home" computer center.

Enjoy free use of the supplied televisions and personal computers.

The Family Technology Center is located right next to Shades of Green's Ticket Office.

Kid's Playground

The kid's playground in located by the Mill Pond Pool and Evergreens. The playground features a soft rubber surface surrounding a modern jungle gym with ladders and a slide.

Kid's Activities

Shades of Green offers occasional activities for kids, but they are not on a standard daily schedule that you can plan on like the Disney resorts. Rather they are occasional events that just have to happen to fall on your vacation dates or just happen a couple days a week.

Shades of Green Transportation

Shades of Green offers free bus transportation to Disney World' theme parks, water parks, and Disney Springs.

Shades of Green has a multi-level parking garage, which currently costs $7.00 per night to use.

Shades' guests may use the entire Walt Disney World Transportation System and Disney's Polynesian Village Resort and its Monorail station is just a short walk from Shades of Green. The Bellhops will even drive you to the edge of Shades' property, which is half way there in a golf cart called the Shady Shuttle.

Guests flying into Orlando for their Disney vacation are responsible for finding and paying for their own transportation to Shades of Green from the Orlando International Airport.

Those desiring to visit SeaWorld or Universal Studios Orlando during their vacation can use a round trip, fee based shuttle service from Shades of Green. Reservations are required the day prior at the Ticket Sales Office. The round trip cost is $ 10.00 per adult (12+) and $ 5.00 per child (4-11), under age 4 is free. There is only one run each way per day so you need to stick to their times. The shuttle departs Shades at 8:15 am, it leaves Universal at 6:30 pm and SeaWorld at 6:45.

Alamo Car Rental has a kiosk just off the left side of the lobby and down the ramp.

Uber – Get a free ride up to $15 by signing up with this promo code: steveb14703ue this promo is for your first ride only, any value not used expires so this is not good for a quick hop across WDW property, but it is perfect for a ride from Orlando International to Shades of Green. The one-way fare from the airport is about $25. If you are already a member, have someone else in your party sign up.

Disney Benefits at Shades of Green

While not a Disney Resort, Shades of Green affords some of the same benefits that you would receive if you were staying at a Disney owned resort, however there are some benefits that you will miss out on.

The benefits that you will receive as a Shades of Green guest are: 60-Day FastPass Plus reservations; Participating in Disney's Extra Magic Hours (early arrival or late departure at selected parks on selected days), merchandise package delivery to your resort, guaranteed theme park entry on high attendance days, full use of the Disney Transportation system.

Benefits that you **will not receive** as a Shades of Green guest: Free theme park parking, as a Shades of Green guest you will have to pay to park at the Disney World theme parks (currently autos are $22 standard/$45 preferred per day), should you decide to drive to the parks. You are unable to participate in the Disney Dining Plan. You may not charge any of your Disney meals/purchases to your room.

Shades of Green's History

The resort that is Shades of Green was originally opened at Walt Disney World as a Disney-owned resort called the Golf Resort in December 1973. The Golf Resort was located in the middle of the Palm and Magnolia golf courses across the street from the Polynesian Village Resort. The Golf Resort was built in the style of a country club and featured 151 guest rooms.

The core building of the resort was originally opened in 1971 as a two-story clubhouse for the golf courses and did not actually have guest rooms. Guest wings were added to the original clubhouse in 1973 to add more guest room capacity to WDW's existing Contemporary and Polynesian Resorts and Fort Wilderness Campground.

One of the major drawbacks to the resort was its location. The resort was not located on the monorail loop. The nearest monorail station was a half-mile away at the Polynesian.

The resort was expanded and renamed The Disney Inn in February 1986 to try to appeal to a wider guest base than just golfers. It received an additional 150 rooms with a new Snow White theme during that renovation. The resort was still small though by Disney standards, with only 301 rooms.

Enter the Military

By the early 1990s, Army officials had decided that it was time to build an Armed Forces Recreation Center in the continental United States. Orlando was the top choice in a market survey of soldiers.

During 1992 in the aftermath of Desert Storm Army MWR placed an ad in the Orlando Sentinel inquiring if anyone in the local business community would be interested in leasing a resort property to the Army. The desired number of rooms and required amenities, such as a pool, restaurant and lounge were listed.

There were 40 responses to that ad. It was decided that the offer from the Walt Disney World Company to lease the Disney Inn was the right offer. After negotiations were completed the Shades of Green Resort opened its doors on 1 February 1994. The Department of Defense leased the resort and the land it sits on with a 99 year lease.

There was a long process for deciding what to call the new resort. The new name had to be acceptable to both Disney and MWR. At the time all branches of the military wore some form of green utility/battle dress uniform. It was decided to call the resort the Shades of Green to refer to the different shades of green in the various services' uniforms thus encompassing all branches of the military. Plus Shades sits between two of Disney's lush green golf courses. It seemed the perfect name.

The resort was so successful and popular that MWR decided to purchase the resort. In 1996, it was purchased outright from Disney, for $43 million, although Disney still owns the land on which the resort sits.

Shades of Green is a self-sustaining resort, **no outside/taxpayer funds are used in its operation or upkeep.**

A Very Popular Resort

In the following years the huge popularity of Shades caused it to fill to capacity often and early. Reservations were hard to get in busy seasons. So in 2002 the resort closed its doors for almost two years for a total remodel and expansion.

During this time Shades of Green's guests were housed in Disney's Contemporary Resort North Garden Wing (now replaced by the Disney Vacation Club, Bay Lake Towers). This section of the Contemporary was totally turned over to Shades of Green. They set up their front desk, ticket sales office and gift shop in some of the guest rooms.

This was a fantastic opportunity; military families were able to stay in a Disney Deluxe resort for Shades of Green prices.

The aim of the renovation was to create an even better resort that included more guest room options, meeting space, additional dining capacity and more guest amenities. The renovation remodeled the guest rooms in the Magnolia Wing, doubled the number of guest rooms with the addition of the Palm Wing, and added ten family suites. Additional restaurants, a fitness center, and a multi-level, 500 space parking garage were added as well as 7,500 square feet of meeting facilities.

The resort reopened in March 2004 with a total of 586 guest rooms, a new Italian restaurant, guest gym, as well as roomier ticket sales and gift shop areas.

In recent years Shades has offered many varied discounts to military members in order to keep their rooms filled in the face of Disney's Armed Forces Salute, which offers steeply discounted resort rooms.

You'll find more information on the Shades of Green resort rooms in the Where to Stay at Walt Disney World chapter.

Wrap Up

Shades of Green is a great, moneysaving alternative to staying at a Disney Resort. I hope this chapter gave you the knowledge of what is and isn't different about staying on Disney property in this Armed Forces Recreation Center.

Ready for More?

Shades of Green can be a huge moneysaving benefit for military families! You should definitely consider it in your WDW vacation planning.

In the following chapters we are going to get more in-depth into areas like tickets, rooms, and dining. In each of the following chapters, where applicable, we'll start off with what Disney and others have to offer military families.

4. Walt Disney World Tickets

What's This Chapter About?

In this chapter we will be discussing several different types of Walt Disney World tickets that are available to you as a military family.

We'll discuss each type, where and how you can get them, and then wrap up with a discussion of how to decide what type would work the best for your situation.

Disney Armed Forces Salute Tickets

In an earlier chapter we learned about the Disney Armed Forces Salute tickets. We learned what a great deal they are and also that there are a lot of restrictions on how and when they can be used.

As a quick refresher, these are 4-Day and 5-day tickets at about half off the comparable regular price. They come in two varieties: Park Hopper and Park Hopper Plus. You are limited to a total of 6 tickets per military member during the 2018 Salute offer period, which started on 1 January 2018 and runs through 19 December 2018.

There are blockout dates for theses tickets:

- There are no Ticket Blockouts for 2018

In some circumstances these Salute tickets are not your best choice, so there are other options for you to consider. Those being: Magic Your Way Tickets (Military Discounted) and Shades of Green Stars and Stripes Passes.

Magic Your Way Tickets

Walt Disney World's Magic Your Way Tickets are what Disney calls their tickets, these are what are available to the general public.

Military Resellers (Base Ticket Offices and Shades of Green) offer these at a slight discount. There is no official name for these other than the street name so **I call them Regular Military Discounted Magic Your Way Tickets** to distinguish them from the more highly discounted Disney Armed Forces Salute Tickets.

Magic Your Way Tickets come in one to ten day lengths. The Base Ticket, as it is called, allows entry into one theme park per day for the specified number of days. You may leave and re-enter the same park as many times as you'd like during the same day.

The more days that you purchase, the lower the price per day (when averaged), for days five and up you are paying very little per additional day. This is to entice you to stay longer and spend more on other things, like your room, food, and other purchases.

One-day tickets expire whether used or not. Current tickets expire 31 December 2018.

Multi-day tickets and any options purchased must be used within 14 days of first use, except for Florida Resident 3-Day and 4-Day Tickets. Florida Resident 3-Day and 4-Day Tickets expire 6 months after first use. First use must occur on or before 31 December 2018.

There are both adult (age 10+) and children's (ages 3-9) versions of these tickets.

There is two options that you can add on to your Base Ticket, these are the Park Hopper Option and the Park Hopper Plus option.

Park Hopper Option: Allows guests to visit multiple parks on the same day. You may enter as many theme parks (Magic Kingdom, Epcot, Disney Hollywood Studios, or Animal Kingdom) as many times as you'd like each day for the number of days on the ticket.

Park Hopper Plus Option: The Park Hopper Plus Option allows a specific number of entries into the following locations:

- Typhoon Lagoon
- Blizzard Beach
- General admission into the Wide World of Sports Complex
- 9 Holes of Golf at Disney's Oak Trail 9-Hole Golf Course
- One round of Miniature Golf per day prior to 4pm at Disney's Fantasia Gardens Miniature & Disney's Winter Summerland Miniature Golf Courses.

Plus entries are separate from the Theme Park Days on your ticket.

Think of them as two separate tickets in one. One with the number of theme park days purchased and a second with the same number of Plus entries.

Your Plus entries can be used on the same or different days as theme park days and can be used multiple times on the same day if you wish.

An Example - You could go to a theme park in the morning (using up a theme park day), then after lunch go to Blizzard Beach Water Park (using 1 Plus Entry), then prior to 4pm play a round of mini golf at Fantasia Gardens (using a 2nd Plus Entry).

Plus entries are for the day, you may leave and then return the same day.

Regular Military Discounted Magic Your Way Tickets

Disney World sells all varieties of these tickets at full price at all of their ticket windows. **It is not possible to get a military discount on these tickets directly through Disney at the ticket window.**

The MWR system sells Magic Your Way Tickets at a slight discount through Base Ticket Offices and Shades of Green. The military discount amount is about four to eight percent off of the full price, depending on the length and options that you desire.

Some ticket offices maintain a good variety of Magic Your Way tickets in stock, while others only keep a few types on hand. Some ticket offices don't keep any in stock. If you desire tickets that they do not carry, they may be able to order exactly what you want.

Be sure to check on purchasing your tickets at least 2 weeks or more prior to when you want to have them in hand, as it may take a week or so to order them if needed.

Shades of Green's Stars and Stripes Passes

These Passes are sold only by Shades of Green only to those staying on Walt Disney World property.

These passes are available to anyone staying anywhere on Walt Disney World property, you do not have to stay at Shades of Green.

These special tickets are a length of stay pass which include theme park admission for the number of days on the ticket, the ability to park hop, and a limited Plus option (they do not include Mini Golf).

These tickets are great if you want to have a vacation filled with things to do!

You can pack your days with visiting the parks each day of your visit while also fitting in some of the other WDW recreation options like WDW's two water parks.

Stars and Stripes Passes are available in 2-day through 10-day increments. They expire one day after the number of days purchased, so a 5-day ticket would expire 6 days after first use. The number of days on your ticket must match your length of stay.

Stars and Stripes Tickets offer admission for the specified number of days to the Magic Kingdom Park, Epcot, Disney's Hollywood Studios, Disney's Animal Kingdom Theme Park, as well as an equivalent number of entries into Typhoon Lagoon, Blizzard Beach, Wide World of Sports Complex.

There are both adult (10+) and children's (3-9) versions of these tickets.

Pluses

Great for maxing out your vacation
Cheaper than Magic Your Way with similar options
You may pre-purchase prior to your arrival and make your FastPass Plus Reservations at the 30 day mark

Minuses

Do not allow for multiple non-park down days (without losing money)
Can only be purchased from Shades of Green

Florida Residents

Those stationed in or who are still Florida residents should be aware that there are special Florida Resident tickets and passes which could be a great option for you. These Florida Resident tickets and passes can be purchased at Shades of Green and other Florida Base Ticket Offices for even more savings! I myself have used the Silver Annual Pass (formerly the Florida Resident Seasonal Pass), it is about the same price as buying two Disney Armed Forces Salute Tickets and is good all year except during the busiest times (2.5 months of Summer, 1 week at Spring Break, and Christmas week).

Florida Resident Ticket Types

- One, three, and four day Magic Your Way Tickets in all combos of: Base, Hopper, & Water Park Fun and More
- Weekday Select Pass

- Epcot after 4 Pass
- Silver Annual Pass
- Gold Annual Pass
- Platinum Annual Pass
- Platinum Plus Annual Pass

A valid military identification card and proof of residency are required at the time of purchase.

Acceptable forms of residency are: a Florida driver's license, Florida state issued ID card (must have a Florida address), or a Florida based military ID. Or one of the following dated within the previous two months showing a Florida residential address: a monthly mortgage statement, Florida Vehicle Registration or Title; homeowner's insurance policy or bill, an automobile Insurance policy or bill; a utility bill; mail from a financial institution, including checking, savings, or investment account statement; or mail from a Federal, State, County or City government agency.

Note: FL residents stationed outside of Florida have experienced issues obtaining FL Annual Passes directly from Disney using a credit card with a billing address outside of Florida. Cash is recommended if this is an issue for you.

One Ticket Per Person

All Disney tickets, no matter what type (military or otherwise) are non-transferable. The person who first uses a ticket for entry is then the only person who can use that ticket on return visits.

For example you cannot buy one 4-day ticket and use it to get four people into a Disney World Park on the same day. Instead, you'd have to buy four 1-day tickets.

Only one "day" on a ticket may be used per calendar day.

For example, you cannot buy a 2-day base (non-hopper) ticket and use it for entrance at a second theme park on a day that you have used it previously.

Where can I buy my Military Discounted Tickets?

While the general public has the option of purchasing their tickets right from Disney online or via phone while making their resort reservations, the military population has to jump through some hoops to get their discounted ones.

These are the locations at which you may purchase the various types of military discounted tickets.

Walt Disney World Ticket Booths

Types of tickets available: Disney Armed Forces Salute, Mickey's Not-So-Scary Halloween Party Tickets, and Mickey's Very Merry Christmas Party Tickets. *You will find more about these special Parties in the Other Things to Do at Walt Disney World chapter.*

Walt Disney World will add sales tax to your purchase.

Shades of Green's Ticket Sales Office

Types of tickets: Disney Armed Forces Salute, Regular Military Discounted Magic Your Way Tickets, Shades of Green's Stars and Stripes Passes, Military Discounted Disney Water Park Tickets, Mickey's Not-So-Scary Halloween Party Tickets, Mickey's Very Merry Christmas Party Tickets. Other Orlando and Central Florida attraction tickets may also be purchased here.

Anyone, whether staying there or not, may buy tickets ahead of time and have Shades FedEx you the physical tickets for a $10 fee.

Orlando ITT Ticket Sales Office

Orlando used to be the home to two military bases, McCoy Air Force Base and Naval Training Center Orlando.

The Orlando International Airport began life as McCoy Air Force Base in the 40s. In 1962 McCoy AFB began sharing its runways with the new Orlando Jetport and then in 1975 McCoy closed down.

Naval Training Center Orlando was established in 1968, it served as a Basic Training base along with hosting other schools.

When McCoy AFB closed NTC Orlando took over portions of the base west of the runways and re-designated it the NTC Orlando Annex. They operated an old small commissary on the site.

The NTC closed in 1999.

Today, while NTC Orlando is long gone due to the BRAC, the Annex still remains and there is a beautiful, large, well maintained Commissary and Navy Exchange, as well as a Subway and ITT Ticket Office.

Contact Info:

Phone: 407-855-0116/407-851-4396
 email: mwrorl@gmail.com
Text MWROrlando to 30364 for MWR Specials

Directions:

 GPS Address: 8717 Avenue C, Orlando, FL 32827

From WDW: take I-4 east toward Orlando exit 72 (528 Expressway), go to exit 9 (Tradeport Dr.), turn right onto Tradeport Dr. The NEX is 1 mile ahead on the right.

From Orlando International Airport: Take the North airport exit and follow 436 north for 2 miles, turn left at first light (Frontage Road), and turn left at next light (Tradeport Dr.) The NEX is 1 mile ahead on the right.

Types of tickets: Disney Armed Forces Salute, Military Discounted Magic Your Way Tickets, Military Discounted Disney Water Park Tickets. Other Orlando and Central Florida attraction tickets may also be purchased here.

Your Local Base Ticket Office

Most base ticket offices sell Disney Armed Forces Salute Tickets and some of all varieties of the Magic Your Way Tickets. They may not stock all or any varieties, so be sure to check well in advance of the date you would like to have them in hand in case they need to order your tickets.

Base ticket offices' prices can vary from the Shades of Green prices, usually by just a couple of dollars, but reports say some bases have been charging as much as ten to eleven dollars more per ticket.

Types of tickets: Disney Armed Forces Salute, Military Discounted Magic Your Way Tickets, Military Other Local attraction tickets may also be purchased here.

Via Phone, Email, FedEx

Most bases require you to come in person, but there are some ticket offices which have procedures in effect to sell to you over the phone and ship via FedEx. There will be an additional charge for shipping.

This list is a list of some of the ticket offices that I am aware of that will assist you long distance, but please note that they could change their policies with time.

Camp Pendleton, CA
Patrick AFB, FL

U.S. Coast Guard Academy, CT
Scott AFB, IL
Fort Knox, KY
Shades of Green Resort at Walt Disney World, FL

Using Your Tickets

When you buy your Disney Armed Forces Salute tickets from a military reseller, such as your Base Ticket Office, you often will receive paper vouchers (called Exchange Vouchers in Disney speak) rather than your actual tickets, although some Bases do still issue non-functional plastic Salute tickets.

In either case the tickets or vouchers may be linked to your My Disney Experience account so that you can make your FastPass Plus reservations.

An important consideration if you will be using Magic Bands and multiple tickets per person is that the last ticket linked to a person's account will be the first one used. This is important if you will be using two or more different tickets during your trip.

If you need to adjust or just to be sure which ticket will be used for entry on a particular day, just drop by the Guest Relations window PRIOR to entering a park that day, or use the physical ticket for entry instead of your magic band.

Disney Armed Forces Salute tickets purchased on base require activation in person after arrival with your whole party present.

Military Discounted Magic Your Way Tickets do not need to be activated.

Ticket Safety

Before I close this chapter I want to talk a little about ticket safety.

Please, only buy your Disney tickets from Disney or Military Resellers (Shades of Green, Orlando ITT or Base Ticket Offices) this is the only way to know that you are getting what you are paying for.

There are sites (Ebay, Craig's List, etc.) where you can buy cheap(er) Disney tickets, military or otherwise, but I encourage you not to do so. You could find yourself in a very awkward position at the park entry tapstiles, when the allegedly unused (or ticket with 2 days left on it) has actually been totally used up.

Also it is stated expressly that all Disney tickets are non-transferable, meaning that the person who first uses a ticket is the only person who can use it on subsequent entrances. Disney has measures in place to ensure this.

At Walt Disney World each time you use your ticket your fingerprint is scanned. The first time is for reference; on follow-on visits the user's print is compared to the original.

Timeshares… There are Orlando Timeshares which offer "Free Disney Tickets" after you sit through their high pressure sales pitch. This will waste your time and you could end up with the cost of a timeshare too. Plus as you have to wait till after the pitch to get the tickets, advance FastPass Plus is then out of the question.

Magic Bands – the same caution goes for Magic Bands, I do not recommend buying them from Ebay, Craigs List, etc. you have no way to guarantee that the previous owner has unlinked them from their account. If they haven't they will be unusable to you.

Physical Ticket Security

With the advent of My Disney Experience accounts the worry of physical ticket security has become much less.

If you link have linked your Disney Armed Forces Salute exchange vouchers purchased on base to you're my Disney Experience account and have Magic Bands, you will not be given physical tickets upon ticket activation at Disney World (unless you ask for one).

But if you don't have or want a My Disney Experience account, will not be linking your physical tickets to the account, or are not using magic bands be sure to read the following about securing your tickets.

What If Your Disney Tickets Were Lost or Stolen?

I ask because this has happened to military families.

One group had arrived in Orlando for their long awaited vacation and stopped at a local grocery store for some supplies. While in the store, their vehicle was broken into and their luggage was stolen along with their WDW tickets, which were inside the luggage.

What an awful situation!

They were a large multi-military member party using an assortment of military discounted ticket types purchased at different bases. Some of their tickets they were able to have replaced for free (because their ITT/ITR kept good records), but others could not be and they had to buy replacements.

In another recent instance a family stationed in Hawaii departed home for a Disney trip and realized once they were in California that they'd left their Armed Forces Salute tickets at home. With a receipt from their Base ITT and pictures of the ticket ID numbers they could have gotten replacement tickets from Disney at no cost.

What You Can Do To Protect Yourself

Don't count on others to maintain your ticket records!

If you have a My Disney Experience account with your tickets linked, you can just log in or go to a Disney ticket booth or Guest Services location and deactivate the tickets. Then request a replacement from Disney.

But if you don't have a My Disney Experience account with your tickets linked:

If you are purchasing your Disney tickets (Disney World or Disneyland) from a Military Reseller (Shades of Green, your Base Ticket Office, or the Orlando ITT) you should follow these procedures in case your tickets are lost or stolen.

- Save your receipt! Put it in your wallet, even if it is months till your vacation.
- Take a picture of your receipt
- Take pictures of the barcode/ID numbers of each ticket or exchange voucher
- Print one set of photos
- Keep another set on your camera/phone
- Send the pictures to someone else in your party
- Keep the tickets/prints/digital copies all in different locations

When leaving for your vacation:

Keep the tickets with you!

Keep the tickets, prints, and digital copies separate. Bring your receipt too. Don't leave them all together in the car or room! Pack some in carry-on, some in checked luggage, and some on your person.

Then if your tickets are lost or stolen you can use the pictures/prints and the receipt to get replacement ones from Disney ticket booths at no cost.

Finger Prints and Pictures, Oh My!

Disney uses 2 methods to identify multi-day ticket holders. This is to prevent ticket sharing or scalping. All Disney tickets are non-transferable. It also prevents a stolen ticket or band from being used.

At Disney World, as you enter a park for the first time you will place your finger on a scanner. The machine will store data points from your fingerprint, which it will then use on your return visits to ensure that it is actually you trying to use your ticket.

If there you have technical issues with the fingerprint scanner a cast member will take your picture with an iPad and tie it to your ticket. This image may then be checked on your return visits.

What's the right ticket?

So what's the right ticket for you?

That is a question which is highly personal and depends on your party makeup, length of stay, the resort at which you will stay, and your desired touring habits. Park hopping vs non-hopping makes a big difference in the price of Magic Your Way tickets.

Here is some general advice to guide you on how to make your own decision. Be sure that you check prices and compute the total for all combinations of tickets possible to find your lowest price.

Note: Disney Armed Forces Salute Ticket prices are announced and set prior to the start of the offer in question and do not change for the life of the offer. Regular Military Discounted Magic Your Way Tickets and Stars and Stripes Passes follow the general public equivalent and will increase when the general public prices do. This is usually once per year (in February the last few years, August prior to that) though there have been two increases in some years. The different price increase dates will affect your ticket decision. **Always check the price for all ticket options!**

One Theme Park day: the Military Discounted Magic Your Way Ticket is the way to go.

Two to five theme park days: The Disney Armed Forces Salute Tickets are the right choice. These 4 or 5-day tickets both cost less than the comparable 2-day tickets. Small parties can use these tickets back-to-back for longer trips.

Six to eight theme park days: This length is where things are the most confusing!

You will need to price out all of your options based upon your preferences and decide on the right choice for you.

Compare:

- Back to back use of Disney Armed Forces Salute tickets (up to the offer limit) for all or some in the party.
- Military Discounted Magic Your Way Ticket for the entire number of days needed. Price all options: Base, Hopper, and Hopper Plus. Most people look as Base vs Hopper.
- A combination of Salute and Magic Your Way tickets for all members or just some in the party.

All members of smaller parties (two or three) or some members of larger parties can use Disney Armed Forces Salute Tickets back-to-back for up to ten days in the parks.

If your party is large, as many adults as possible should use back to back Salute tickets, then the rest of the party can use the next cheapest option.

Consider buying non-Hopper Magic Your Way tickets to mix with your Salute tickets as they are cheaper. You'll have to decide which days of your trip that you do not want to park hop and use the non-Hoppers those days.

For those on longer stays (5+ days) it is almost always cheaper to buy one Military Discounted Magic Your Way Ticket for the whole time, than to buy both a Disney Armed Forces Salute Ticket and a shorter Military Discounted Magic Your Way Ticket to reach the desired length. But check both ways as there are a couple of instances where 2 different tickets will be cheaper!

If just some in your party will be using Magic Your Way tickets, any members of the party who are between three and nine years old should use these before adults do, as the child's MYW tickets are cheaper than adult's.

The **Shades of Green Stars and Stripes Passes** could also be an option. These passes are a slightly cheaper option to longer Regular Military Discounted Magic Your Way tickets with the Park Hopper Plus Option minus Mini Golf.

Wrap-up

Making the decision on just which ticket or ticket combo is right for you can be a daunting task. Hopefully I've given you the information that you'll need to make a great choice.

Ready for More?

Now that we've discussed the military specific items it's time to talk about deciding when is the best time for you to go to Walt Disney World.

5. When to Go to Walt Disney World

What's This Chapter About?

In this chapter we'll be discussing the many things to consider when deciding the best time for your military family to visit Walt Disney World.

Because this book was created exclusively for the military family this chapter presents a lot of information which applies only to the military community.

Other Disney World Guide Books are designed for the general public and start their discussion of when to go with things like crowds, cost, and weather.

Military families have other things to consider first, like block leave, deployments, PCS moves, and the availability of military discounts before ever getting to the point where the general public starts their Disney World planning.

Military Considerations

We'll first discuss the military centric items and then move on to the general topics. The two military centric areas we will cover are Ability to Go and Discount Availability.

Leave - Military Schedules

Perhaps the biggest consideration for military families is leave!

First and foremost, when will you be allowed to take leave?

Are you in a situation where you can take leave whenever you'd like? Awesome!

But perhaps you're in a situation where you have to take block leave at the same time with your whole unit on specific dates. Or does a six month or longer deployment dictate when you would be able to go, either prior to, mid deployment break, or after? What about a PCS move into or out of the continental US? Is there a mandatory formal school in your future, which would prevent leave?

Because of these things your timetable may be set for you or be very limited.

If your timeframe is dictated for you, then you will have to deal with all of the following considerations based upon those dates.

On the other hand if you can go whenever you'd like your next consideration will be to ensure that you go during a timeframe when the Disney Armed Forces Salute discounts are available!

Salute Discount Availability

If you do have the ability to choose when you'll go or are trying to choose between times that you are allowed to take leave, your primary consideration is the availability of the Disney Armed Forces Salute discounts for your potential dates.

There are three things which can affect the availability of the Disney Armed Forces Salute, these are: Blockout Dates, the Salute Changeover Period, and the possibility that the Salute offers will not be continued.

Armed Forces Salute Blockout Dates

These are dates on which the Salute ticket and room discounts are not available for use. They coincide with the very busiest times of the year, which are coincidentally when the majority of US schools happen to be on vacation.

You should avoid the Disney Armed Forces Salute Blockout Dates! This is in order to make use of the huge savings afforded by the Salute discounts and to miss the worst crowds.

Disney blocks these days from use for the Salute discount because they already have way too many people coming at the full rate, so they do not want to encourage any more to come by offering a discount.

Blockout dates for rooms and tickets are often the same, but not always. At times they have been a few days off from each other.

The Blockout dates for the 2018 Salute are:

Salute Resort Rooms Only – No Ticket Blockouts for 2018

- 25 March - 5 April 2018

Salute Changeover Periods

New Calendar Year Salutes

In 2016 Disney switched to offering the Salutes on a calendar year basis vesus the old fiscal year Salutes of the past.

With the switch to calendar year offers the old Christmas/New Year's Blockout dates are built into the offer end and beginning dates and create a roughly 2-week long buffer period between the Salute offers.

The 2018 Armed Forces Salute runs through just before Christmas (19 December 2018), and a new 2019 Armed Forces Salute has not been announced.

Just be aware that the 2018 Salute tickets will not be usable starting on 20 December and that any days remaining on them expire. If you'll be going during this timeframe you'll need to use other ticket options and there will be no room discounts.

Salute Termination

The end of each Disney Armed Forces Salute offer could potentially be the end of an era if Disney decides not to continue the program. Planning a trip in a period with no Salute offer would more than double your ticket cost!

It is not known if our community would receive any advance indication that the Salutes would be coming to an end, or if they would just run out with no news of a follow-on. But as of right now we are all set through December 2018!

Considerations for Dates Without a Salute Offer

If you must go during a timeframe that contains dates without a Salute offer consider the following:

- Disney Armed Forces Salute tickets will not work on Blockout Dates or dates between Salute end and start dates – Any theme or water park days during that timeframe will require a separate or entirely different (close to full price) ticket. *See the Walt Disney World Tickets chapter on how to decide what the right ticket is.*
- If you are mixing tickets (Salute and non-Salute) do not leave unused days on your Salute tickets, this is a waste of highly discounted days! Unless of course you **will** use those days on another trip prior to the end of the Salute offer period in question.
- Disney Armed Forces Salute room rate discounts are not available during Blockout dates or dates between Salute end and start dates – Nightly room charges for the period without a Salute will be at full price. You may need to make two or more separate reservations in order to get the Salute rate on nights that it is available. This means multiple deposits of one night's rate.

Note: Shades of Green does not have Blockout Dates, their room rates are the same low price even on these dates. You could make your entire stay at Shades or do a Split Stay (some nights at a Disney Resort, some at Shades), switching to Shades during the blocked out dates.

My Suggestions

Here are my thoughts on Blockout dates and Christmas.

Christmas - While you might think spending Christmas at Walt Disney World would be Magical… it really isn't, because: the crowds are at times unbearable!!! And the resort prices are the highest of the year!!!

Imagine being in the middle of tens of thousands of people all shoulder to shoulder, all trying to move in different directions… And keep your kids with you! We experienced this Christmas Eve 2014 in the Magic Kingdom.

The Magic Kingdom will begin attendance control measures at about 10 in the morning on Christmas Day! The line of traffic waiting to get into the paring lot will be backed up for many miles!

Instead go prior to Christmas

Disney begins decorating for Christmas the day after Halloween. They are finished within days. They hold special after hours Christmas parties all through November and most of December.

If you'd like a special, magical Disney World experience, go during the first couple weeks of December, crowds are much lighter and you'll get all the benefits of the Disney Armed Forces Salute! Then have a nice, quiet Christmas at home with the family.

Spring Break – Disney determines the peak of Spring Break for Blockout Dates each year based upon many factors, chief among these being when the majority of US schools are on break. Please be advised, many of these people will converge on Central Florida and Walt Disney World at the same time!

This time period will be as miserable as Christmas. The crowds won't be *quite* as bad, but the temperatures will be higher.

Avoid this timeframe

I know going when the kids are out of school is the easy solution, but attempt to find another option, take schoolwork and homework if needed, but avoid Spring Break Blockout days for the big savings and a much less stressful vacation.

If you have to go when the kids are out of school, go the day after they get out for summer vacation. The first half of June is much better crowd wise than much of the summer. Plus the temperatures are not a high as later in the season.

Alternately, go the second half of August as crowds are again lower than mid-summer and the Disney resort rates are lower than the rest of the summer. But it will be hot then!

Planning Your Disney Vacation Timeframe

So, how do you put all of the above information to use?

There are two things to consider.

1. When will you be able to take leave for your WDW vacation? Are you limited to a specific time or times, or can you take leave whenever you'd like?

2. If you can choose your dates and if possible, consider avoiding the Disney Armed Forces Salute blockout dates and the dates between offers. I know that is when the kids are out of school, but the volume of

people in the parks will be at the very highest of the year and you'll get no Salute discounts and it will be crowded! *See more info on Crowds below.*

But if you must go during one of these times, the issues you may encounter and some suggestions to help follow.

Resort Rooms

During blockout dates your Disney Resort room will cost 30% to 40% more than using the Disney Armed Forces Salute room discounts. The dates that are blocked out have some of the very highest full price rates of the year!

Your rate at check in does not carry through; rather each night is charged at the rate for that day. So eliminate or minimize your stays on blockout dates.

Shades of Green is not affected by the blockout dates and will have rooms available at their normal rates. *Note: They do have length of stay requirements during the Christmas and New Year's holidays.*

Park Ticket

Disney Armed Forces Salute tickets are non-functional during blockout dates. Mixing various types of tickets or leaving unused days on a Salute ticket is costly!

If possible plan to finish your vacation before a blockout period or start it after. If it is necessary to have some of your vacation in a blockout period, try to minimize the number of days. The same goes for the timeframe between offers.

Don't leave days on a Salute ticket unless you plan to return prior to the end of the *current offer*.

Disney tickets for the military is a very complex topic which we've covered elsewhere, please check out the Walt Disney World Tickets Chapter for an overview of ticket types.

General Public Considerations

We've now reached the part of deciding "When should I plan to go to Disney World?" where the general public starts…

After considering the military specific areas above, continue on with these general considerations.

Next you'll need to consider:

The cost for your room, which depends on the time of year, the length of your stay, and where you'll stay.

The cost for your tickets, the length of your stay (4 or 5 park days vs longer), and where you stay.

Crowds, which vary by the time of year.

Weather, which varies by the time of year.

Special Events, which you might want to attend or avoid.

How Much Will Your Room Cost?

Shades of Green – The price for your Shades of Green room rate will be based upon your military/civilian pay grade and is constant all through the year, except when they are offering discounts during the slower months.

Disney Resorts - Keep in mind that Disney World has many different "price seasons" for their resort rooms throughout the year, as well as two different prices during most weeks no matter the price season. Friday and Saturday nights as well as special or high volume nights (Long Weekends, Christmas, etc.) are priced at a higher rate.

The price for your room, even with the military discount, can vary greatly based upon the time of year that you go to Disney World.

There are numerous different room types differentiated by resort type and view. The type of resort, i.e. value, moderate, or deluxe, affects the size of the rooms and the amenities offered by the resort as well as the price. The room view also affects your price as rooms with parking lot views are cheaper than one's looking out on greenery, or water (pool, lake, or river), or those that are closer to the lobby.

Disney World's resort rates are complex and vary greatly depending on the time of year. There are eight major price seasons during the year, there are nine short periods within the major price seasons during which the price bumps up, and then six price seasons have weekday night (Sunday-Thursday) and weekend night (Friday & Saturday) prices.

Below are typical Disney World's Value Resort Price Seasons just to show how much prices vary from the lowest price of the year, which is the "Value Season Weekday" rate. You will see that even within each season there are price differences for weekend nights, long weekends, and high volume dates.

Please note that price seasons vary, sometimes considerably between the resort Categories i.e. the start and end dates are sometimes different between resort categories. The purpose in showing the price seasons table and chart below is not for actual date planning, rather to show the degree to which prices can fluctuate.

Date Range	Price Season	Standard Room M-W	% More Expensive	Standard Room Th & Su	% More Expensive	Standard Room F & Sa	% More Expensive
1-Jan	New Years	$208	89%	$208	89%	$208	89%
Jan 2-Jan 6	Marathon	$159	45%	$159	45%	$159	45%
Jan 7-Jan 11	Value	$110	0%	$121	10%	$152	38%
Jan 12-Jan 14	MLK Day	$158	44%	$158	44%	$158	44%
Jan 15-Feb 10	Value	$110	0%	$121	10%	$152	38%
Feb 11-Feb 14	Regular	$138	25%	$150	36%	$186	69%
15-Feb	Spring	$166	51%	$177	61%	$207	88%
Feb 16-Feb 18	Presidents Day	$208	89%	$208	89%	$208	89%
Feb 19-Feb 24	Spring	$166	51%	$177	61%	$207	88%
Feb 25-Mar 8	Regular	$138	25%	$150	36%	$186	69%
Mar 9-Mar 24	Spring	$166	51%	$177	61%	$207	88%
Mar 25-Apr 5	Easter	$208	89%	$208	89%	$208	89%
Apr 6-Apr 7	Spring	$166	51%	$177	61%	$207	88%
Apr 8-May 24	Regular 2	$137	25%	$149	35%	$186	69%
May 25-May 27	Memorial Day	$186	69%	$186	69%	$186	69%
May 28-Aug 11	Summer	$162	47%	$162	47%	$193	75%
Aug 12-Aug 25	Summer 2	$138	25%	$150	36%	$179	63%
Aug 26-Sep 15	Value 2	$121	10%	$133	21%	$149	35%
Sep 16-Oct 4	Fall	$138	25%	$150	36%	$185	68%
Oct 5-Oct 7	Columbus Day	$185	68%	$185	68%	$185	68%
Oct 8-Oct 27	Fall	$138	25%	$150	36%	$185	68%
Oct 28-Nov 8	Fall 2	$121	10%	$133	21%	$149	35%
Nov 9-Nov 11	Veterans Day	$158	44%	$158	44%	$158	44%
Nov 12-Nov 16	Fall 2	$121	10%	$133	21%	$149	35%
Nov 17-Nov 23	Thanksgiving	$163	48%	$163	48%	$163	48%
Nov 24-Dec 8	Fall 2	$121	10%	$133	21%	$149	35%
Dec 9-Dec 13	Winter	$138	25%	$138	25%	$138	25%
Dec 14-Dec 20	Peak	$166	51%	$166	51%	$208	89%
Dec 21-Dec 31	Holiday	$210	91%	$210	91%	$210	91%

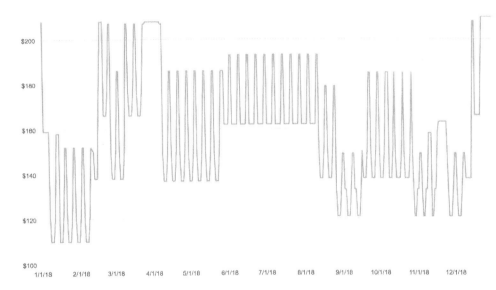

Example of fluctuating prices at a typical Disney Value Resort

By studying the numbers and chart above you'll see that the highest WDW resort prices are during the periods when most people have the availability or biggest desire to go to Disney World. Prices are generally lower during times that people travel less, because Disney is trying to attract vacationers. The chart above depicts the price differences visually; a typical Disney Value Resort is shown.

The prices at other non-Disney hotels in the area will also vary during the year so be sure to check on their websites or with their reservations departments.

For much more on deciding which resort or hotel you'd like to stay at see the chapter on Where to Stay at Walt Disney World. There we take into consideration price, amenities, extras, and FastPass Plus eligibility windows.

How Much Will Your Tickets Cost?

Next figure out the cost for your tickets. If you are considering different timeframes, are they all at a time when you can use the Disney Armed Forces Salute Tickets? Or will you find yourself having to travel when they are not available?

Make sure you do a comparison calculation of how much tickets would cost for each of your timeframes.

Keep in mind, the Salute Tickets do expire at the end of the offer period, they are 4-day or 5-day tickets, there is a limit of six tickets per military member during each year's Salute offer, but they may be used back to back.

Your length of stay and the size of your party can affect your ticket choice.

If your vacation length only includes two to four or five days in the theme parks, then the Armed Forces Salute tickets are the best, cheapest choice. But if you'd like to spend more than four/five days in the parks, you'll need to carefully evaluate what is the correct ticket or ticket combo for you.

For much more on deciding which ticket or ticket combo is right for you see the Walt Disney World Tickets Chapter. There we take into consideration party size, length of stay, price, ticket extras, and FastPass Plus.

How Crowded Will It Be?

Crowd levels can be a big consideration for your Walt Disney World vacation. If you have the ability to select when you will visit WDW you should plan to avoid the busiest times of the year.

When are the busiest times of the year?

When the kids are out of school!

Spring Break, Thanksgiving weekend, Christmas through New Year's, and summer see the very highest crowds.

This presents a quandary for parents with kids in school. Should you go during Spring Break, Christmas vacations (the two worst times crowd wise), during the very crowded summer months when it is very busy and also very hot in Central Florida, or pull the kids out of school?

I recommend the latter!

But, if you must go when the kids are on vacation from school, I recommend doing so as early as possible in June or during the second half of August, the second half of August being the cheaper period of the two, Disney resort room price wise.

During the rest of the year attendance can fluctuate widely. Below is a general depiction of typical WDW monthly attendance levels. Even during individual months attendance can vary greatly, a month with generally low attendance can have a long holiday weekend with peak attendance.

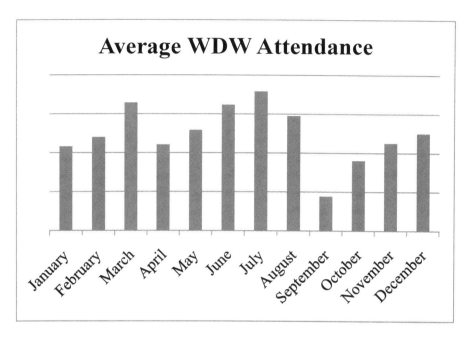

General Crowd Patterns

Lower Crowds

- The first week of January until President's week
- The end of February
- Second week of April through Memorial Day
- Mid-August through September
- Mid-October through Thanksgiving
- The week after Thanksgiving through the week before Christmas

Medium Crowds

- Marathon Week (in January)
- First half of October
- Thanksgiving week

Highest Crowds

- President's Week
- March through the first week of April

- Memorial Day through Mid-August
- Christmas through New Year's Day

What Will the Weather Be Like?

Temperature - One of the many reasons Walt Disney decided to locate Disney World in Orlando was the year-round generally nice weather. This allows for year-round operation without shut downs for the winter season.

Generally there are two distinct "seasons." summer-like weather can stretch from May through October, with the highest temperatures being in June through September. Cooler fall-like weather can be expected in November through April.

Early November to early December is my favorite time to go. While usually temperate there can be days or periods when it can get quite cool or even cold in December through February. While very, very rare Orlando has seen temperatures near or below freezing.

Rainfall – Rain is a big concern in the summer. During the summer it rains most afternoons in Central Florida. Not all over Central Florida, but in isolated areas or lines of storms. This is a function of the heat, humidity, and moist air moving inland from the Gulf of Mexico.

Being a very large area, somewhere on Disney property will get wet almost daily. Disney World sells rain ponchos in every theme park gift shop or you can bring your own cheaper ones. If it is just rain, you can keep pressing on with your planned activities, but if the rain is associated with thunder and lightning you should hole up somewhere (gift shop, restaurant, or other indoor area) until it passes.

Orlando Monthly Average Temperatures and Rainfall in Inches

	Jan	Feb	Mar	Apr	May	Jun	Jul	Aug	Sep	Oct	Nov	Dec
High Temp	71	72	78	83	88	90	92	91	90	84	78	73
Low Temp	47	49	54	59	65	71	73	73	72	65	57	50
Rainfall	2.35	2.47	3.77	2.68	3.45	7.58	7.27	7.13	6.06	3.31	2.17	2.58

Hurricanes and Thunderstorms at Walt Disney World and Shades of Green

Hurricane Season is 1 June through 30 November. Hurricanes affecting Central Florida are typically rare, though there have been years when several have blown through.

Disney World rarely closes for inclement weather and rest assured that they have plans in place to shelter their guests if it is required! Shades of Green, which is a military facility, also has plans for these situations.

If a hurricane is heading somewhere near Central Florida the Disney World area will be in store for very heavy winds and lots of rain at the least!

If you decide to continue with your vacation plans you can expect lots of hard driving rain and probably very low attendance in the Disney theme parks.

Now rain isn't out of the ordinary at Disney World during the summer and fall. In the summer it can rain every day in the afternoon. But a hurricane will dump lots more water than the Orlando afternoon rainstorms can. So you should be prepared to be very wet all day!!!

There are things you can do to prepare for rain at Disney World and work with it.

- Bring or buy ponchos or rain gear for in your backpack – Disney sells ponchos as well
- Pack lots of socks and extra footwear, you'll want to start the day with your feet dry
- Bring ball caps or hats
- Hole up in a restaurant or shop during the worst of the rain
- Ride the rides – While others are holed up in restaurants & shops
- See a movie at the Disney Springs AMC Theatre
- Spend time having a table service meal in a theme park restaurant
- Most importantly though, stay inside if there is any lightning! You can spend that time shopping, eating, or enjoying a beverage.

What if it's so bad that I want to cancel my vacation?

Disney World has established policies for just this situation. Disney's Hurricane Policy says:

That it is a temporary policy that is effective in the event a hurricane warning is issued no more than 7 days before your scheduled arrival date by the National Hurricane Center for the Orlando area or for your place of residence.

You may call in advance to reschedule or cancel your Walt Disney Travel Company Magic Your Way vacation package and most room only reservations (booked directly with Disney), without any cancellation or change fees imposed by Disney.

If you have products and services provided by third-party suppliers included in your vacation-such as airlines, hotels, car rental agencies or vacation insurance companies you will continue to be responsible for any non-refundable payments, as well as cancellation or change fees assessed by those suppliers. The policy does not apply to certain special events or dining experiences.

You may call in advance to reschedule without a Disney imposed change fee. All amounts you paid to Disney for rooms, Theme Park tickets, Disney Dining Plans and other Disney products and services will be applied toward your new reservation. Any discounts or free offers applicable to your original vacation will not apply to the rescheduled vacation. They cannot guarantee availability of similar accommodations for the new travel dates.

If you made your reservations through a travel agent versus through Disney you should contact your travel agent or tour operator directly for information relating to the cancellation and change policies that apply to your package.

Some key info in Disney's policy that you should be aware of is that if you are on a special rate like the Armed Forces Salute room discounts, those rates are not guaranteed on dates or at the same resort that you may reschedule to, as they are based upon availability.

Keep Informed

Hurricanes are unpredictable, so be sure to keep checking to see what the latest info is. Then decide what you think is right for you and your family!

Weather Advice

If you'll be touring in the summer months you will be very hot! You will be soaked with sweat by mid-day and by the afternoon rains. Make sure to bring plenty of changes of clothes, or be prepared to do laundry while there.

Take a break! Nothing beats coming back to your resort mid-day when you are hot, tired, and soaked with sweat. You can hop in the pool, take a nap on the bed under the ceiling fan to get yourself cooled off, or both!

Then in the early evening, after any rain has passed by you can head back to the parks in clean, dry clothes and shoes. This mid-day break gives the kids a chance to rest too, hopefully avoiding the "Disney Meltdown" which plagues young, tired and over stimulated kids in the happiest place on earth.

In the cooler months be sure to pack some long pants and a light coat such as a windbreaker, maybe even some hats and gloves if the forecast suggests very cold temps during your visit. You can always buy sweatshirts there if you need them.

The key here is to be prepared. Watch the weather forecasts as your trip approaches and pack accordingly.

Special Events

Disney World has many special events throughout the year. Some are big multi-month events, while others are small isolated events.

Here is a list of the big annual events that you might want to attend. Our favorite is the Epcot International Food and Wine Festival.

- Walt Disney World Marathon Weekend – Early January
- Princess Half Marathon Weekend – Late February
- Epcot's Flower and Garden Festival – Early March – Mid-May
- Star Wars Half Marathon – Mid-April
- Star Wars Weekends – Mid-May to Mid-June
- Mickey's Not-So-Scary Halloween Party – September and October
- Epcot International Food and Wine Festival – Late September through Mid-November
- Mickey's Very Merry Christmas Party – November through Mid-December

Refurbishments and Construction

Disney World gets a lot of wear and tear and requires a lot of upkeep. Much of this is done daily after hours while the rest of the world sleeps, but all attractions and areas need to have more extensive work done on a regular basis. This involves taking the attraction, restaurant, or area off-line for refurbishment. During this period the location will be totally closed to the public.

Refurbishments usually occur during January through mid-February. Generally, about three rides Walt Disney World wide will be closed for upkeep and modifications.

From time to time more extensive work is planned, whether a total remodel or construction of an entirely new area is required. These projects could be multi-month to well over a year or more long. Some recent examples are: Camp Minnie – Mickey at Animal Kingdom was closed to be turned into Pandora, the entire central hub of the Magic Kingdom recently went through a year plus long redesign, and recently the Maelstrom log ride at Epcot's Norway was closed for what was be a very extended period to be turned into the Frozen Ever After attraction.

Currently large sections of Disney's Hollywood Studios have been closed for the construction of the Star Wars themed land and the Toy Story land. At Epcot Ellen's Energy Adventure closed to be turned into a Guardians of the Galaxy attraction.

All of this is a lot to take in, but now you are armed with the knowledge that you will need to make an informed decision on when to go to Walt Disney World based on your unique circumstances.

Wrap Up

I hope that this chapter helps you with deciding the best time for you to go to Walt Disney World. It is such a personal decision for your family's specifics that there is no one right answer that I could give you. But you should now be armed to make the decision yourself.

Ready for More?

Next we'll be taking a look at the many varied options that are available when deciding where to stay at Walt Disney World.

6. Where to Stay at Walt Disney World?

What's This Chapter About?

In this chapter we'll discuss the many different options that are available to you when you are trying to decide where to stay for your Walt Disney World vacation. For each we'll discuss price, available discounts, the resorts and rooms themselves, dining options, amenities, features, locations, and the pluses and minuses of the resort.

Your options for where to stay during your Walt Disney World Vacation fall into two basic categories: on Disney World property and off Disney World property. On property locations fall into three sub-categories: Disney Resorts, Shades of Green, and other Non-Disney Resorts.

There are advantages and disadvantages to staying either on or off property and you'll also see that all of the options in each category are not equal, they all have different strengths and weaknesses.

In general, staying on property offers in varying degrees depending on the resort, both higher convenience and quality, as well as a more immersive experience, but often at a higher price. While many off property locations offer you cheaper prices, they are lacking in convenience, an immersive experience, and at times quality.

The Disney owned resorts offer a long list of benefits that are included as part of your stay which are hard to pass up. Other on property resorts offer some, but not all of these benefits as well. Your desire to take advantage of some of these benefits may affect your decision. I'll detail these later in the chapter.

Every family is different in their needs and preferences and there is no one overall right or best choice. You should weigh all of the various options and select what you think would be the best resort for your situation.

I do however recommend staying on property versus off, it just makes things so much easier from a convenience and time management standpoint. That is unless you have found a deal that is just too good to pass up, which will offset the inconvenience.

Staying On Walt Disney World Property

There are numerous Disney owned resorts in several different price/amenity categories. Staying at a Disney owned resort comes with many benefits, the most intangible of which is that you will feel like you are at Disney during your entire trip, not just while at the parks. Staying at a Disney owned resort is an immersive experience and so much more convenient.

Check out this list of amenities that you'll receive when you stay in a Disney Resort:

- Free Disney provided roundtrip transportation to your resort from the Orlando International Airport (Disney's Magical Express).

- Free transportation from your resort to all WDW destinations via Disney's fleet of buses, boats, monorails, and in the future gondolas.

- Free theme park parking, should you decide to drive your car.

- Participation in Extra Magic Hours – early entry and late stays at designated parks on designated days. The general public is not allowed in during Extra Magic Hours.

- Property wide charging of your Disney purchases (Merchandise, Dining, etc.) to your room.

- Disney Merchandise delivery to your resort (from the theme parks or Disney Springs)

- Guaranteed theme park entry on high attendance days when the parks close due to nearing capacity

- Booking FastPass Plus reservations 60 days prior to check in

- The ability to add the various Disney Dining Plans to your vacation

- The ability to book Advance Dining Reservations for your entire trip (up to 10 days) at the 180-day mark.

Now let's take a look at all the Disney resorts and what they have to offer.

Walt Disney World Owned Resorts

The Disney look. Walt Disney was a stickler for details and theming at the Disney Resorts runs from the most grand, down to the smallest detail. The Value Resorts are the most over the top with huge icons outside each building relating to the theme of the resort section. When strolling around the Moderate Resorts, be sure to notice the sidewalks. They are not your average flat cement; rather designs were crafted into the cement when it was poured which fit the resort's theme, such as palm fronds, leaves, sea shells, or horseshoe tracks. Look at your bedspread in the deluxe resorts, do you see a hidden Mickey? Note the background music, it matches the theme where you are standing. These are but a few examples of what you will find all through Disney's various resorts.

What's a Hidden Mickey? It is the traditional shape of the Mickey Mouse icon (three circles, one head and two ears) hidden in plain sight by Disney's Imagineers.

You'll find the above type of detail and more in most places around WDW if you take the time to look.

Resort Areas – Walt Disney World divides its resorts into groupings called Resort Areas. This is to give you the guest a quick sense of what the resort is near. There are five resort areas, they include The Magic Kingdom, Epcot, Animal Kingdom, ESPN Wide World of Sports, and the Disney Springs Resort Areas.

The Magic Kingdom Area has four Deluxe Resorts and a campground with campsites and Moderate level Cabins. They are the Contemporary Resort, Grand Floridian Resort & Spa, Polynesian Village Resort, Wilderness Lodge, and Fort Wilderness Resort and Campground.

As you would imagine the Magic Kingdom Resorts are closest to the Magic Kingdom. The two original resorts (Contemporary and Polynesian) as well as the newer Grand Floridian are "Monorail Resorts." They are located on the Magic Kingdom monorail line that makes the transit to the park a snap. They are also some of the most expensive rooms on property because of this. All Magic Kingdom Resorts have boat service to the Magic Kingdom as well and bus service property wide. The Contemporary is close enough to walk to the Magic Kingdom!

Note Shades of Green, the DoD owned and operated resort on WDW property is also a Magic Kingdom Area Resort, but more on that later.

The Epcot Area has three Deluxe Resorts and one Moderate. They are the Yacht Club, Beach Club, BoardWalk Inn, and the Caribbean Beach Resort. The first three, all Deluxes are located adjacent to Epcot and offer boat service to the Epcot International Gateway and Disney Hollywood Studios entrances. You can also easily walk to Epcot, while the Studios is a bit longer walk. The Caribbean, the Moderate is located across a major street from Epcot and only has bus service to all WDW destinations.

Note the Walt Disney World Swan and Dolphin Resorts, which are non-Disney owned resorts are also Epcot Area Resorts, we'll cover these later in this chapter.

The Animal Kingdom Area has one Deluxe, one Moderate, and three Value Resorts. They are in order the Animal Kingdom Lodge, Coronado Springs, and the three All-Star Resorts (Movies, Music, and Sports). The only transportation method available for all of these resorts is the WDW bus system.

The ESPN Wide World of Sports Area has two Value Resorts. They are the Pop Century and the Art of Animation Resorts. These two Values are the newest of all Disney's Resorts, Animation being the newest. The only transportation method available for these resorts is the WDW bus system.

Disney Springs Resort Area has two Moderate Resorts. They are the Port Orleans - Riverside and the Port Orleans - French Quarter. These resorts have boat service between each other and Disney Springs as well as bus service to all WDW destinations.

These Resorts were originally separate resorts named the Dixie Landings and Port Orleans Resorts, in 2001 they were both combined under the Port Orleans umbrella with hyphenated names and a change to Riverside for Dixie Landings.

Disney Resort Types

Disney World offers several categories or levels of resort services. I use the word services rather than quality, as all Disney resorts are high quality. Following you'll see the different ways that Disney categorizes its resorts and the typical amenities you'll find at each.

Value Resorts – The Values are the least expensive option when selecting a resort. Here you'll find:

- Small rooms (260 Sq Ft)
- Outdoor room entries
- Limited luggage service
- Food courts
- Pizza delivery
- Heated pools
- Bus transportation

Moderate Resorts – The middle of the road price wise. (Except for Fort Wilderness Cabins, which cost more)

- Medium sized rooms (314 Sq Ft)
- Outdoor room entries
- Business Class rooms (at the Coronado)
- Luggage service
- Food courts
- Table service restaurants (except French Quarter)
- Limited room service
- Pizza delivery
- Heated pools with water slide and hot tub
- Additional Quiet pools (standard rectangular pools located through the resort)
- Bus or boat transportation
- On site recreation

Deluxe Resorts – The most expensive Disney resorts

- Biggest rooms (344-440 Sq Ft)
- Indoor (hallway) room entries
- Concierge/Club level floors/sections
- Luggage service
- Valet Parking
- Food courts
- Multiple table service restaurants
- Fine Dining
- Room service

- Pizza delivery
- Heated pools with water slide and hot tub
- Additional Quiet pools (Except the Animal Kingdom Lodge) these are standard rectangular pools located through the resort
- Beach Access (Except the Animal Kingdom Lodge)
- A variety of bus, boat, and monorail transportation
- On site recreation
- Onsite Childcare (at 4 of them)

Disney Vacation Club Resorts – The Disney vacation Club is Disney's timeshare program. DVC locations are either co-located with some of the Deluxe resorts and share amenities, or in a couple instances are totally separate resorts.

DVC properties offer studio, one-bedroom, and 2 bedroom condo type rooms with kitchen facilities. These resorts are more expensive than the Deluxes but could be an option for big parties. You may pay by the night just as you would for any other WDW resort, or rent points to use for your stay from a DVC owner through a third party.

A small number of DVC rooms may at times be available for the Disney Armed Forces Salute room discount.

Disney Room Types

As you read through the following resort descriptions you will see many different room views and room types. Some are self-explanatory, but others need a little explaining. The "Views" are either out your front opening door and window in the Values and Moderates, or from your patio/balcony in the Deluxes.

Here are some basic definitions:

Standard View – This view is a parking lot, roof, or otherwise unappealing view. They are the least expensive category.
Garden View – This is a view of greenery, it could be flowerbeds, interior

courtyards, or a wall of trees.

Water View – A generic term for any view where you can see some type of water. It could be a pond, stream, lake, lagoon, river, or pool. Although there are some resorts where they have more than one water view category, each with specific names i.e. Lagoon vs Pool Views.

Adjoining vs Connecting – In Disney speak, adjoining rooms means that the rooms are nearby each other, while connecting rooms have a physical door connecting the two rooms. Be sure to ask for what you need.

Club Level includes access to a concierge lounge offering snacks of varying options throughout the day. Breakfast is often offered and adult beverages are on hand too.

Childcare

Walt Disney World offers several Children's Activity Centers, where your little ones can be dropped off so Mom and Dad can have some adult time.

Note: Disney recently announced that Simba's Clubhouse, Lilo's Playhouse, and the Sandcastle Club will close by 1 August 2018.

Camp Dolphin will remain open.

And Pixar Play Zone opens 13 April at the Contemporary Resort.

Kids ages 3-12 may take part. Services vary, but children generally can be left between 4:30 PM and midnight. Milk and cookies and blankets and pillows are provided at all centers, and dinner is provided at most. Play is supervised but not organized, and toys, videos, and games are plentiful. Guests at any Disney resort or campground may use the services. Age limits are 3-12 years old (4-12 at Camp Dolphin and Pixar Play Zone).

Rates vary by location:

- Camp Dolphin and Simba's Clubhouse Are $15 per hour, per child (2-hour minimum)
- Lilos Playhouse and Sandcastle Club charge a flat $55 plus tax per child per evening
- Pixar Play Zone is $65 plus tax per child

All of the childcare clubs accept reservations (some six months in advance!) with a credit card guarantee and are highly recommended.

The Clubs and phone numbers are:

Animal Kingdom Lodge - Simba's Clubhouse, Ages: 3-12, 407-938-4785, or 407-WDW-DINE

Polynesian Resort - Lilos Playhouse, Ages: 3-12, 407-824-1639, or 407-WDW-DINE

Yacht and Beach Club Resorts - Sandcastle Club, Ages: 3-12, 407-934-3750, or 407-WDW-DINE

Dolphin and Swan - Camp Dolphin, Ages: 4-12, 407-934-4241

Contemporary Resort - Pixar Play Zone, Ages: 4-12, 407-934-KIDS, or 407-WDW-DINE

Disney Room Pricing

All Disney prices listed under each individual Resort in this chapter are 2018 prices with tax added and rounded to the nearest dollar (prices are subject to change by Disney).

Prices vary greatly based upon retort type and price season. Standard Value Resort rooms range in price from $110 per night on weeknights at the All-Stars during Value Season to $260 per night at Art of Animation over Christmas. Standard rooms at the Deluxe Resorts start at $366 per night at the Wilderness Lodge for weeknights in the Value Season up to $934 per night for a Standard View at the Grand Floridian over

Christmas. If you'd like a larger room, better locations, or better views it will cost you even more.

The prices listed here are before any discounts, military or otherwise. The highest prices are for Christmas week and the lowest prices are weekdays in January and February following Christmas pricing, the rest of the year varies somewhere in-between.

There are numerous Disney price seasons through the year. **The more popular a time period is, the more expensive it is!** To get a feel for the various price seasons here are some of them: New Years, Value, Marathon, Martin Luther, Peak, President's Day, Regular, Easter, Summer, Value II, Fall, Columbus Day, Thanksgiving, Holiday. Value is the cheapest rate followed by Value II and Holiday is the most expensive, some rates are used at several times of the year, some only one weekend. Pretty complex isn't it?

During most weeks of the year Friday and Saturday nights and often Thursday and Sunday are more expensive than the rest of the week.

Starting in 2018 Disney World has introduced a new third price period for most weeks, that being Thursday and Sunday. This price period falls between Monday through Wednesday and Friday/Saturday rates. Only a couple of weeks have the old Sunday through Thursday and Friday/Saturday pricing.

Also, the start and end dates of the various price periods are different depending on which resort category you are talking about.

Below to illustrate how Disney's prices fluctuate are the daily 2018 prices for a standard view room at a typical Value Resort, the All-Star Movies. The numerous little spikes are weekend (Thurs/Sun & Fri/Sat) rates.

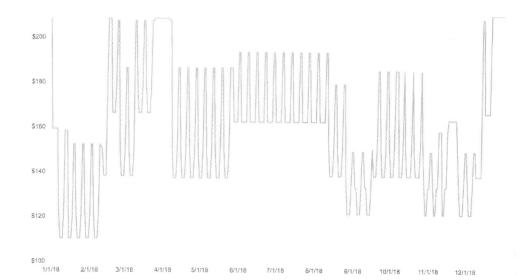

Using the Disney Armed Forces Salute will reduce these Value rates by up to 30%.

Disney Resort Dining

You will find various dining options at the Walt Disney World Resorts, everything from food courts to fine dining. The level of your resort will determine what options are available to you. At the Value Resorts you'll find food courts, the Moderates have food courts but also offer table service locations (except Port Orleans French Quarter), while the Deluxe Resorts offer both types often with multiple locations and fine dining as well.

All Disney resorts have Pizza Delivery. There are plusses to this, one for you and one for Disney. The big plus for you is security. Disney asks that you use their Pizza Delivery, this keeps a horde of external individuals from roaming the hotels at night. Your pizza will also be hotter and probably will taste better! For Disney the plus is additional income.

In this chapter look for these keys to the rough cost of restaurants and meals they offer:

- $ = Less than $15 per adult
- $$ = $15 - $30 per adult
- $$$ = $30 - $60 per adult
- $$$$ = $60 plus
- B = Breakfast
- L = Lunch
- D = Dinner
- S = Snack

General Information

Recently Disney made a surprise announcement that they would begin charging Walt Disney World Resort Guests for the privilege of parking their car while staying at their WDW Resort. This came as a shock to the WDW fan community, as parking at the Resorts had been free for the last 47 years (since 1971).

Disney says that, "This change is to bring their Florida hotels more in line with industry standards. Disney Springs Resort Area Hotels, the Swan & Dolphin, Universal Orlando on-property hotels, and most Orange County Convention Center area-hotels charge for overnight parking."

Parking charges are for reservations made after 21 March 2018, for any date of stay. If you made your reservation before 21 March, no parking fee.

Disney World Resort Parking Rates:

Standard Overnight Parking charges per Resort Category:

- Disney Value Resorts: $13 per night
- Disney Moderate Resorts: $19 per night
- Disney Deluxe and Deluxe Villa Resorts: $24 per night

Exceptions - DVC Members will not be charged for standard overnight self-parking when staying at a DVC Deluxe Villa, regardless of whether they use vacation points or another form of payment. Members also will not be charged to park when using vacation points to stay at a Walt Disney World Resort hotel.

Check in time at the Disney resorts is either 3 or 4 pm depending on resort and check out is 11 am. You may check in online ahead of time using your My Disney Experience account to speed up the check in process. Head to the Online Check In line upon your arrival for a shorter wait.

You may check in at your resort at any time during the day, but if you arrive early your room may not be ready. In this case the bellhops will store your luggage and deliver it to your room later, after you call for it. The front desk will get your cell phone number and you'll receive an automated text when your room is ready.

There is Free Wi-Fi throughout Disney World's Resorts and Parks.

Wheelchair accessible rooms are available

Disney resorts offer airline check in for domestic flights on some airlines right at your hotel.

All rooms have a mini fridge, flat panel TV, small in room safe, iron, and ironing board. Moderates and Deluxes have a coffee maker.

Disney Resorts have quite extensive recreation options such as, outdoor movies, equipment rental (varies: fishing poles, bikes, boats, etc.), campfires (with S'mores), organized pool activities for the kids, trivia, and Resort tours to name a few. The options are limited at the Value Resorts and more plentiful at the more expensive Moderate and Deluxe Resorts.

Disney resorts sell Refillable Mugs, which you can use for coffee, tea, hot chocolate, and fountain drinks, juice, and milk. You can purchase these plastic mugs for your length of stay. **They can only be used at the WDW resorts, not in the theme parks.**

All Disney resorts have a merchandise location where you can purchase WDW souvenirs, food, beverages, wine, beer, liquor, OTC medicines, and baby necessities.

Family Pets – At press time Disney World has announced a trial pet-friendly program allowing dogs in some of their Resorts. Resorts participating are: The Cabins at Fort Wilderness, Disney's Art of Animation Resort, Disney's Port Orleans Riverside Resort, and Disney's Yacht Club Resort. Note, The Campsites at Disney's Fort Wilderness Resort have allowed dogs for a long time. Certain floors or sections of a hotel will be designated as dog-friendly, while the majority of areas will remain canine-free to accommodate guests with allergies or other concerns.

- Notify Disney of your dog(s) when making your reservation
- Pet-friendly rooms in the four pilot resorts will cost an additional $50 ($75 at the Yacht Club) per night. The pet fee is not added to your room bill until check in as Disney leaves you the option to make other arrangements prior to arrival if desired.
- Two dogs maximum per room
- Guests are responsible for their dog's behavior and waste disposal
- Dogs must be well behaved and not allowed on furniture in common areas
- Dogs should remain silent if left unattended in the room. You will be called to address any noises
- Dogs should not be left unattended in the room for more that 7 hours
- A special sigh must be hung on your room door to advise staff that dogs are present
- Housekeeping is only available when you are present
- Leashes required in public areas
- Dogs are allowed on Disney's Magical Express and Minnie Vans in carriers only
- Vaccination records must be provided upon request

For more information about the new dog-friendly trial program, including other restrictions and policies, guests may contact 407-W-DISNEY.

The Resorts

And now what you've been waiting for, here are the Disney resorts listed by category.

Value Resorts

There are five different Value Resorts on Walt Disney World Property. These are the lowest priced of Disney's resorts and understandably have the lowest level of amenities.

The Disney Value Resorts are: All-Star Movies, All-Star Music, All-Star Sports, Pop Century, and the Art of Animation Resorts.

The Value Resorts are each decorated in a big way based on the theme they represent, with large exterior icons decorating the buildings, themed pools, and bright color schemes throughout.

The Value rooms have a small price (by Disney standards) and are small in size too. Standard size rooms offer 2 double beds, which sleep four (a crib may be requested for children under 3), a small table and two chairs, dresser, TV, and small fridge. The bathroom proper is separated from the single sink vanity area. Set a few suitcases out and it gets "very cozy" in these rooms.

Family Suites are available at the All-Star Music and Art of Animation for a higher rate. These suites offer twice the room and sleep six, plus a crib.

Being entry level resorts, they have entry level amenities such as: Quick Service food courts, limited pizza delivery, an arcade, playground, heated pools, pool bar, scheduled (hourly) luggage service, in room safe, iron and board, and coffee makers (only in suites). These resorts all have exterior hallway room entry doors.

These resorts are very large, from 1600 to about 3000 rooms each. Due to the lower price younger families, children's athletic teams participating in competitions at Disney's ESPN Wide World of Sports Complex, and South American vacationers, mostly frequent them. They can at times be hectic and noisy in general, **especially the food courts in the morning!**

The Values each have one Disney Transportation bus stop located near the lobby. *Note that at some of the rooms furthest to the north from the All-Star Resort's lobby (by the Mighty Ducks pool), the closest bus stop is at the lobby for the All-Star Music Resort next door.*

During slower times of the year all three All Stars share a bus to most destinations, the order of pickup being: Music, Sports, and then Movies. During busier times additional buses will be used and some or all of the Resorts will have their own route.

Preferred rooms at the Values are in buildings that are closer to the lobby.

Value Resort room rates (except for Little Mermaid rooms) are eligible for up to a 30% Disney Armed Forces Salute discount based upon availability and Blockout Dates.

At all Values extra adults are an additional $10 per night, kids under 18 are free.

Disney's All-Star Movies Resort

Description

The theme of the All-Star Movies is, as you'd expect, Disney Movies!

Each section of the resort has its own theme: Toy Story, 101 Dalmatians, Fantasia, The Mighty Ducks, and Herbie the Love Bug. Large 25-40 foot tall icons (statues) decorate the exterior of each building. You'll see Buzz Lightyear, Woody, a broom from Fantasia, and Pongo to name a few.

Dining

The only dining location at the All-Star Movies is the World Premiere Food Court (BLD $) - Features American cuisine at various stations: Soup/Salad, Pizza, Entrees, and Bakery. You then pay at a central location.

Menus change for all three meals. Breakfast items are standard (eggs, meats, Mickey waffles), lunch features sandwiches and burgers, while for dinner you can have items like pot roast, lasagna, baked chicken, or shrimp creole.

Silver Screen Spirits is the Pool Bar at Movies.

All Star Pizza Delivery – Have pizza and salads delivered to your room.

Features

Two pools – Fantasia and Duck Pond

Fantasia - Sorcerer Mickey sprays water at this expansive pool inspired by the classic Disney film.

Duck Pond Pool - The Duck Pond Pool is a hockey rink-styled pool based on The *Mighty* Ducks film series.

Kiddy Pool/Water Play Area - For the little ones, a smaller Kiddy pool and water play area are located near the Fantasia Pool.

Movies Under the Stars - Watch complimentary screenings of Disney films on select nights by the Fantasia Pool.

Arcade - Reel Fun Arcade, play video and pinball games at this arcade in the Cinema Hall building, near the food court.

Playground - Kids can climb, slide and play at this area found between the Fantasia and Toy Story sections.

Guest Laundry - 24-hour self-service laundry rooms are available near Duck Pond Pool and Fantasia Pool.

Jogging Trail – 1 mile long around the resort.

Location

An Animal Kingdom Area Resort

Transportation

Bus transportation is available to all Disney World guest areas

Price

Standard Room: $110 to $210

Preferred Room: $127 to $233 (Closer to the lobby)

Room Notes

Standard Room sleeps up to 4 with 2 Double Beds.

Preferred Room sleeps up to 4 with 2 Double Beds. Preferred room locations at All-Star Movies are the Fantasia, Toy Story and 101 Dalmatians buildings.

Disney's All-Star Music

Description

The theme of the All-Star Music is of various types of music!

Each individual building has its own theme: Calypso, Jazz, Rock, Country, and Broadway. Large 25-40 foot tall icons (statues) decorate the exterior of each building. You'll see giant cowboy boots, jukeboxes, and electric guitars to name a few.

The All-Star Music along with the Art of Animation are the two Value Resorts that have family Suites. Prices for the suites are about $75-$115 less per night here at the All-Star Music!

Dining

The only dining location at the All-Star Music is the Intermission Food Court (BLD $) Quick Service – Features American cuisine at various stations: Soup/Salad, Pizza, Entrees, and Bakery. You then pay at a central location.

Menus change for all three meals. Breakfast items are standard (eggs, meats, Mickey waffles), lunch features sandwiches and burgers, while for dinner you can have items like London broil, lasagna, baked chicken, or pepper steak.

Singing Spirits is the Pool Bar at Music.

All Star Pizza Delivery – Have pizza and salads delivered to your room.

Features

Two pools – Calypso and Piano

Calypso Pool - This guitar shaped, heated pool is home to a fountain with the Three Caballeros—Donald Duck, José Carioca and Panchito—playfully spraying water at swimmers.

Piano Pool - A grand piano-shaped watering hole featuring a deck of black and white keys is also available for families looking to play it cool throughout the day.

Kiddy Pool - For the little ones, a Kiddy pool is located near the Calypso Pool.

Arcade - Note'able Games Arcade, fine-tune your gaming skills at this arcade in the Melody Hall building, adjacent to the food court.

Playground - Little musical prodigies can swing and slide at the play area located near the Jazz Inn section.

Guest Laundry - 24-hour self-service laundry rooms are available near Piano Pool and Calypso Pool.

Jogging Trail – 1 mile long around the resort.

Location

An Animal Kingdom Area Resort

Transportation

Bus transportation is available to all Disney World guest areas

Price

Standard Room: $110 to $210

Preferred Room: $127 to $233 (Closer to the lobby)

Family Suite: $269 - $484

Room Notes

Standard Room sleeps up to 4 with 2 Double Beds.

Preferred Room sleeps up to 4 with 2 Double Beds. Preferred room locations at All-Star Music are the Calypso buildings.

Family Suite: Sleeps up to 6 with 1 Queen Bed and 1 Twin-Size Sleeper Chair and 1 Double-Size Sleeper Sofa and 1 Twin-Size Sleeper Ottoman.

Disney's All-Star Sports Resort

Description

The theme of the All-Star Sports is of course various Sports!

Each individual building has its own theme: Football, Baseball, Basketball, Tennis, and Surfing. Large 25-40 foot tall icons (statues) decorate the exterior of each building. You'll see giant tennis racquets, surfboards, and football helmets to name a few.

Dining

The only dining location at the All-Star Sports is the End Zone Food Court (BLD $) Quick Service – Features American cuisine at various stations: Soup/Salad, Pizza, Entrees, and Bakery. You then pay at a central location.

Menus change for all three meals. Breakfast items are standard (eggs, meats, Mickey waffles), lunch features sandwiches and burgers, while for dinner you can have items like roast turkey, lasagna, baked chicken, or penne Alfredo.

Grandstand Spirits is the Pool Bar at Sports.

All Star Pizza Delivery – Have pizza and salad s delivered to your room.

Features

Two pools – Surfing and Baseball themed.

Surfboard Bay - Giant-sized surfboards line one sprawling pool area perfect for catching some rays or taking a dip.

Grand Slam - Grand Slam Pool is shaped like a baseball diamond, and it features a Goofy fountain that squirts water at swimmers.

Kiddy Pool - For little ones, a Kiddy pool is located behind Stadium Hall adjacent to Surfboard Bay Pool.

Movies Under the Stars - After the game is won and the day is done, take in a Disney movie outdoors at Surfboard Bay Pool.

Arcade - Game Point Arcade, compete in a variety of video and pinball games at this arcade in Stadium Hall, by the food court.

Playground - Little athletes can climb and slide at the playground located near the Touchdown! hotel area.

Guest Laundry - 24-hour self-service laundry rooms are available near Grand Slam Pool and Surfboard Bay.

Jogging Trail – 1 mile long around the resort.

Location

An Animal Kingdom Area Resort

Transportation

Bus transportation to all Disney World guest areas

Price

Standard Room: $110 to $210

Preferred Room: $127 to $233 (Closer to the lobby)

Room Notes

Standard Room sleeps up to 4 with 2 Double Beds.

Preferred Room sleeps up to 4 with 2 Double Beds. Preferred room locations at All-Star Sports are Surfs Up buildings 1 & 6.

Disney's Pop Century Resort

Description

The theme at the Pop Century Resort is the fads of the 1950s through the 1990s!

Each individual building has its own theme which is from a different decade: 50s, 60s, 70s, 80s, and 90s. Large 25-40 foot tall icons (statues) decorate the exterior of each building. You'll see giant yo-yos, Play-Doh®, Rubik's Cube®, and rollerblades to name a few.

Note: there was originally going to be a second section of Pop Century featuring the 00s through the 40s, but the downturn in the travel industry after 9/11 caused its construction, which had just started, to cease for many years. The project was later restarted as the new Art of Animation Resort. The opening of Pop Century was also delayed for years even though it had been finished.

Dining

The only dining location at Pop Century is the Everything Pop Food Court - BLD $ - Quick Service – Features American cuisine at various stations: Soup/Salad, Flatbreads, Entrees, and Bakery. You then pay at a central location.

Menus change for all three meals. Breakfast items are standard (eggs, meats, Mickey waffles), lunch features sandwiches and burgers, while for dinner you can have items like pot roast, nachos, rotisserie chicken, or shrimp and cheesy grits.

Petals is the Pool Bar at Pop Century.

Pop Art Pizza Delivery – Have pizza and salads delivered to your room.

Features

Three Pools – Hippy Dippy, Computer, and Bowling

Hippy Dippy Pool – Is a pool with Water Jets. Immerse yourself in the spirit of the 1960's at the sprawling Hippy Dippy Pool, which features flower-shaped water jets.

Two more pools, the smaller 1950's Bowling Pool and the 1990's Computer Pool, are also on hand for Guests looking to take the pop-culture plunge.

Kiddy Pool - For the little ones, a Kiddy pool is located behind Classic Hall, just behind the Hippy Dippy Pool.

Movies Under the Stars - Disney movies are screened on select nights at the Hippy Dippy Pool.

Arcade – At the Fast Forward Arcade play video games old and new, in the Classic Hall building, adjacent to the food court.

Playground - Children can climb, slide and play at the fun play area located in the '60s section.

Guest Laundry - 24-hour self-service laundry rooms are available near Bowling Pool, Computer Pool and Hippy Dippy Pool.

Jogging Trail – 1 mile long around the resort.

Location

An ESPN Wide World of Sports Area Resort

Transportation

Bus transportation is available to all Disney World guest areas

Pop Century is one of the resorts that will have Disney Skyliner gondola system added in the future for transportation to Epcot and Disney Hollywood Studios. Construction has started with no announced completion date announced, but it could be in late 2018. **Expect rates at this resort to be increased when service starts!**

Note - The Pop Century Resort is located right next door to the Art of Animation Resort, take the short walk to see the neat exterior decorations at AoA or try the Landscape of Flavors Food Court, which is different than Pop's food court.

Price

Standard Room: $126 to $238

Standard Pool View: $132 - $250

Preferred Room: $140 to $258

Preferred Room Pool View: $150 - $263

Room Notes

Standard room sleeps up to 4 with 2 double beds or 1 king bed.

Standard pool view sleeps up to 4 with 2 double beds or 1 king bed.

Preferred room sleeps up to 4 with 2 double beds or 1 king bed.

Preferred pool view sleeps up to 4 with 2 double beds or 1 king bed.

Preferred rooms at Pop Century are located in selected sections of the 1950s, 1960s and 1970s buildings.

Disney's Art of Animation Resort

Description

Art of Animation is Disney World's newest Value resort. The theme of the resort is straight out of some of Disney's most famous animated movies: *Cars, The Lion King, Finding Nemo,* and *The Little Mermaid*. Each movie has its own section with big icons from the movies and buildings painted to match.

Art of Animation offers four person rooms and family suites.

The four person rooms are located in the *Little Mermaid* section.

The family suites will comfortably accommodate up to 6 Guests. Suites are located in the Nemo, Cars and Lion King sections. The suites include:

2 separate bathrooms

A master bedroom with Queen-size bed

A main living space with a pullout double size sleeper sofa. A work/dining table that includes a Murphy bed that can sleep 1 or 2.

Mini-kitchen with microwave, coffee maker, sink, and small refrigerator

The Art of Animation along with the All-Star Music are the two Value Resorts that have family Suites. Prices for the suites are about $75 – $115 more per night here than at the All-Star Music.

Dining

Landscape of Flavors - BLD $ - Quick Service – This is the food court at the Art of Animation. Just like all the other Value food courts, there are several stations offering various items, you'll gather what you'd like and pay in one central location. This is the best of the Value food courts quality and taste wise. Representative menu selections are Tandoori Boneless Chicken Thigh, Buffalo-Style Turkey Sandwich, Meatball Sandwich, Create Your Own Pasta, and Pizzas.

Pop Art Pizza Delivery

The Drop Off Pool Bar

Features

Three Pools – the Big Blue Pool, Cozy Cone, and Flippin' Fins

The Big Blue Pool - Take the plunge in the largest resort pool in Walt Disney World Resort. Inspired by the Disney Pixar movie *Finding Nemo*, the pool features state-of-the-art underwater speakers—a first for Disney Resort hotels.

Cozy Cone Pool – Is inspired by the Cozy Cone Motel in the Disney Pixar film Cars.

Flippin' Fins Pool - features the "Under the Sea Orchestra" conducted by Sebastian from The Little Mermaid.

Kiddy Pool and Water Play Area - An interactive water play area for little ones is located near the Finding Nemo Pool.

Movies Under the Stars - Watch some of your favorite Disney films outside in the fresh evening air at the Big Blue Pool Deck.

Arcade - Pixel Play Arcade, catch up on video games both classic and new at this arcade located in the Animation Hall building.

Playground - Children can climb and slide at Righteous Reef playground, located in the Finding Nemo courtyard.

Guest Laundry - 24-hour self-service laundry rooms are available near The Big Blue Pool, Flippin' Fins Pool and Cozy Cone Pool.

Jogging Trail – 1.38 mile long around the resort.

Location

An ESPN Wide World of Sports Area Resort

Transportation

Bus transportation is available to all Disney World guest areas

Art of Animation is one of the resorts that will have Disney Skyliner gondola system added in the future for transportation to Epcot and Disney Hollywood Studios. Construction has started with no announced completion date announced, but it could be in late 2018. **Expect rates at this resort to be increased when service starts!**

Price

Little Mermaid Standard Room: $148 to $260

Lion King, Cars, or Finding Nemo Family Suite: $354 to $596

Room Notes

The Little Mermaid standard room sleeps up to 4 with 2 double beds or 1 king bed.

Family suites sleep up to 6 with 1 queen bed and 1 double-size table fold out bed and 1 double-size sleeper sofa.

Value Resort Wrap Up

These Value Resorts are great for those on a budget, younger families, solo travelers, or those who will not be spending very much time in their room or at the resort. I often stay in these when I am on solo research trips.

You'll find prices at the Disney Values using the Disney Armed Forces Salute comparable to Shades of Green's Category 2 and 3 during the more expensive times of Disney's price year. During the rest of the year the Values are well below Shades of Green Cat. 2 & 3 and equivalent to the Category 1 rate.

Moderate Resorts

There are five different Moderate Resorts on Walt Disney World Property. These resorts come in at a price point between the Values and the Deluxes.

The Disney Moderate Resorts are: the Caribbean Beach, Coronado Springs, Port Orleans Riverside, Port Orleans French Quarter, and the Cabins at Fort Wilderness Resorts.

The Moderate Resorts are each decorated in various facets of an overall resort theme. For example, the Port Orleans Riverside Resort has two different sections, Magnolia Bend and Alligator Bayou. Each is themed differently both inside and out. Magnolia Bend has large three story buildings, which look like New Orleans style mansions with elegant interiors, while Alligator Bayou has a more rustic feel with smaller tin roofed, wood sided, two story buildings with simulated roughhewn interiors.

The Moderates fill the needed middle of the road in both price and amenities between the Value and Deluxe resorts. Standard size rooms (Except Pirate Rooms at the Caribbean Beach Resort) offer two queen beds that sleep four (a crib may be requested for children under three). Some rooms in Port Orleans Riverside and the Caribbean Beach sleep five with a fold down single Murphy bed. The Moderates all have exterior room entry doors. The Wilderness Cabins sleep six with one double, one bunk, and one double Murphy bed.

The Pirate Rooms at the Caribbean Beach Resort have double (full) sized beds.

Disney Moderate rooms are somewhat larger that the Value rooms (on average 315 square feet compared to 260). They offer a small table and two chairs, dresser, TV, and small fridge. The bathroom proper is separated from the double sink vanity area, while the vanity area can be separated from the room with a curtain or door. Even with your suitcases out you'll still have room to move around.

These are mid-level resorts and as you expect have mid-level amenities such as: Table Service dining (except French Quarter), Quick Service food court, pizza delivery, room service at Coronado, an arcade, playground, heated pools, hot tub, a gym at Coronado, Indoor and pool bars, luggage service, in room safe, iron and board, and coffee makers.

These resorts except for French Quarter are very large and spread out, they have from 1000 to over 2100 rooms each. The Moderates all have a lake or river where you can rent various watercraft and even fish. The food courts, which are the primary breakfast dining locations, can be hectic in the morning!

All the Moderates except French Quarter have numerous Disney Transportation bus stops located through the resort so you won't have to walk too far. French Quarter, which is the smallest moderate, has one bus stop near the lobby.

In general the preferred rooms at the various Moderates are either in buildings that are closer to the lobby or specially decorated rooms. For example royal rooms at Riverside are decorated in splendor for Tiana's (from the *Princess and the Frog*) guests; other princesses are featured to a lesser extent. Pirate rooms at the Caribbean Beach are decorated in pirate fashion.

The Moderate room rates are eligible for up to a 35% Disney Armed Forces Salute discount based upon availability and Blockout Dates.

Extra adults are an additional $15 per night, kids under 18 are free.

Disney's Caribbean Beach Resort

Description

Huge changes are underway at the Caribbean Resort!

During 2017 through 2019 lots of construction projects are ongoing at the Caribbean Beach.

- *Old Port Royale and Centertown renovation*
- *Disney Skyliner gondola station construction*
- *Construction of Disney's Riviera Resort which won't open until Fall 2019*
- *Expected demolition of the Custom's House as part of the Riviera construction*

Old Port Royale is the "main Building" of the resort where all non-Front Desk functions take place (restaurants, shops, etc.). It has been totally closed for a total renovation. Temporary (think trailers and tents) locations have bee set up to take its place during this renovation.

See Transportation further down in this section and our Transportation chapter for more on Disney's Skyliner. This construction is taking place between the Aruba and old Barbados sections of the Caribbean Beach.

Disney's Riviera Resort is to be the newest Disney Vacation Club Resort. The Barbados section of the Caribbean Beach was demolished and will be the location of the Riviera.

Many experts assume the Custom's House will be done away with as it will then be closer to the Riviera than the remaining parts of the Caribbean. It's assumed that check in and out will move to the newly renovated Old Port Royale.

Until the majority of Old Port Royale construction is complete (late 2018 to 2019) it might be best to avoid the Caribbean Beach.

Also Expect rates to rise here once the Skyliner construction is completed!

The Caribbean Beach Resort is the oldest Moderate and is themed on the Caribbean Islands. The resort is divided into six sections, each with a different theme, the sections are: Aruba, Jamaica, Barbados (now gone), Martinique, and Trinidad North and South. Each section has its own quiet pool if you don't feel like making the trek to the main pool.

The Caribbean offers Pirate Rooms, your little swashbuckler will love the skull and cross bones and pirate ship décor.

Rooms at the Caribbean are priced at the lowest end of the Moderate scale that is until the Disney Skyliner gondola system begins service; expect it to then be the most expensive Moderate.

Dining

Notice from WDW: Beginning in May 2017, the following venues will be unavailable due to refurbishment: Old Port Royale Food Court, Shutters at Old Port Royale, Banana Cabana Pool Bar and Calypso Trading Post.

During this time, there will be a variety of dining options available to you for breakfast, lunch and dinner. Centertown, a dining location, will serve an all you care to enjoy buffet for breakfast and dinner. A selection of grab and go meals will be conveniently available for purchase in 3 new island markets located in the Aruba, Jamaica and Martinique regions of the Resort. Additional à la carte offerings will be available at mobile food vending locations. Our in room dining will remain available. Disney dining plans will be accepted. We will make every effort to assist you with your dietary needs.

Pizza Delivery

Banana Cabana Pool Bar

Features

Six Pools

Main Pool with Water Slide and Hot Tub – At the Fuentes del Morro Pool you can hold the fort at this Old Spanish citadel with a zero-entry pool, 2 slides and water cannons. Climb a spiral staircase to the top of a turret for an 82-foot trip down the larger slide, which penetrates the fortress wall! Enjoy two relaxing spas with the capacity for 12.

Five Quiet Pools - One in each village, offer escape for the less boisterous buccaneers of your crew.

Kids Water Play Area - Kids less than 48 inches tall will love being marooned at the nearby shipwreck play area, where a barrel periodically dumps a deluge and 3 small slides delight little scallywags.

Movies Under the Stars - Watch some of your favorite Disney films outside in the fresh evening air at Caribbean Cay Island.

Caribbean Beach Campfire Activities - Gather 'round as the sun goes down for old-fashioned family fun as you roast marshmallows by a crackling fire.

Pirate Adventure Cruise - Scallywags 4 to 12 years of age can set sail on a pirate adventure, following clues to discover hidden treasure.

Fishing - Experience catch-and-release fishing at its finest with a guided excursion leaving from the Marina

Bike and Surry Bike Rentals - Embark on a leisurely bicycle outing along the island promenade.

Arcade - Goombay Games Arcade, for video games, air hockey and more, visit this arcade located in the Old Port Royale complex.

Four Playgrounds – There is a playground at Caribbean Cay and there are small playgrounds located on the village beaches of Barbados, Jamaica and Trinidad South.

Guest Laundry - 24-hour self-service laundry rooms are located in each of the 6 villages.

Jogging Trail - 0.6-mile course with views of Barefoot Bay.

Lakeside Beaches are available for you to enjoy at each village. Grab a hammock and kick back.

Location

An Epcot Area Resort

Transportation

Bus transportation is available to all Disney World guest areas

The Caribbean Beach is one of the resorts that will have Disney Skyliner gondola system added in the future for transportation to Epcot and Disney Hollywood Studios. Construction has started with no announced completion date announced, but it could be in late 2018. **Expect rates at this resort to be increased when service starts!**

Price

Standard View: $187 - $314

Water or Pool View: $215 - $338

King Bed: $220 - $343

Preferred Room: $259 - $366

Pirate room: $259 - $359

Pirate Room Water View: $264 - $400

Room notes

Standard view sleeps up to 4 with 2 queen beds.

Water or pool view sleeps up to 4 with 2 queen beds.

King bed sleeps up to 2 with 1 king bed.

Preferred room sleeps up to 4 with 2 double beds. Preferred location at Caribbean Beach resort applies to Martinique and Trinidad North buildings.

Pirate standard view sleeps up to 4 with 2 double beds.

Pirate water view sleeps up to 4 with 2 double beds.

Disney's Coronado Springs Resort

Description

The Coronado Springs Resort is the newest Moderate and is the only one in this category which has convention facilities. Due to this the clientele tends to be weighted more towards the adult side of the age spectrum and the atmosphere a little more laid back.

Business class rooms with a club lounge and other upgrades are offered at the Coronado.

The theme at the Coronado is Southwestern, with three different themed groups of buildings. Casitas is modeled after a Southwestern urban area, Rancheros, which are themed on Southwest cattle ranches, and Cabanas, which represent Mexican coastal villages.

In 2017 Disney World began construction of a new 15-story tower adjacent to the resort's main building that will add 500 rooms, including suites and concierge-level services. Additionally, the resort will be transforming its landscape with floating gardens and an island that connects the resort through a series of bridges as well. The new tower will also feature rooftop dining with panoramic views of nighttime fireworks from Epcot and Disney's Hollywood Studios. **Expect this section of Coronado Springs to be priced at the Deluxe level when it opens.** Construction of the tower should continue through 2019.

Dining

Maya Grille – D $$ - Table Service – Southwestern cuisine is featured here, with offerings like San Antonio Fajitas Skillet, Chicken Enchiladas, Shrimp Tacos, and a Vegetarian Skillet.

Pepper Market Food Court – BLD $ - Quick Service – Pepper Market is an oddity on Disney property, while it is a quick service restaurant food wise, the wait staff will bring and refill your beverages. Sandwiches, burgers, nachos, and flatbread pizzas are offered.

Las Ventanas – BLD $$ - Table Service – Enjoy a classic American breakfast: from "ancient grain" whole wheat pancakes to steak and eggs. Lunch offers healthy fare like mahi mahi sandwiches and hearty favorites such as our signature crab cakes. For dinner choose from our specialties, including seared pork loin medallions and hand-cut ribeye steak.

Café Rix – BLD $ - Quick Service - Grab and Go items. Sandwiches, salads, fruit.

Pizza Delivery

Rix Lounge is the main bar off the lobby

Siestas Cantina Pool Bar and Laguna Bar are the outdoor bars

Features

Four Pools

Main Pool with Water Slide and Hot Tub - Worship the sun at an awesome aquatic area built around a 50-foot replica of a Mayan pyramid. Watch water stream down the steps of the massive stone structure into the Lost City of Cibola pool or plunge headlong into it on the spitting Jaguar Slide. This complex, known as the Dig Site Pool, is also home to the largest outdoor hot tub at Walt Disney World Resort, with room for 22 people!

Three Quiet Pools - One located at each settlement—the Casitas, Ranchos and Cabanas—provide Mayan civilization.

Playground with "Dig Site" - Kids can climb, slide and play on an archaeologically themed playground near the Dig Site complex.

Movies Under the Stars - Watch some of your favorite Disney films outside in the fresh evening air near the Lost City of Cibola pool.

Coronado Springs Campfire Activities - Gather 'round as the sun goes down for old-fashioned family fun as you roast marshmallows by a crackling fire.

Arcade - Iguana Arcade for video games, air hockey, pinball and more, visit this arcade beside the Dig Site pool complex.

Jogging Trail – 0.9 miles along the scenic trail that loops around 22-acre Lago Dorado.

Guest Laundry - A 24-hour self-service laundry room is adjacent to each of the 3 quiet village pools.

Fitness Center – Revitalize your spirits at La Vida Health Club—a full-service facility featuring exercise equipment, massages and more.

Business Center - Fax, print, ship and more at the Business Center inside Disney's Coronado Springs Resort Convention Center. The Business Center also provides a full range of office services and supplies.

Location

An Animal Kingdom Area Resort

Transportation

Bus transportation is available to all Disney World guest areas

Price

Standard View: $201 - $315

Water View: $242 - $348

King Bed: $276 - $362

Preferred Room: $276 - $362

Preferred Room King: $281 - $368

Water View King: $289 - $402

All Suite Types (sleep 4-6): $483 - $778

Room Notes

Standard view sleeps up to 4 with 2 queen beds.

Water view sleeps up to 4 with 2 queen beds.

King bed sleeps up to 2 with 1 king bed.

Preferred room sleeps up to 4 with 2 queen beds.

Preferred room king sleeps up to 2 with 1 king bed.

Water view king sleeps up to 2 with 1 king bed.

Junior suite sleeps up to 6 with 2 queen beds and 1 queen-size sleeper sofa.

Junior suite king sleeps up to 4 with 1 king bed and 1 queen-size sleeper sofa.

Disney's Port Orleans Riverside Resort

Description

Riverside is themed on the Mississippi River communities in Antebellum Louisiana. It is divided into two sections that display the opposite ends of the spectrum. There is Magnolia Bend, where the buildings look like Southern Plantation Mansions and then there is Alligator Bayou, which, has tin roofed wood plank, sided buildings.

Dining

Boatwright's Dining Hall – D $$ - Table Service – Offers up food with a Cajun Flare. Offerings include: Andouille-Crusted Catfish or Jambalaya with Chicken and Andouille Sausage, Crescent City Gumbo, and N'awlins Barbecued Shrimp.

Riverside Mill Food Court - BLD $ - Quick Service – A typical WDW Resort food court with different stations serving things like Freshly Carved Meats (Beef, Turkey, Ham), Baked Ziti, Sandwiches, Soups, and Pizza.

Pizza Delivery

The Rivers Roost Lounge is the indoor bar off the lobby. Enjoy entertainment with Ye Haa Bob most nights of the week.

Muddy Rivers is the outdoor pool bar

Features

Six Pools

Main Pool with Water Slide and Hot Tub - Cross the bridge to a 3.5-acre hideaway with an old-fashioned swimmin' hole and a sawmill slide. Inspired by the story of Tom Sawyer, Ol' Man Island even features a catch-and-release fishing hole and stories told around an evening campfire. The nearby Muddy Rivers pool bar and a hot tub provide fun for grown folks.

Five Quiet Pools - 3 in Alligator Bayou and 2 in Magnolia Bend—are also available throughout the Resort.

Movies Under the Stars - Watch some of your favorite Disney films outside in the fresh evening air in the courtyard at Oak Manor.

Horse-Drawn Carriage Rides - Relax on a horse-drawn carriage ride as you travel along the scenic banks of the Sassagoula River.

Pirate Adventure Cruise - Scallywags 4 to 12 years of age can set sail on a pirate adventure, following clues to discover hidden treasure.

Bike and Surry Bike Rentals - Embark on a leisurely bicycle outing along the Resort's scenic waterfront promenade.

Fishing - Catch and release fish with an old-fashioned cane pole at the rustic wooded alcove on Ol' Man Island.

Arcade - Medicine Show Arcade show off your gaming skills at this video arcade located in the Colonel's Cotton Mill building.

Playground - Kids can climb, slide and play at this themed area near the main pool at 3.5-acre Ol' Man Island.

Jogging Trail - 1-mile course along the lushly landscaped banks of the Sassagoula River.

Guest Laundry - 24-hour self-service laundry rooms are adjacent to each of the 5 quiet pools dotted around the Resort hotel.

Location

A Disney Springs Area Resort

Transportation

Bus transportation is available to all Disney World guest areas. Boat transportation is available to Port Orleans French Quarter, Disney's Old Key West DVC Resort, Disney's Saratoga Springs DVC Resort, and Disney Springs.

Price

Standard View: $224 - $340

Garden View: $236 - $345

Pool View: $242 - $351

King Bed: $276 - $367

Preferred Room: $276 - $376

River View: $276 - $378

Royal Room Preferred View: $278 - $390

Royal Room River View: $284 - $410

Room Notes

Standard view sleeps up to 5 with 2 queen beds and 1 bunk-size pull down bed or 2 queen beds.

Garden view sleeps up to 5 with 2 queen beds and 1 bunk-size pull down bed or 2 queen beds.

Pool view sleeps up to 5 with 2 queen beds and 1 bunk-size pull down bed or 2 queen beds.

King bed sleeps up to 3 with 1 king bed or 1 king bed and 1 bunk-size pull down bed.

Preferred room sleeps up to 5 with 2 queen beds and 1 bunk-size pull down bed.

River view sleeps up to 5 with 2 queen beds and 1 bunk-size pull down bed or 2 queen beds.

Royal guest room preferred view sleeps up to 4 with 2 queen beds.

Royal guest room river view sleeps up to 4 with 2 queen beds.

Disney's Port Orleans French Quarter Resort

Description

French Quarter as the name suggests is themed after New Orleans. As the smallest Moderate, French Quarter is much less busy. There are no sections due to the resorts size.

Dining

Sassagoula Float Works - BLD $ - Quick Service – A typical WDW Resort food court with different stations serving things like Burgers, Sandwiches, Fried Shrimp, Po' Boys, Muffaletta, and Pizza.

Pizza Delivery

Scat Cat's Club is the indoor lobby bar.

Mardi Grogs is the outdoor pool bar

Features

Pool with Water Slide and Hot Tub - Parade around a Mardi Gras-themed Doubloon Lagoon pool area where King Neptune sits astride a giant sea serpent. Scale "Scales," as he's affectionately known, and slide down his tongue for a splash landing. Jazz-loving gators and clamshell water features add more poolside panache while a hot tub and the nearby Mardi Grogs pool bar let the good times roll.

Guests may also swim in the pools at nearby Disney's Port Orleans Resort – Riverside.

Kiddy Pool – Little Cajuns can enjoy the nearby Kid's pool.

Movies Under the Stars - Watch some of your favorite Disney films outside in the fresh evening air between buildings 5 & 6 on the French Quarter green.

Cajun Campfire Activities - Gather 'round as the sun goes down for old-fashioned family fun as you roast marshmallows by a crackling fire.

Horse-Drawn Carriage Rides - Relax on a horse-drawn carriage ride as you travel along the scenic banks of the Sassagoula River.

Bike and Surry Bike Rentals - Embark on a leisurely bicycle outing along the Resort's scenic waterfront promenade.

Arcade - South Quarter Games for video games, pinball, air hockey and more, stop by this arcade at Port Orleans French Quarter.

Playground – Can be found near the Doubloon Lagoon pool area.

Jogging Trail - 1-mile course along the lushly landscaped banks of the Sassagoula River.

Guest Laundry - A 24-hour self-service laundry room is located near the Doubloon Lagoon pool, behind Mardi Grogs.

Location

A Disney Springs Area Resort

Transportation

Bus transportation is available to all Disney World guest areas. Boat transportation is available to Port Orleans Riverside, Disney's Old Key West DVC Resort, Disney's Saratoga Springs DVC Resort, and Disney Springs.

Price

Standard View: $224 - $340

Garden View: $230 - $345

River View: $244 - $357

Pool View: $244 - $366

King Bed: $254 - $371

Room notes

Standard view sleeps up to 4 with 2 queen beds.

Garden view sleeps up to 4 with 2 queen beds.

River view sleeps up to 4 with 2 queen beds.

Pool view sleeps up to 4 with 2 queen beds.

King bed sleeps up to 2 with 1 king bed.

The Cabins at Disney's Fort Wilderness Resort

Description

The Fort Wilderness Cabins fall into the Moderate Resort classification. The rest of this large resort is comprised of campsites for RVs, campers, and even tents.

You can rough it in comfort with these cabins, which are 50% larger than the other Moderate category rooms and come with a kitchen. These suites, which resemble log cabins on the outside, are situated along winding roads running through the piney woods.

Each of the Fort Wilderness Resort Cabins is furnished with the following:

- One double bed
- One pull-down Murphy bed
- One bunk bed
- Dresser with 4 small-size drawers
- One small couch
- Table with 3 chairs and a long bench
- Nightstand digital alarm clock
- Full-length mirror (on bath door)
- WiFi wireless Internet access
- Flat-panel TV
- Full-sized fridge
- Microwave
- Coffee Maker
- Ironing board and iron
- Hair dryer
- Digital thermostat
- In-room safe
- Tiny bottle of H2O-brand shampoo, and bar soap
- Dishwasher
- Stove

- A limited collection of pots, pans, plates, glasses and silverware.
- Toaster

Dining

Trail's End – BLD $$ - Table Service - Lunch includes chili, pan-seared catfish, spicy grilled shrimp and andouille sausage as well as s'mores and warm sticky-bun sundaes. For dinner fried chicken, ribs, pasta, fish, carved meats, pizza, and fruit cobbler. There is also a take away counter at Trail's End.

P & J's Southern Takeout - BLD $$ - Quick Service – Breakfast sandwiches, burritos, and waffles. Lunch and dinner include chicken and rib meals, burgers, and sandwiches.

Crockett's Tavern – S $$ - Quick Service - Pizza, wings, and loaded nachos. Draft and bottled beer and wine.

Meadow Snack and Pool Bar – BLD $ - Quick Service – Sandwiches, Hot Dogs, and Pizza.

Hoop-Dee-Doo Musical Review - D $$$$ - Table Service – the Hoop Dee Doo is a nightly Dinner Show with a set price and menu. The all you care to eat menu features Garden Salad, Fried Chicken, BBQ Pork Ribs, Mac 'n Cheese, and PBJs. Sides include Corn Bread, Mashed Potatoes, and Cowboy Beans. Strawberry Shortcake is for desert.

While you eat, enjoy the "Wild West Show" full of corny jokes interspersed with song and dance.

Mickey's Backyard Barbeque Dinner Show – D $$$$ – Character Meal – Features Mickey, Minnie, Chip 'n' Dale, and Goofy. Offerings include: Smoked BBQ chicken, BBQ spare ribs, hot dogs, hamburgers, jambalaya, and honey-mustard baked chicken. Sides include: salads, slaw, cowboy beans, mac n cheese, corn on the cob, cornbread, watermelon, and ice-cream bars for dessert. Enjoy live country band and line dancing.

Features

Two Pools - Meadow Swimmin' Pool and Wilderness Swimmin' Pool

Main Pool with Hot Tub - Barrels of water-filled fun, Meadow Swimmin' Pool features a corkscrew waterslide, whirlpool spa and Kiddy pool.

Quiet Pool - You can also take a dip at Wilderness Swimmin' Pool, the all-ages quiet pool with a whirlpool spa.

Kiddy Pool/Kiddy Water Play Area - Young cowpokes can even cool off in the fort-themed water play area with tot-friendly slides or splash it up in the kiddy pool.

Chip 'N' Dale's Campfire Sing-A-Long - Join nutty friends Chip 'n' Dale for some old-fashioned family fun as you roast marshmallows around a crackling fire.

Movies Under the Stars - Cozy up for complimentary screenings of popular Disney films at the outdoor theater of Meadow Recreation Area.

Water Sports - Motorized boat, canoe, and kayak rentals, waterskiing, and fishing.

Bike Rentals - Ride through pine forests and meadows teeming with wildlife. Rentals are available from the Bike Barn.

Two Arcades - Daniel Boone's Wilderness Arcade delight in games both classic and contemporary at this arcade near the Meadow Swimmin' Pool.

Davy Crockett's Wilderness Arcade - Head on down to Pioneer Hall for a variety of video and pinball games.

Playgrounds - Kids can climb, slide and swing to their hearts content at playgrounds located throughout Disney's Fort Wilderness Resort, including ones at Clementine's Beach and the Meadow Recreation Area.

Jogging Trail - 2.5 miles through lush meadows and pine and cypress groves. Or explore the 0.75 mile shaded fitness trail and bike path that connects the Wilderness Lodge and Fort Wilderness.

Guest Laundry - Self-service laundry rooms are available at Comfort Stations throughout Disney's Fort Wilderness Resort & Campground.

Location

A Magic Kingdom Area Resort

Transportation

Bus transportation is available to all Disney World guest areas. Boat Transportation is also available to the Contemporary Resort, Wilderness Lodge, and the Magic Kingdom

Price

Wilderness Cabins: $364 - $637

Room Notes

Wilderness cabin sleeps up to 6 with 1 double bed and 1 bunk bed and 1 double-size pull down bed.

Moderate Resort Wrap Up

The Moderate Resorts are great for those who would like a little bit bigger room with upgraded resort amenities.

You'll find prices at the Disney Moderates using the Disney Armed Forces Salute comparable to Shades of Green's Category 2 and 3 only during the cheaper half of Disney's price year. During the rest of the year, on most weekends, and always at Fort Wilderness Cabins the Moderate's prices are more expensive.

Deluxe Resorts

There are eight different Deluxe Resorts on Walt Disney World Property.

The Deluxe Resorts are the premier hotels of Walt Disney World. They are decorated exquisitely based upon their overall resort theme.

These hotels are for those who really want to splurge on their accommodations. They are high in both price and in services.

Standard size rooms offer 2 queen beds and in some a sofa bed, which will sleep four to five (a crib may be requested for children under 3). The Deluxe Resorts all have room entry doors from an interior hallway.

Disney Deluxe rooms are larger that the Moderate rooms and fall into 3 size groupings: 400 square feet plus (Contemporary, Polynesian, Grand Floridian), 370-380 square feet (BoardWalk, Beach Club, Yacht Club), and 344 square feet (Wilderness and Animal Kingdom Lodges). Prices in this category fall in a larger range than in the others due to the different room sizes and special amenities offered.

The Wilderness and Animal Kingdom Lodges are sometimes referred to as Moderate Plus or Deluxe Minus, due to their room size and price.

Deluxe Resorts offer a table and two chairs or a desk and chair, dresser, TV, and small fridge. The bathroom proper is separated from the double sink vanity area.

These resorts are at the top of the Disney World lineup! You'll find all the amenities that you would expect at a first class resort, such as: Fine Dining, Table Service dining, Quick Service food court, room service, an arcade, playground, the best heated pools with slides, hot tub, a full service Spa at most, a gym, indoor and pool bars, luggage service, valet parking, balconies or porches, in room safe, iron and board, and coffee maker.

The Deluxe Resorts are all near at least one of the theme parks, which gives you easy access to that park.

All the Deluxe Resorts have a single Disney Transportation bus stop located near the lobby.

The Deluxe room rates are eligible for up to a 40% Disney Armed Forces Salute discount based upon availability and Blockout Dates.

Extra adults are an additional $25 per night, kids under 18 are free.

Disney's Animal Kingdom Lodge and Villas

Description

The Animal Kingdom Lodge and Villas is a joint property. It is both a Disney World Resort and a Disney Vacation Club property. There are two buildings, the first is called Jambo House, it is the original building and contains all of the Resort rooms as well as some DVC villas. The second newer building is called Kindani Village and is entirely comprised of DVC villas.

The majority of rooms in either building have views of the Lodge's savannas, areas where African animals live. You'll enjoy watching animals such as giraffes and zebras right outside your balcony window.

The Animal Kingdom Lodge and Villas is themed after East African hunting lodges.

Dining

Boma, Flavors of Africa - B$$ D$$$ – Buffet Service – African and American all you can eat buffet, featuring salads, roasted meats, and interesting sauces.

Jiko, The Cooking Place - D $$$$ – Table Service – One of Disney World's premier restaurants (an AAA's Four Diamond Award winner).

Specialties include wood-fired flatbreads; a trio of dips with house-made naan (Indian flatbread); oak-grilled filet mignon with red-wine sauce and sweet-corn risotto.

Sanaa - LD $$ – Table Service – Indian-African cuisine featuring Tandoori meats, grilled lamb, and steak.

The Mara - BLD $ – Quick Service – A typical Disney Resort Food Court with various stations. Sandwiches, Pitas, Flatbreads, and Salads.

Pizza Delivery

Room Service

Victoria Falls Lounge

Uzima Pool Bar

Maji Pool Bar

Features

Animal Viewing (Day and Night) - Discover over 30 species of African wildlife, including zebras, giraffes, gazelles, kudu and flamingos, from your room or common areas. At night enjoy the night vision goggle animal viewing.

Two Pools – Uzima and Samawati Springs

Uzima Pool - The Jambo House pool with water slide and 2 Hot Tubs – Enjoy a 11,000-square-foot pool with an exciting water slide and gently sloping, zero-depth entry point similar to that of a natural watering hole. Surrounded by large canopy trees and Floridian palms.

Samawati Springs Pool - located just a short walk away at Disney's Animal Kingdom Villas – Kidani! Featuring an exciting 128-foot waterslide and zero-depth-entry, this 4,700-square-foot, 118,138-gallon pool is the perfect place to cool off and have fun.

Hot Tubs – Both pool areas have a hot tub.

Kiddy Pools – Both pool areas include a children's wading pool.

Bus transportation is available to all Disney World guest areas

Water Play Area - Uwanja Camp; the Samawati Springs pool area also includes Uwanja Camp, a water playground with 3 distinct zones to please kids of all ages. At Observation Station, children 4 years of age and younger can climb through cargo crates, unscramble animal images and frolic through a gently bubbling geyser and shallow cistern pool—while their parents watch from nearby.

Playground – Hakuna Matata Playground. Kids can monkey around at this 24-hour playground overlooking the flamingo area and savanna.

Jambo House Campfire Activities - Gather 'round as the sun goes down for old-fashioned family fun as you roast marshmallows by a crackling fire.

Arcade - Pumbaa's Fun and Games Arcade, conquer classic arcade games and popular video games at this arcade near The Mara café.

Guest Laundry - Enjoy 24-hour self-service laundry rooms, as well as dry cleaning and valet laundry services.

Fitness Center - Service your spirit at Zahanati Massage & Fitness Center, a workout facility featuring equipment, massages and more.

Simba's Clubhouse - Disney Childcare. (Closes 1 August 2018)

Location

An Animal Kingdom Area Resort

Transportation

Bus transportation is available to all Disney World guest areas

Price

Standard View: $378 - $605

Pool View: $412 - $646

Pool View Bunk Bed: $438 - $740

Savanna View: $548 - $817

Savanna View Bunk Bed: $570 - $846

Savanna View Club Level: $632 - $903

Various Suites: $1051 - $2871

Room Notes

Standard view sleeps up to 4 with 2 queen beds or 1 queen bed and 1 bunk bed or 1 king bed and 1 day bed.

Pool view sleeps up to 4 with 2 queen beds or 1 king bed or 1 king bed and 1 day bed.

Pool view bunk bed sleeps up to 4 with 1 queen bed and 1 bunk bed.

Savanna view sleeps up to 4 with 2 queen beds or 1 king bed and 1 day bed.

Savanna view bunk bed sleeps up to 4 with 1 queen bed and 1 bunk bed.

Savanna view club level sleeps up to 4 with 2 queen beds or 1 queen bed and 1 bunk bed or 1 king bed and 1 day bed.

Standard view 1 bedroom suite club level sleeps up to 6 with 2 queen beds and 1 queen-size sleeper sofa.

1 bedroom suite club level sleeps up to 6 with 2 queen beds and 1 queen-size sleeper sofa.

2 bedroom suite – club level sleeps up to 8 with 1 queen bed and 1 bunk bed and 1 king bed and 1 queen size sleeper sofa or 1 king bed and 2 queen beds and 1 queen-size sleeper sofa.

Disney's Beach Club Resort

Description

You'll enjoy the beach/ocean theming in this beautiful resort. The Beach Club is also collocated with the Disney Yacht Club and they share many facilities including Stormalong Bay, the awesome sand bottomed, zero entry pool with pirate ship water slide and kids water play area.

The Beach Club Villas, a Disney Vacation Club property, is attached to the Beach Club Resort and they share all facilities.

Dining

Cape May Café – BD$$$ - Buffet Service - Here you'll find a Character Buffet Breakfast featuring Goofy, Minnie, and Donald, and a Buffet Dinner (without characters). Dinner includes Strip Loin, Snow Crab Legs, Steamed and Fried Clams, Fried Shrimp, Steamed Mussels, Paella, Salmon, and a kiddy menu for the little ones too.

Beaches & Cream Soda Shop – LD$ - Table Service - Burgers, Hot Dogs, Sandwiches, and awesome Ice-cream Treats, including the kitchen sink, a huge portion of ice cream with every topping imaginable.

Beach Club Marketplace – BLD$ - Quick Service - A small counter service restaurant with a limited menu, located in the Beach Club Marketplace Gift Shop. Sandwiches and Flatbreads.

Hurricane Hanna's Grill – LD$ - Quick Service, Pool Bar – Located by Stormalong Bay, the main pool shared with the Yacht Club Resort. Burgers, Lobster, Shrimp and Scallop Roll.

Pizza Delivery

Room Service

Martha's Vineyard Lounge – Indoor Bar

Features

Four Pools

Stormalong Bay is the main pool with water slide, sand bottom, and zero entry - Explore Stormalong Bay, a 3-acre water wonderland! Climb the mast of a life-size shipwreck and zip down one of the highest hotel water slides at Walt Disney World Resort. Float down a lazy river, unwind in one of 3 whirlpool spas and soak up the sun on the elevated tanning deck. A kid's shallow area offers the little ones a place to play in the sand. Stormalong Bay is shared with the Yacht Club.

Hot Tubs - At all pools

Three Quiet Pools - Disney's Beach Club Resort pool—the 43,000-gallon Tidal pool is located in a garden area on the far end of the resort facing Crescent Lake. Disney's Yacht Club Resort pool—the 54,000-gallon Admiral pool—can be found in its own quiet garden area. A third pool—the 55,350-gallon Dunes Cove pool—is located at Disney's Beach Club Villas. Though it is situated for the convenience of Guests staying at the Disney Beach Club Villas, all Resort Guests are welcome to enjoy it. All pools also include steaming whirlpool spas.

Kiddy Pool - Children can make a splash in the Kiddy pool complete with a miniature water slide—and delight in the sand beach that slopes gently into the main pool.

Playground - Children can climb, slide and play in the sand at this playground near the Kiddy pool.

Pirate Adventure Cruise - Scallywags 4 to 12 years of age can set sail on a pirate adventure, following clues to discover hidden treasure.

Movies Under the Stars - Head to Crescent Lake Beach on select nights for a campfire and complimentary screenings of Disney films.

Beach Club Campfire Activities - Gather 'round as the sun goes down for old-fashioned family fun as you roast marshmallows by a crackling fire.

Motorized Boat Rentals - Captain your own adventure when you rent a motorboat from Bayside Marina.

Fishing - Enjoy a guided bass fishing excursion—perfect for amateur wranglers and seasoned fishermen alike.

Bike Rentals - Breeze around Crescent Lake on a bicycle from Bayside Marina.

Arcade - Score big on a variety of video games at this arcade near Stormalong Bay.

Jogging Trail - Your pick of several jogging paths, including a loop around Crescent Lake.

Guest Laundry - Enjoy 24-hour self-service laundry rooms near Tidal Pool, plus dry cleaning and valet laundry services.

Fitness Center and Spa - Get toned at Ship Shape Massage Salon Fitness—a full-service facility featuring equipment, massages and more.

Sandcastle Club - Disney Childcare (Closes 1 August 2018)

Lakeside Beach – Enjoy the chaise lounges, swings, or hammocks on the white sandy beach.

Location

An Epcot Area Resort

Transportation

Bus transportation is available to all Disney World guest areas except Epcot and Hollywood Studios. Boat Transportation to: Disney's Yacht Club and BoardWalk Resorts, the Walt Disney World Swan and Dolphin Resorts, Epcot's International Gateway, and Disney's Hollywood Studios. Epcot's International Gateway is also a short walk away and Hollywood Studios just a little farther in the opposite direction.

Price

Standard View: $441 - $732

Garden/Woods View: $479 - $759

Lagoon or Pool View: $567 - $810

Standard View Club Level: $662 - $1041

Garden View Club Level: $670 - $1046

Deluxe Room Club Level: $694 - $1099

Lagoon or Pool View Club Level: $720 - $1117

One to Two Bedroom Suites: $828 - $2856

Room Notes

Standard view, Garden view, Lagoon or pool view, and Standard view club level rooms sleep from 2 to 5 people with the following options:

- 1 king bed
- 2 queen beds
- 1 queen bed and 1 twin-size sleeper chair and 1 day bed
- 2 queen beds and 1 day bed

Garden view club level sleeps up to 4 with 2 queen beds and 1 day bed.

Lagoon or pool view club level sleeps up to 5 with the following options:

- 1 king bed
- 2 queen beds
- 2 queen beds and 1 day bed
- 1 queen bed and 1 twin-size sleeper chair and 1 day bed

Deluxe room club level sleeps up to 5 with 2 queen beds and 1 day bed.

1 bedroom suite club level sleeps up to 3 with 1 king bed and 1 day bed.

2 bedroom suite club level sleeps up to 7 with 2 queen beds and 1 king bed and 1 day bed.

Disney's BoardWalk Inn

Description

The BoardWalk Resort represents Atlantic City (before the casinos) and the East Coast in general from the 1930s era. Behind the resort buildings is an actual BoardWalk like the famous one in Atlantic City. Along it you'll find restaurants, shops, and clubs. During the evening street performers will be on hand to entertain you.

The BoardWalk and other resorts in the area are conveniently located between Epcot's World Showcase and Disney's Hollywood Studios. Both are accessible by walking or Disney water craft.

The BoardWalk Villas, a Disney Vacation Club property is collocated with the BoardWalk Resort and they share all facilities.

There is also a Convention Center located at this resort.

Dining

Flying Fish Café – D $$$ - Table Service - The menu includes Fish of the Day, Grilled Steak, Potato-Wrapped Snapper, and Florida Rock Shrimp.

Big River Grille & Brewing Works – LD$$ - Table Service - Hand crafted Beers are on hand here. Steaks, Pasta, Chicken, Seafood, and the famous Grilled Meatloaf.

Trattoria al Forno - BD $$ – Table Service – Mediterranean food, Lasagna, Lamb Shank, Braised Beef Bolognese, and Chicken Parm are a few of the entrees.

ESPN Club – LD $$ – Table Service – A Sports Fan's Sports Bar. Burgers, Sandwiches, Wings, and Nachos

BoardWalk Bakery – BLD $ - Quick Service – Bakery items, Sandwiches (breakfast and others), and Grab and Go Items.

AbracadaBar – S $$ - The new magic themed cocktail bar located next to Trattoria al Forno, a great place to wait on your Advance Dining Reservation. "Curious Cocktails, Worldly Wines, Baffling Beers, and Ciders" are served up by a wait staff who perform magic tricks.

BoardWalk Joes – S$ - Quick Service -Margaritas and snacks.

BoardWalk Pizza Window – LD $ – Quick Service - Pizzas whole or by the slice.

BoardWalk To Go – LD $ – Quick Service - Hot Dogs, Corn Dogs, Ravioli, Mozzarella Sticks, Meatball Subs, and Nachos.

Pizza Delivery

Room Service

Belle Vue Lounge is the indoor bar

Leaping Horse Libations is located by the main pool

Features

Three Pools

Main Pool with Water Slide - Clown around at the carnival-themed Luna Park Pool. Glide down the Keister Coaster waterslide, cool off under the spouting trunks of grinning elephant statues and sink into the whirlpool spa.

Two Quiet Pools - For a more tranquil experience, relax at 2 all-ages leisure pools—each with a whirlpool spa.

Kiddy Pool - Children can even splash about in their own Kiddy pool.

Hot Tubs – There are hot tubs at all pools.

BoardWalk Campfire Activities - Gather 'round as the sun goes down for old-fashioned family fun as you roast marshmallows by a crackling fire.

Movies Under the Stars - Watch a favorite Disney film by the Ferris W. Eahlers Community Hall when night falls.

Bike and Surrey Bike Rentals - Breeze down Disney's BoardWalk on a bicycle from the Community Hall.

Fishing - Enjoy a guided bass fishing excursion—perfect for amateur wranglers and seasoned fishermen alike.

Arcade - Side Show Games Arcade - Discover action-packed video games at this lively arcade near the Luna Park Pool.

Playground - children can climb, slide and have a ball at the Luna Park Crazy Play Area.

Jogging Trail - Your pick of several jogging paths, including a loop around Crescent Lake.

Guest Laundry - Enjoy a 24-hour self-service laundry room near the 3rd-floor elevators, as well as dry-cleaning and valet laundry services.

Fitness Center - Pump it up at Muscles & Bustles Health Club—a full-service facility with workout equipment, massages and more.

Business Center - Ship packages—plus print, copy and fax documents—at the Business Center inside the Conference Center.

Location

An Epcot Area Resort

Transportation

Bus transportation is available to all Disney World guest areas. Boat Transportation to: Disney's Yacht Club and Beach Club, the Walt Disney World Swan and Dolphin Resorts, Epcot's International Gateway, and Disney's Hollywood Studios. Epcot's International Gateway is also a short walk away and Hollywood Studios just a little farther in the opposite direction.

Price

Standard View: $483 - $767

Garden View - $511 - $795

Water View: $611 - $835

Standard View Club Level: $702 - $1056

BoardWalk View Club Level - $820 - 1171

Deluxe Room Club Level: $847 - $1303

Outer Building Garden Room Club Level: $919 - $1401

Room Notes

Standard view sleeps up to 5 with 2 queen beds and 1 day bed or 1 king bed or 2 queen beds or 1 king bed and 1 day bed.

Garden View sleeps up to 5 with 2 queen beds and 1 day bed or 1 king bed or 2 queen beds or 1 king bed and 1 day bed.

Water view sleeps up to 5 with 2 queen beds and 1 day bed or 2 queen beds or 1 king bed. Water view rooms overlook a pool, waterway or lake.

Standard room club level sleeps up to 5 with 2 queen beds and 1 day bed or 1 king bed or 2 queen beds.

Deluxe room club level sleeps up to 6 with 2 queen beds and 1 queen-size sleeper sofa.

Outer building garden room club level sleeps up to 2 with 1 king bed.

Disney's Contemporary Resort

Description

The Contemporary Resort is one of the original Resorts that opened at the same time as the Magic Kingdom in October 1971. Just a stone's throw away from the MK's Tomorrowland, the look and feel of the Contemporary used to fit right in with the original theme of Tomorrowland.

The look and feel of Tomorrowland has since moved on to a more 50's retro Sci-Fi look, leaving the Contemporary as the sole version of the classic look that it once shared with Tomorrowland.

The Contemporary is divided into two buildings, the huge main A-frame Tower building and the Garden Wing, a two-story outbuilding.

The Tower has guestrooms on the west and east sides, all with views of the Seven Seas Lagoon and the Magic Kingdom to the west or Bay Lake to the east. The center of the building is all open space with the WDW Monorail Line running right through.

The Garden Wing is a sprawling building which houses cheaper rooms with Standard and Garden Views.

Co-located with the Contemporary resort is the Disney Vacation Club's Bay Lake Towers, which shares amenities with the Contemporary.

Dining

California Grill – D$$$ - Table Service – This exquisite fine dining restaurant sits atop the Contemporary Resort with wonderful views of the Magic Kingdom and surrounding areas. Featuring seasonal produce, fish, and meats, sushi, and flatbreads.

Chef Mickey's – B$$ D$$$ - Buffet Service, Character Meal – Dinner selections include, spiced rubbed sirloin of beef, oven roasted turkey breast or ham, seasoned salmon filet with a mango chutney or dill aioli, mango BBQ pork ribs, and many sides. Featuring Chef Mickey, Minnie, Chip, Dale, Pluto, and Chef Goofy.

The Wave...of American Flavors – B$ L$$ D$$$ - Table Service - Features healthful dining options using local products. Features include, crab cakes, fish tacos, black bean chili, Cobb salads, and more.

Contempo Café – BLD$ - Quick Service – Order your food on touch-screen monitors and then pick up at the window. Lunch and dinner feature, flatbreads, salads, sandwiches, and burgers.

Pizza Delivery

Room Service

The Outer Rim is the indoor Bar

The Sand Bar is the Pool Bar

Features

Two Pools

Main Pool with Water Slide and Hot Tub - Glide down the 17-foot-high, curving waterslide at the feature pool, and relax in one of 2 whirlpool spas.

Quiet Pool - You can also escape to Bay Pool, the all-ages quiet pool that juts out over Bay Lake. Soak up the sun from a lounge chair on the deck, or rent a private cabana for added luxury.

Kiddy Pool - None.

Water Play Area - Children can make a splash in the water playground designed just for kids.

Contemporary Campfire Activities - Gather 'round as the sun goes down for old-fashioned family fun as you roast marshmallows by a crackling fire.

Movies Under the Stars - Enjoy a different Disney film on select nights on the lawn behind the Contemporary Tower.

Arcade - The Game Station Arcade, discover high-octane thrills at this arcade located on the 4th floor of the Contemporary Tower.

Playground – Located near the Garden Wing.

Pixar Play Zone - Beginning 13 April 2018, children ages 4 to 12 can enjoy a Pixar-packed evening of fun, games and Character encounters at Pixar Play Zone at Disney's Contemporary Resort. This kids-only experience also includes dinner and dessert!

- Children must be fully potty-trained.
- Activities, entertainment and menu are subject to change.
- A valid accepted credit card number is required at time of booking. No-shows or cancellations made within 24 hours of the scheduled time will be charged the full price of the experience.

Jogging Trail – 0.9 miles, loops around Bay Lake Tower and the South Garden Wing.

Guest Laundry - Enjoy a 24-hour self-service laundry room on the 2nd floor, plus dry-cleaning and valet laundry services.

Fitness Center and Spa - Shape up at Olympiad Fitness Center—a full-service facility featuring exercise equipment, massages and more.

Business Center - Discover printing, copying and shipping services at the Business Center inside the Convention Center.

Motorized Boat Rentals - Cruise around Bay Lake and Seven Seas Lagoon aboard a motorized boat from the Boat Nook Marina.

Sammy Duvall Watersport Center, featuring waterskiing, wake boarding, parasailing, and tubing.

Location

A Magic Kingdom Area Resort

Transportation

Bus transportation is available to all Disney World guest areas. Monorail Transportation is available to the Magic Kingdom, Epcot, Transportation and Ticket Center, Polynesian Village Resort, and the Grand Floridian Resort. Boat service to the Magic Kingdom. The Magic Kingdom is also just a short half-mile walk away.

Price

Garden Wing Standard View: $450 - $708

Garden Wing Garden View: $456 - $773

Garden Wing Deluxe Room: $544 - $818

Tower Bay Lake View: $639 - $876

Tower Magic Kingdom View: $711 - $962

Standard Room Club Level: $818 - $1106

Magic Kingdom View Club Level: $868 - $1304

One to Two Bedroom Suites: $1249 - $2157

Room Notes

Garden wing standard view sleeps up to 5 with 2 queen beds and 1 day bed or 1 king bed and 1 day bed.

Garden wing garden view sleeps up to 5 with 2 queen beds and 1 day bed or 1 king bed and 1 day bed.

Garden wing deluxe room sleeps up to 4 with 1 king bed and 1 queen-size sleeper sofa.

Tower bay lake view sleeps up to 5 with 2 queen beds and 1 day bed or 1 king bed and 1 day bed.

Tower theme park view sleeps up to 5 with 2 queen beds and 1 day bed or 1 king bed and 1 day bed.

Standard room atrium club level sleeps up to 5 with 2 queen beds and 1 day bed or 1 king bed and 1 day bed.

Theme park view atrium club level sleeps up to 5 with 2 queen beds and 1 day bed or 1 king bed and 1 day bed.

Garden wing 1 bedroom suite sleeps up to 5 with 1 king bed and 1 queen-size sleeper sofa and 1 twin-size sleeper chair.

Garden wing hospitality suite sleeps up to 7 with 1 king bed and 1 queen-size sleeper sofa and 1 day bed or 2 queen beds and 1 queen-size sleeper sofa and 1 day bed.

Bay lake view 1 bedroom suite club level sleeps up to 6 with 2 queen beds and 1 queen-size sleeper sofa.

Bay lake view 2 bedroom suite club level sleeps up to 8 with 4 queen beds and 1 queen-size sleeper sofa or 2 queen beds and 1 king bed and 1 queen-size sleeper sofa.

Disney's Grand Floridian Resort & Spa

Description

Inspired by Florida's grand Victorian seaside resorts from the turn of the last century, the Grand Floridian is the Walt Disney World Flagship Resort!

The Grand Floridian theming features pristine white wood sided buildings with multiple porches, latticework, dormers, and turrets beneath a red-shingle roof.

There is also a Disney Vacation Club building which offers studios and suites.

Dining

Victoria & Albert's – D$$$ - Table Service - This is Disney World's premier fine dining restaurant. It is the only restaurant in Central Florida to hold the AAA Five-Diamond Award. Victoria and Albert's is a lavish and expensive experience. The menu changes daily in this very small restaurant.

There is a required dress code: Men: Dinner jackets with dress pants/slacks and shoes. Ties are optional (Please no jeans, shorts, sandals, flip-flops, or tennis shoes) Ladies: Cocktail dress, dressy pantsuit, skirt/blouse or nice dress. (Please no jeans, shorts, Capri pants, sandals, flip-flops or tennis shoes)

Citricos – D$$$ - Table Service - Selections include sautéed shrimp with lemon, feta cheese, tomatoes, and white wine; oak-grilled filet of beef; braised veal shank.

Grand Floridian Café – B$ LD $$ - Table Service – An upscale coffee shop. Typical breakfast items, for lunch, there's Cobb salad and the Grand sandwich with ham, turkey, and Boursin-cheese sauce. For dinner, choose from salmon, shrimp pasta, or grilled pork chop.

Narcoossee's –D$$$ - Table Service – Narcoosess's offers a sea food centric menu featuring, lobster and shrimp fettuccine, pan-seared scallops, grilled filet mignon, and a two-pound steamed Maine lobster.

1900 Park Fare – B$$ D$$$ - Buffet Character Meals – Dinner offerings include, spicy Durban chicken, pork pot stickers, chicken marsala, and peel-n-eat shrimp. Breakfast features Mary Poppins, Alice in Wonderland, and the Mad Hatter while at dinner you'll see Cinderella and Prince Charming, Lady Tremaine, Anastasia, Drizella, and the Fairy Godmother (some characters may only be in the lobby for photos).

Garden View Tea Room – Afternoon Tea $$ to $$$ - Table Service - The menu includes a selection of international teas and an assortment of sandwiches and pastries.

Gasparilla Island Grill – BLD$ - Quick Service – Featuring Burgers, Flatbreads, and Sandwiches.

Pizza Delivery

Room Service

Mizner's Lounge is the indoor Bar

The Courtyard Pool Bar and Beaches Pool Bar and Grill are the two Pool Bars.

Features

Two Pools

Main Pool – Relax at the Courtyard Pool, the all-ages quiet pool that includes an adjacent kiddy pool and whirlpool spa.

Beach Pool - Water Slide and Hot Tub - Make a splash at Beach Pool! Breeze down the 181-foot-long waterslide as it curves down the mountain, zips past trees and slips under a walking bridge before plunging you into the pool. Sunbathe in a poolside lounge chair, or rent a plush cabana for added luxury. Just steps from the white-sand shore of Seven Seas Lagoon, Beach Pool features a gently sloping entry similar to that of a natural beach.

Kiddy Pool/Kiddy Water Play Area by the Beach Pool.

Grand Floridian Campfire Activities - Gather 'round as the sun goes down for old-fashioned family fun as you roast marshmallows by a crackling fire.

Motorized Boat Rentals - Cruise around the lagoon aboard a motorized boat, available from the Marina.

Pirate Adventure Cruise - Scallywags 4 to 12 years of age can set sail on a pirate adventure, following clues to discover hidden treasure.

Movies Under the Stars - Watch favorite Disney films at complimentary movie screenings on the beach near Beach Pool.

Fishing - Experience bass fishing at its finest with a guided excursion departing from the Marina.

Arcade - Delight in arcade games both classic and contemporary, as well as quick-service snacks and meals.

Jogging Trail – 1.0 mile, runs along the Seven Seas Lagoon.

Guest Laundry - 24-hour self-service laundry rooms are available on the second floor of the main building, as well as on the ground floors of most buildings with Guest Rooms.

Business Center - Fax, print, ship and more at the Business Center inside Disney's Grand Floridian Convention Center.

Fitness Center and Spa - Invigorate your spirits at Senses—a Victorian-themed, full service spa offering massages, body treatments and more.

Beach – Enjoy the swings, chaise lounges, and hammocks for a relaxing afternoon or watch the Electric Water Pageant at night.

Location

A Magic Kingdom Area Resort

Transportation

Bus transportation is provided to all Disney World guest areas. Monorail Transportation is available to the Magic Kingdom, Epcot, Transportation and Ticket Center, Polynesian Village Resort, and the Contemporary Resort. Boat transportation is available to the Magic Kingdom.

It is not possible to walk directly to the Magic Kingdom as a waterway with no bridge is between the Grand Floridian and the Magic Kingdom.

Price

Outer Building Garden View: $646 - $934

Outer Building Lagoon or Pool View: $658 - $1002

Outer Building Deluxe Room Garden View: $706 - $1061

Outer Building Deluxe Room Theme Park View: $770 - $1217

Outer Building Standard Room Club Level: $774 - $1217

Main Building Standard View Club Level: $1018 - $1591

Main Building Deluxe King Room Club Level: $1076 - $1747

Main Building Theme Park View Club Level: $1148 - $1817

Outer Building 1 – 2 Bedroom Suites: $1413 - $3583

Room Notes

Outer Building garden view sleeps up to 5 with 2 queen beds and 1 day bed or 2 queen beds or 1 king bed and 1 day bed or 1 king bed and 1 double-size sleeper sofa.

Outer Building lagoon view sleeps up to 5 with 2 queen beds and 1 day bed or 2 queen beds or 1 king bed or 1 king bed and 1 double-size sleeper sofa.

Outer Building deluxe room garden view sleeps up to 4 with 2 queen beds.

Outer Building theme park view sleeps up to 5 with 2 queen beds and 1 day bed or 2 queen beds or 1 king bed and 1 double-size sleeper sofa.

Outer Building standard room club level sleeps up to 5 with 2 queen beds and 1 day bed or 2 queen beds or 1 king bed and 1 day bed or 1 king bed and 1 double-size sleeper sofa.

Main Building standard room club level sleeps up to 5 with 2 queen beds or 2 queen beds and 1 day bed or 1 king bed.

Main Building deluxe king room club level sleeps up to 3 with 1 king bed or 1 king bed and 1 day bed.

Main Building theme park view club level sleeps up to 5 with 2 queen beds and 1 day bed.

Outer Building – 1 bedroom suite – club level: sleeps up to 6 with 2 queen beds and 1 double-size sleeper sofa.

Disney's Polynesian Village Resort

Description

The Polynesian Village Resort is also one of the original WDW Resorts, opening in October 1971 with the Magic Kingdom. The "Poly" is both a Disney World Resort and a Disney Vacation Club property. The theme here is the South Pacific tropic islands. Celebrate the spirit of the South Pacific at this oasis of tropical palms, lush vegetation, and white-sand beaches. From moonlit nights on torch-lined waterfront to the exotic tastes of our world-class restaurants, discover the signature tropical ambience that's made Disney's Polynesian Village Resort a favorite Disney destination since 1971.

Guests stay in two and three-story Hawaiian "longhouses" situated around the four-story Great Ceremonial House.

Dining

Spirit of Aloha Dinner Show – D$$$ - Table Service - Features South Seas-island native dancing followed by an all-you-can-eat "Polynesian-style" meal.

'Ohana – B$$ D$$$ - Table Service - 'Ohana's meals are all served "Family Style." Platters and bowls are delivered to the table for you to serve yourselves and are refreshed as often as you'd like. Dinner features, Sweet-n-Sour Pork Loin, spicy grilled peel-n-eat shrimp, Szechuan sirloin steak, noodles, tossed in a teriyaki sauce with fresh vegetables, and stir-fried vegetables. 'Ohana bread pudding à la mode with bananas-caramel sauce is for desert!

Kona Café – BLD$$ - Table Service – Enjoy great Pan-Asian specialties including, grilled kona coffee-rubbed pork chop, togarashi spiced ahi tuna, pan-Asian noodles, and sesame seared sea scallops.

Kona Island – A small sushi counter next to the Kona Café.

Capt. Cook's – BLD$ - Quick Service – Typical breakfast items plus Tonga Toast (banana stuffed sourdough bread, battered and deep fried), lunch and dinner many types of sandwiches and flatbreads with a Polynesian flair: aloha pork sandwich, teriyaki chicken sandwich, coconut curry meatballs, the big kahuna, and Hawaiian flatbread to name a few.

Pineapple Lanai – S$ - Quick Service – Offers Dole Whip soft serve, a WDW cult favorite. Frozen pineapple slush, served by itself or with vanilla soft serve swirl (my favorite!). Pineapple juice floats are also available.

Trader Sams Grotto and Tiki Bar– S$ - Explore the whimsically themed lounge—overrun with ancient artifacts and exotic treasures—or set sail for the open-air Tiki Terrace for a relaxing sip or nibble under the starry sky, complete with the melodious sounds of live Hawaiian-themed musical entertainment. Tropical drinks and small plates.

Room Service

Pizza Delivery

Trader Sams Grogg Grotto is a new casual bar located off of the lobby. They serve fruity Polynesian drinks, beers (including Kona), and Pacific/Asian style appetizers all while you enjoy live music.

The Tambu Lounge is located on the second floor of the lobby area near the restaurants.

The Barefoot Pool Bar is right by the main pool.

Features

Two Pools – Lava Pool and Oasis Pool

Lava Pool - Make a splash at this pool, which features a towering volcano, a waterfall and a thrilling 142 foot-long waterslide. A zero-depth entry point, similar to a beach, slopes gently into the pool making for easy entry and exit. Nearby, a lounge and bar offer refreshments and snacks.

Oasis Pool, is the quiet pool which is nestled amid a garden, this all-ages leisure pool promises a more tranquil swim for those looking to relax and unwind.

Kiddy Pool - None

Kiddy Water Play Area – A small "Splash Pad" rubberized flooring with water squirting up from spouts.

Movies Under the Stars - Watch favorite Disney films at complimentary screenings on the beach nearest Lava Pool.

Polynesian Village Campfire Activities - Gather 'round as the sun goes down for old-fashioned family fun as you roast marshmallows by a crackling fire.

Jogging Trail – 1.0 mile, runs along the Seven Seas Lagoon.

Guest Laundry - A 24-hour self-service laundry room is available near Lilo's Playhouse. For dry cleaning and valet laundry service, please select "Housekeeping" on your Guest Room phone.

Motorized Boat Rentals - Cruise around Seven Seas Lagoon aboard one of the motorized boats from Seven Seas Marina.

Fishing - Experience bass fishing at its finest with a guided catch-and-release excursion.

Lakeside Beach – The perfect spot to watch Wishes, the Magic Kingdom fireworks and the Electrical Water Pageant or chill out on the chaise lounges during the day.

Never Land Club - Disney Childcare

Location

A Magic Kingdom Area Resort

Transportation

Bus transportation is available to all Disney World guest areas. Monorail Transportation is available to the Magic Kingdom, Epcot, Transportation and Ticket Center, Contemporary Resort, and the Grand Floridian Resort. Boat Transportation is available to the Magic Kingdom.

It is not possible to walk past the Grand Floridian and on to the Magic Kingdom as a waterway with no bridge is between the Grand Floridian and the Magic Kingdom.

Price

Standard View: $568 - $836

Lagoon View: $683 - $1059

Garden View Club Level: $732 - $1076

Theme Park View: $768 - $1130

Lagoon View Club Level: $908 - $1325

Theme Park View Club Level: $999 - $1403

One Bedroom Suite Club Level: $1338 - $1918

Room notes

Standard view sleeps up to 5 with 2 queen beds.

Lagoon view sleeps up to 5 with 2 queen beds and 1 day bed.

Theme park view sleeps up to 5 with 2 queen beds and 1 day bed.

Garden view club level sleeps up to 5 with 2 queen beds and 1 day bed.

Lagoon view club level sleeps up to 5 with 2 queen beds and 1 day bed.

Theme park view club level sleeps up to 5 with 2 queen beds and 1 day bed.

1 bedroom suite club level sleeps up to 5 with 2 queen beds and 1 day bed.

Disney's Wilderness Lodge

Description

The Wilderness Lodge is a joint property. It is both a Disney World Resort and a Disney Vacation Club property. There are two buildings and a collection of cabins along the lakefront. The original main building, the Wilderness Lodge has been divided into regular guest rooms and DVC wings, the DVC wing being called Cooper Creek Villas. The newer building, originally the only DVC rooms in the resort is called Boulder Ridge Villas. Then there are a collection of new cabins along the lakeside which are DVC properties called the Cascade Cabins.

All major common areas (front desk/bellhop services, dining, and merchandise) are in the original main building.

The look and feel of the Wilderness Lodge was inspired by national-park lodges of the early 20th century. There is lots of stone work and exposed timber. The lobby soars eight stories and has huge totem poles and a stone fireplace, which represent the various levels of the Grand Canyon strata as it rises through the lobby.

Dining

Artist Point – D$$$ - Table Service – This fine dining restaurant features dishes inspired by the Pacific Northwest. A few of the offerings are, cedar plank-roasted king salmon, hickory char-crusted filet mignon, roasted Berkshire pork loin, and artist point vegetarian lo mein.

Whispering Canyon Café – B$ LD$$ - Table Service - This rowdy location is just off the lobby and offers both family style and individual meals. Grilled western buffalo meatloaf, citrus-glazed rainbow trout, oak-roasted pork loin chop, and grilled New York strip steak are some of the dinner offerings. *Note Servers are known to engage in over the top guest interactions when "set off" by such things as: asking for ketchup, informing them of a birthday in the party, dropping your silverware, or asking where the bathroom is.*

Roaring Fork – BLD$ - Quick Service – You will find typical breakfast items available and the lunch/dinner menu offers items such as: Soups, salads, pasta of the day, sandwiches, burgers, chicken nuggets, and pizza.

Geyser Point Bar & Grill – BLD$ - Quick Service – This poolside eatery offers Scrambled eggs, pancakes, and wraps among other things. For lunch and dinner enjoy burgers, sandwiches, and salads with specialty cocktails, beer, wine, and sangria.

Room Service

Pizza Delivery

The Territory Lounge is the Lobby Bar

Trout Pass is the Pool Bar

Features

Two Pools – Copper Creek Springs Pool and Hidden Springs Pool

Copper Creek Springs Pool - Follow the bubbling Silver Creek to discover a dazzling heated pool surrounded by pine trees and boulders. Zip down the exciting 67-foot waterslide built into the rocks, and relax in the hot and cold whirlpool spas.

Boulder Ridge Cove Pool - Retreat to this leisure pool which, along with a whirlpool spa, is nestled amongst the Villas.

Kiddy Splash Area – Children can even enjoy a bubbling, squirting play area adjacent to the Copper Creek Springs Pool.

Bus transportation is available to all Disney World guest areas

Playground - Children 5 to 12 years of age can climb and slide to their hearts' content on the beach playground.

Bike and Surrey Bike Rentals - Enjoy meandering woodland trails on a bicycle from Teton Boat & Bike Rentals.

Movies Under the Stars - Watch favorite Disney films on the moonlit shores of Bay Lake.

Wilderness Lodge Campfire Activities - Gather 'round as the sun goes down for old-fashioned family fun as you roast marshmallows by a crackling fire.

Arcade - Buttons and Bells Arcade. Aim for the high score at this exciting arcade, offering games both classic and contemporary.

Jogging Trail - 2.5 miles through lush meadows and pine and cypress groves. Or explore the 0.75-mile shaded fitness trail and bike path that connects the Wilderness Lodge and Fort Wilderness.

Guest Laundry - A 24-hour self-service laundry room is available just beyond Roaring Fork. For dry cleaning and valet laundry service, please select "Housekeeping" on your Guest Room phone.

Spa & Fitness - Soothe your mind at Sturdy Branches Health Club—a full-service facility and sauna with massage and facial services.

Motorized Boat Rentals - Cruise around Seven Seas Lagoon aboard a motorized boat from Teton Boat & Bike Rentals.

Sailboat Rentals - Zip around Bay Lake on a 12-foot sailboat, available from the Marina, Teton Boat & Bike Rentals.

Fishing - Reel in the fun with a guided excursion—perfect for seasoned sportsmen and amateur wranglers alike!

Location

A Magic Kingdom Area Resort

Transportation

Bus transportation is available to all Disney World guest areas. Boat Transportation is also available to the Contemporary Resort, Fort Wilderness, and the Magic Kingdom

Price

Standard View: $336 - $649

Courtyard View: $457 - $669

Courtyard View Bunk Bed: $482 - $724

Standard Room Club Level: $611 - $911

Deluxe Room Club Level $777 - $1262

Room Notes

Standard view sleeps up to 4 with 2 queen beds or 1 king bed.

Courtyard view sleeps up to 4 with 2 queen beds or 1 king bed.

Courtyard view bunk bed sleeps up to 4 with 1 queen bed and 1 bunk bed.

Standard room club level sleeps up to 4 with 1 queen bed and 1 bunk bed or 2 queen beds.

Deluxe room club level sleeps up to 6 with 2 queen beds and 1 queen-size sleeper sofa.

Disney's Yacht Club Resort

Description

You'll enjoy the nautical theming in this beautiful resort. The Yacht Club is also co-located with the Disney Beach Club Resort and they share many facilities including Stormalong Bay, the awesome sand bottomed, zero entry pool with pirate ship water slide and kids water play area.

The Yacht Club Resort is also home to a large convention center.

Dining

Yachtsman Steakhouse – D$$$ - Table Service - Steak, steak, and more steak as well as buffalo, chicken breast, and halibut.

Captain's Grille – B$ L$$ D$$$ - Table Service – For lunch sandwiches and salads, for dinner chicken, pork, beef, and fish.

Pizza Delivery

Hurricane Hanna's Grill – LD$ - Quick Service Pool Bar – Located by Stormalong Bay the main pool shared with the Yacht Club Resort. Burgers, lobster, shrimp and scallop roll.

Ale and Compass Lounge – Indoor Bar

Crew's Cup Lounge – Indoor Bar

Features

Four Pools

Stormalong Bay is the main pool with water slide, sand bottom, and zero entry - Explore Stormalong Bay, a 3-acre water wonderland! Climb the mast of a life-size shipwreck and zip down one of the highest hotel water slides at Walt Disney World Resort. Float down a lazy river, unwind in one of 3 whirlpool spas and soak up the sun on the elevated tanning deck. A kid's shallow area offers the little ones a place to play in the sand. Stormalong Bay is shared with the Beach Club

Hot Tubs at all pools

Three Quiet Pools - Disney's Beach Club Resort pool—the 43,000-gallon Tidal pool—is located in a garden area on the far end of the resort facing Crescent Lake. Disney's Yacht Club Resort pool—the 54,000-gallon Admiral pool—can be found in its own quiet garden area. A third pool—the 55,350-gallon Dunes Cove pool—is privately located at Disney's Beach Club Villas. Though it is situated for the convenience of Guests staying at the Disney Beach Club Villas, all Resort Guests are welcome to enjoy it. All pools also include steaming whirlpool spas.

Kiddy Pool - Children can make a splash in the Kiddy pool—complete with a miniature water slide—and delight in the sand beach that slopes gently into the main pool.

Playground - Climb, slide and play to your heart's content at this 24-hour playground near Stormalong Bay.

Pirate Adventure Cruise - Scallywags 4 to 12 years of age can set sail on a pirate adventure, following clues to discover hidden treasure.

Movies Under the Stars - Head to Crescent Lake Beach on select nights for a campfire and complimentary screenings of Disney films.

Motorized Boat Rentals - Captain your own adventure when you rent a motorboat from Bayside Marina.

Fishing - Enjoy a guided bass-fishing excursion—perfect for both amateur wranglers and seasoned fishermen!

Arcade - Score big with a variety of video games at this arcade near Stormalong Bay.

Jogging Trail - Your pick of several jogging paths, including a loop around Crescent Lake.

Guest Laundry - Enjoy 24-hour self-service laundry rooms near Admiral Pool, plus dry cleaning and valet laundry services.

Fitness Center and Spa - Ship Shape Health Club. Enjoy a workout or indulge in a massage at this full-service fitness center.

Business Center - Fax, copy, print, ship and more at the Business Center, located just inside the Convention Center.

Lakeside Beach – Enjoy the chaise lounges, swings, or hammocks on the white sandy beach.

Location

An Epcot Area Resort

Transportation

Bus transportation is available to all Disney World guest areas. Boat Transportation to: Disney's Beach Club and BoardWalk Resorts, the Walt Disney World Swan and Dolphin Resorts, Epcot's International Gateway, and Disney's Hollywood Studios. Epcot's International Gateway is also a short walk away and Hollywood Studios just a little farther in the opposite direction.

Price

Standard View: $441 - $732

Garden/Woods View: $457 - $706

Lagoon or Pool View: $559 - $810

Standard View Club Level: $652 - $994

Garden View Club Level: $682 - $1033

Lagoon or Pool View Club Level: $770 - $1148

Deluxe Room Club Level: $804 - $1288

Two Bedroom Suite Club: $1868 - $2936

Room Notes

Standard view sleeps up to 5 with 2 queen beds and 1 day bed or 1 queen bed and 1 twin-size sleeper chair and 1 day bed or 1 king bed or 1 king bed and 1 day bed.

Garden/Woods view sleeps up to 5 with 2 queen beds or 2 queen beds and 1 day bed or 1 queen bed and 1 twin-size sleeper chair and 1 day bed or 1 king bed.

Lagoon or pool view sleeps up to 5 with 2 queen beds or 2 queen beds and 1 day bed or 1 queen bed and 1 twin-size sleeper chair and 1 day bed or 1 king bed or 1 king bed and 1 day bed.

Standard view club level sleeps up to 5 with 2 queen beds and 1 day bed or 2 queen beds or 1 queen bed and 1 twin-size sleeper chair and 1 day bed or 1 king bed.

Garden view club level sleeps up to 4 with 1 king bed or 2 queen beds or 2 queen beds and 1 day bed.

Lagoon or pool view club level sleeps up to 4 with 1 king bed or 2 queen beds and 1 day bed or 2 queen beds or 1 king bed and 1 day bed.

Deluxe room club level sleeps up to 4 with 2 queen beds.

2 bedroom suite club level sleeps up to 4 with 2 king beds.

Deluxe Resort Wrap Up

The Disney Deluxe Resorts are great for those who'd like the best room and amenities possible and don't mind paying for it. You should plan to spend some time in your room and at the resort enjoying all it has to offer if you opt for this level of accommodations.

Even using the Disney Armed Forces Salute the Deluxe Resorts do not compare to Shades of Green's rates. The Disney Deluxe rates are quite a bit more.

The Disney Vacation Club Resorts

The Disney Vacation Club is Disney's take on timeshares. Members buy into a property and use points for stays at DVC properties worldwide.

DVC resorts offer Deluxe accommodations in studio, one, two, and three bedroom suites. These suites can also be rented through the regular Walt Disney World reservation process and are eligible for the Disney Armed Forces Salute 40% off room discount, though the number available is very limited.

There are currently nine DVC resorts at Walt Disney World, many of which are co-located with a Deluxe Resort and share facilities with that resort. They are: Animal Kingdom Lodge Villas, Bay Lake Tower, Disney's Beach Club Villas, Disney's BoardWalk Villas Resort, The Villas at Disney's Grand Floridian Resort and Spa, Disney's Old Key West Resort, Disney's Polynesian Villas and Bungalows, Saratoga Springs Resort and Spa, and Cooper Creek & Boulder Ridge Villas and Cascade Cabins at Disney's Wilderness Lodge.

Disney Resort Wrap Up

That's it for our tour of the Walt Disney World owned resorts. In the next section of this chapter we'll cover the other on property resorts that are not owned by Disney.

There are eleven non-Disney owned resorts at different locations around Walt Disney World property. Some are just as convenient as staying at a Disney resort and some are not.

Your stay at a non-Disney resort may or may not come with some of the Disney Resort amenities mentioned previously in this chapter depending on which resort that you will be staying at. You'll find specifics on this under each individual resort.

On Property, Non-Disney Resorts

Next we come to a review of the non-Disney resorts that are located on Walt Disney World property. One of these is a Department of Defense owned Armed Forces Recreation Center and the rest are owned by national chains, some under their regular brand name, and some with Disney specific names.

The On Property Non-Disney Resorts are:

- Shades of Green – an Armed Forces Recreation Center
- Walt Disney World Swan – a Starwood Resort operated under the Westin brand
- Walt Disney World Dolphin - a Starwood Resort operated under the Sheraton brand
- Four Seasons Resort Orlando at Walt Disney World
- Seven National Chain Resorts collectively called the Disney Springs Resort Area Hotels.
    o B Resort & Spa
    o Best Western Lake Buena Vista Resort Hotel
    o Doubletree Suites by Hilton Disney Springs Area
    o Hilton Orlando Buena Vista Palace Disney Springs Area
    o Hilton Orlando Lake Buena Vista Disney Springs Area
    o Holiday Inn Orlando – Disney Springs Area
    o Wyndham Lake Buena Vista

Shades of Green

Description

Shades of Green, is often considered equivalent to a Disney Deluxe Level Resort, as it once was a Disney owned Deluxe Resort.

Note Shades of Green is covered in even more detail in the Shades of Green Chapter.

The theme of the resort is that of a mountain golf course lodge. Large simulated rock outcroppings dominate the interior and exterior areas of the resort. The grounds are landscaped beautifully with winding paths between the buildings. You'll see the two beautiful golf courses on each side of the property and you'll also see some local wildlife. A few small alligators live in the ponds at Shades of Green and deer and turkeys regularly roam the grounds.

The resort rooms are divided between two wings, the older Magnolia Wing has both of the resort's pools and the newer Palm Wing has the attached parking garage.

Shades of Green's deluxe rooms come at a price well below Disney's Deluxe Resorts and also below the full price rates at the Moderate resorts. Shades of Green's prices, based on your pay grade or status, are the same all year long (except during special promotions) while Disney's vary greatly through the year.

At 480 Square feet Shades of Green's rooms are among the largest to be found on Walt Disney World property. Guest rooms include two queen size beds and a single sleeper sofa. Each guest room features either a private balcony or patio, with two chairs and a table. All of the rooms have main entries that are off of interior hallways.

All rooms include: a refrigerator, in-room safe, free Wi-Fi (in most rooms the signal is just OK), in-room movies/video games, coffee maker, hair dryer, and an iron and ironing board.

Shades of Green also offers Family Suite combinations, sleeping between 5 and 12. Plan far in advance, especially during the busy seasons, if you want one of these suites.

Shades has comparable amenities to those found at the Disney Deluxe Resorts including: Table Service, Buffet Service, and Quick Service Dining, room service, an arcade, playground, heated pools, hot tub, kids splash area, a gym, indoor bar, and luggage service.

With 586 rooms, Shades never feels crowded, except during the breakfast rush at the Garden Gallery Buffet Breakfast, where you'll have to queue up and wait for an open table.

The single resort bus stop is located on the lower front level of the main building. Shades buses run on a set schedule to several WDW destinations.

Disney's Polynesian Village Resort is just a short 10 to 15-minute walk away. There you'll find even more dining options as well as the Magic Kingdom Resort Monorail line.

The transportation and Ticket Center is another five to ten minute walk from the Polynesian. There you can catch the monorail to Epcot.

Check in is after 1500 hrs.

Check out is prior to 1100 hrs.

Disney Benefits:

Disney's Magical Express: No

Disney Transportation from the resort: No

Free theme parking: No

Participation in Extra Magic Hours: Yes

Charging Disney purchases to your room: No

Disney Merchandise delivery to your resort: Yes

Guaranteed theme park entry: Yes

FastPass Plus reservation Window: 60 days prior to check in *(see the Disney Tech Chapter for more on FastPass+)*

Disney Dining Plan: No

Advance Dining Reservations for entire trip: No

Dining

Mangino's Steakhouse – L$ D$$ Table service – Steak, Seafood. To Go Menu for carry out. Room Service is available in the evening.

The Garden Gallery – BD$ - Buffet meal - Rotating themed buffets.

Evergreens Sports Bar & Grill - LD$ - Table service – Typical Bar food.

Express Cafe – BLDS$ - Counter service – Sandwiches, pastries, snacks.

Java Cafe - S$ - Counter Service - Starbucks coffee and assorted pastry items, ice cream, and adult beverages.

On the Greens Grill – S$ - Counter service - Hot dogs, Italian sausage, hamburgers, sandwiches.

Features

Two pools, one with water slide and kids water play area – Spend a quiet afternoon relaxing at these lightly used pools!

Kids Dry and Water Play Areas – The kids will love spending time climbing, sliding, and splashing on these!

Evergreens Arcade - Play video games in this arcade adjacent to the Mill Pond Pool.

Ticket Sales – At the ticket sales office you may purchase military discounted tickets for Disney and the other major Orlando area attractions, as well as some of the minor ones, dinner shows, and out of the area attractions such as Kennedy Space Center and Busch Gardens.

Gym – Get a workout in during your stay with cardio and universal type equipment.

Spa – Pamper yourself in the Magnolia Spa, which offers full day spa services.

Tennis – feel like a round of tennis? Then check out some racquets from Guest Services.

Shopping

Army Air Force Exchange Service (AAFES) Store – Sundries and souvenirs at reasonable prices with no tax.

Location

A Magic Kingdom Area Resort

Transportation

Shades of Green Bus transportation to the Transportation and Ticket Center, Disney Hollywood Studios, Animal Kingdom, Disney Springs, and both Water Parks. Guests have the full use of Disney World's Transportation System once they arrive at a WDW departure location.

Price

Fiscal Year 2018 - 1 October 2017 – 30 September 2018

Standard Room: $115.00 Category #1, $145.00 Category #2, $155.00 Category #3

Poolside Room: $125.00 Category #1, $155.00 Category #2, $165.00 Category #3

Magnolia Suite: $280.00 All Categories

Junior Family Suite: $295.00 All Categories

Family Suite/Garden Suite: $325.00 All Categories

Palm Suite: $445.00 All Categories

Fiscal Year 2019 - 1 October 2018 – 30 September 2019

Standard Room: $119.00 Category #1, $149.00 Category #2, $159.00 Category #3

Poolside Room: $129.00 Category #1, $159.00 Category #2, $169.00 Category #3

Magnolia Suite: $284.00 All Categories

Junior Family Suite: $299.00 All Categories

Family Suite/Garden Suite: $329.00 All Categories

Palm Suite: $449.00 All Categories

Discounts

Shades of Green runs promotions during the slower times of the year, offering a variety of discounted rates, discounted rates with breakfast included and occasionally discounted rates with breakfast and dinner included.

In late 2017 Shades of Green began an 18 – 24 month long renovation (in stages) of the Magnolia Wing, reducing room inventory. Due to this both discount percentages and dates have been negatively effected. Discounts have settled out to be 15% off during 2018.

Room Notes

Shades of Green has two different regular guest room types and several types of suites.

All regular Guest rooms sleep 5 on two queen beds and a fold down single couch. The couch bed is not suited for tall individuals!

Standard Rooms – Are located in both the original Magnolia wing and the newer Palm Wing. The Palm is closer to parking, while the Magnolia is closer to the pools and much of the dining.

Poolside Room – Shades has 46 Poolside rooms, these rooms are an extra $10 per night. These are popular and will fill up early.

All Poolside rooms are located in the Magnolia Wing of the resort. Thirteen rooms face the Magnolia Pool on two sides in an "L" shape, while the remaining 33 face the Mill Pond Pool on three sides in a squared "U" shape.

The Magnolia rooms and the middle Mill Pond rooms are closest to the lobby and the two outer sections of the Mill Pond rooms extend towards the rear of the property and are close to Evergreens and the playground.

Suites – Shades of Green has 12z suites All but one of the Suites are located in the Palm Wing.

Note, Shades does offer connecting rooms and at the Category 1 and 2 rates it is cheaper to get two connecting rooms than it is to get one Junior or Family Suite! While at the Category 3 rates the Junior Suite would be cheaper than two rooms and the Family Suite would still be more expensive.

Junior Suite – Sleeps six in two rooms. The master bedroom has a King bed and full bath. The Living area has two fold out double sized couches, a dining table and chairs, a second full bath, and a kitchenette.

Family Suite – Sleeps eight in two rooms. The master bedroom has a King bed and full bath. The Living area has two fold out double sized couches, a double Murphy Bed, a dining table and chairs, a second full bath, and a kitchenette.

Special Suites:

The Magnolia Suite is a two-room suite that sleeps 5. In the bedroom there is a king bed and a single fold out couch and there is a double sleeper sofa in the living room.

The Garden Suite is a 2 rooms suite that sleeps 4. The master room has 1 king bed with a full bath (stand shower only) The living area has a queen pull out sofa, table and chairs, desk with chair. Please be advised stays may be preempted up to 90 days prior due to a wedding package.

The Palm Suite sleeps 12 with three bedrooms. Two bedrooms each have two queen beds, while the third has two sets of bunk beds. The common area includes a living area with couches and chairs, a dining area, and a kitchen.

The Palm Suite may be preempted for a Wounded Warrior up to 30 days prior to arrival, Shades of Green will accommodate with another room type.

Reservations for these special suites are very hard to obtain. Try exactly 1 year out!

Shades of Green is a fantastic value, especially for those who fall into the price category number 1. Those in category 1 can get a deluxe room on WDW property for under one hundred dollars a night.

Shades offers a much slower pace than the Disney resorts do, which makes for a much more relaxed vacation.

The Walt Disney World Swan and Dolphin Resorts

Description

The Walt Disney World Swan and Dolphin Resorts are not owned by the Walt Disney Company, rather they are owned by Tishman Hotel Corporation and MetLife and are operated by Starwood Hotels and Resorts Worldwide under the Westin and Sheraton brands. Reservations may be made either through Disney's reservation system or through Starwood/Westin/Sheraton. Points may be used for stays here (via the chain websites or phone numbers)!

The Swan and Dolphin are part of the Epcot Deluxe Resort Area and sit on the far side of Crescent Lake from Epcot's International Gateway.

This makes them the furthest resorts from Epcot and the closest to Disney's Hollywood Studios.

As they are not "Disney" Resorts, you will not find much if any Disney theming within these resorts. You could transplant them anywhere else in the world without making any changes.

Both the Swan and Dolphin have large Convention Centers attached. Many Swan and Dolphin guests are staying at the resorts for a convention.

Disney Benefits

Disney's Magical Express: No

Disney Transportation from the resort: Yes

Free theme park parking: Yes

Participation in Extra Magic Hours: Yes

Charging Disney purchases to your room: No (only within the Swan and Dolphin complex)

Disney Merchandise delivery to your resort: Yes

Guaranteed theme park entry: Yes

FastPass Plus reservation Window: 60 days prior to check in

Disney Dining Plan: No

Advance Dining Reservations for entire trip: No

Dining

The Swan and Dolphin have a plethora of restaurants, many of very high quality. They run the full spectrum from Grab-and-Go to Fine Dining.

They do offer character meals at the Garden Grove in the Swan: Garden Grove Cafe Breakfast on Saturday and Sunday! - Features Goofy and Pluto. Garden Grove Dinner has the following character entertainment: Goofy and Pluto every night; Chip and Dale added on Fridays only.

Features

Main Pool with Hot Tub

Two Quiet Pools

Kiddy Pool

Kiddy Water Play Area

Playground

Guest Laundry

Fitness Center and Spa

Lakeside Beach

Camp Dolphin – Child Care

Location

An Epcot Area Resort

Transportation

Disney Bus transportation to all Disney World guest areas. Boat Transportation to: Disney's Yacht Club, Beach Club, and BoardWalk Resorts, Epcot's International Gateway, and Disney's Hollywood Studios.

There is a $20 per day plus tax self-parking fee to park your car in the Swan and Dolphin's lot. Valet parking is $28 per day.

Price

The rates at the Swan and Dolphin do vary depending on the time of year, but not as greatly as the Disney World Resorts do.

Points can be both used and earned here.

Check swananddolphin.com for rates or call (407) 934-4400 or 888-828-8850

There is a mandatory $28 plus tax per day Resort Service Package.

For this fee you will receive:

- Unlimited access to the resort's health club facilities including 24 hour access to Dolphin Health Club
- Unlimited domestic, long distance, and local calls
- 2 bottles of water refreshed daily
- In-room enhanced high speed wireless internet access
- Complimentary daily scheduled fitness classes
- Complimentary daily scheduled recreational resort and pool activities
- $25 off spa services of $100 or more during each day of your visit at Mandara Spa
- Complimentary Swan Paddle Boat rentals
- Complimentary S'mores Fun Kit each day of your stay to be used at our evening Campfire & S'mores event

Discounts

Unfortunately the Swan and Dolphin no longer offer the TROOPS military discount package which started in 2009 and ran through 2016, which included 50% off Food & Beverage and several other amenities.

The Swan and Dolphin do still offer discounts for the military under their government rate code GO1.

Call (888) 828-8850 and ask for the military rate code.

Room Notes

Rooms feature; WiFi/High Speed Internet, mini-fridge, safe, separate vanity in some rooms, hair dryer, iron, and ironing board. All rooms are non-smoking and some are disability accessible.

Guest rooms are 360 square feet will sleep 2 to 5 and feature either:

- King bed with a single or double sleeper sofa
- Two Queen beds (Swan)
- Two Queen beds and a day bed (Dolphin)
- Two full beds (Swan)
- Two full beds and a day bed (Dolphin)

Rollout Beds and cribs are available.

Swan and Dolphin Suites vary greatly, offering single to multi-room suites with minor upgrades like a wet bar, lounge chairs, and table with chairs to numerous rooms and baths with walk-in closets.

The Four Seasons Resort Orlando at Walt Disney World

Description

The Four Seasons is the newest resort on Walt Disney World property. This hotel offers five-star service at a five-star price!

You'll find no Disney theming at this very high end resort.

Disney Benefits

Disney's Magical Express: No

Disney Transportation from the resort: No

Free theme park parking: No

Participation in Extra Magic Hours: No

Charging Disney purchases to your room: No, just within the Four Seasons' complex

Disney Merchandise delivery to your resort: Yes

Guaranteed theme park entry: Yes

FastPass Plus reservation Window: 30 days prior to desired date

Disney Dining Plan: No

Advance Dining Reservations for entire trip: No

Dining

The Four Seasons has numerous restaurants, many of very high quality. They run the full spectrum from Grab-and-Go to Fine Dining.

Features

Huge Pool Complex featuring - Adult Pool, Family Pool, Splash Zone, Lazy River, Water Slide and Explorer Island.

Golf

Tennis

Fitness Facilities

Complimentary Kids' Camp

Location

The Four Seasons does not fall into one of Disney's traditional Resort Areas. It lies on the east side of Fort Wilderness Campground (a Magic Kingdom Area Resort) and on the north side of Port Orleans Resort (an Disney Springs Resort) it is about equidistant to both theme parks on the Northeast part of Disney World's property.

Transportation

Four Seasons buses every half hour to the Transportation and Ticket Center, every hour to the other parks.

All parking at the Four Seasons is Valet Parking

Price

Rates at the Four Seasons vary based upon date and range from around $500 to well over a thousand dollars per night.

See fourseasons.com/Orlando/ or call (407) 313-7777

Discounts

No known military discounts.

Room Notes

Accommodations at the Four Seasons range from Standard rooms sizing in at 500 sq. ft. to nine-room suites!

Standard rooms have either a King and sleeper sofa or two fulls. Also you'll find a table and two chairs, shower and separate tub, vanity in the bathroom.

The Disney Springs Resort Area Hotels

Description

The Disney Springs Resort Area Hotels are a collection of third party hotels located along Hotel Plaza Boulevard, which is adjacent to the Disney Springs Entertainment Area. These hotels have been around (under various individual names/hotel chains) since very early in Walt Disney World's History. When WDW just had three of its own resorts and a campground these hotels provided nearby, cheaper, overflow guest rooms.

The Disney Springs Resort Area Hotels are national chain hotels from brands you'll recognize. They are not owned or operated by Disney World.

These resorts have their own bus system, which has fewer buses and scheduled runs, which causes longer waits than the Disney World bus system.

The Disney Springs Resort Area Hotels are:

B Resort & Spa
Best Western Lake Buena Vista Resort Hotel
Doubletree Suites by Hilton Disney Springs Area
Hilton Orlando Buena Vista Palace Disney Springs Area
Hilton Orlando Lake Buena Vista Disney Springs Area
Holiday Inn Orlando – Disney Springs Area
Wyndham Lake Buena Vista

Disney Benefits

Disney's Magical Express: No

Disney Transportation from the resort: No, the Resorts have their own Shuttle bus to Disney World destinations leaving every 30 minutes.

Free theme park parking: No

Participation in Extra Magic Hours: Yes

Charging Disney purchases to your room: No

Disney Merchandise delivery to your resort: Yes

Guaranteed theme park entry: Yes, if you use the resorts' bus system

FastPass Plus reservation Window: 60 days prior to check in

Disney Dining Plan: No

Advance Dining Reservations for entire trip: No

Dining

There are a wide range of restaurants at these hotels. They run the full spectrum from grab-and-go to table service restaurants.

Features

Because these hotels are owned by different chains the features available vary greatly!

Features that are common to all resorts are:

Heated outdoor pool(s)

WiFi

Fitness Center

Business Center

Location

Hotel Plaza Boulevard, adjacent to Disney Springs (within walking distance)

Transportation

Disney Springs Resort Area Hotel bus system

Price

Prices for these resorts vary greatly; you should check their respective corporate websites.

You do have the ability to stay using points from the hotel chain's loyalty programs.

See disneyspringshotels.com

Discounts

U.S. Military Discount, up to 20% off

Both active and retired U.S. military personnel, including United States Coast Guard and activated members of the National Guard or Reservists, can enjoy this discount. Restrictions and black out dates may apply. Discount is not valid with any other offer.

*Limited availability - Offer only valid for online reservations using the link provided on their website.

With the "Celebrate the U.S. Military" offer, both active and retired U.S. military personnel, including active and retired members of the United States Coast Guard and activated members of the National Guard or Reserve, can enjoy up to 20% off the best available room rate at all of the member hotels, when booking directly.

Room Notes

You'll find all types of rooms available at these different chain hotels. Anything is available, from a standard guest room to, two-room suites, to multi-room suites with kitchens.

On Property Wrap Up

These on property non-Disney non–DoD resorts offer some of the same amenities as the Disney resorts at times at a lower price.

Those with hotel points to spare might consider a stay in one of these.

Staying Off Walt Disney World Property

Now, last on our tour are the off property resorts and other options. This section will be brief as the options are almost limitless and too numerous to list.

Once you exit Walt Disney World property there are literally hundreds, if not thousands of resorts, hotels, vacation homes, and condos to choose from! You'll find all the big national chains, smaller chains and those which are only local.

Off property locations also run the spectrum from five stars to ramshackle and run down, choose wisely!

A particular national chain that you like to use and have points accumulated with would be your best bet.

The closest areas with the most direct access to the Disney theme parks lie along US Highway 192, which runs East-West along the south end of Disney property. World Drive is the main Disney road for three of the four theme parks; it dead-ends at 192. Just to the East and West on 192 are a plethora of places for you to select from. To the West is historically called "Westgate," while to the East is Kissimmee, FL.

There is another area with many hotels located near Disney Springs. It is the area that falls between Disney's Hotel Plaza Boulevard, Interstate-4, and State Route 535. This is on the East side of Walt Disney World property. This area is less convenient due to having to navigate through the Disney Springs traffic (always heavy) and numerous red lights to get to the theme parks themselves.

Driving Northeast along I-4 towards SeaWorld, International Drive, and Universal Studios are many more locations to choose from.

Military Prices Off Property

Most national chains offer some sort of Government Rates. A military/Government ID is required upon check in. You do not usually need to be on travel orders to use these rates, but do check! The rates are most often equivalent to the max allowable rate as set by the Joint Travel Regulation and are also usually for the standard or bottom category room.

Wherever you check off property for rates be sure to ask about military discounts!

The Armed Forces Vacation Club or AFVC is a company which rents to military members unused inventory at low rates for week-long stays. AFVC's current rates are $349 for week long stays, or sometimes lower during sales.

This is a totally legit service for military members and other members of the US Government. Locations are first class, with many great amenities. AFVC has locations nationwide and in fact worldwide as well.

Walt Disney World Gateway Hotels

In Mid-April 2018 Disney World announced Gateway Hotels. "A collection of quality hotels that offer choice proximity to Walt Disney World Theme Parks!" Walt Disney World Gateway Hotels are available to book as part of a Walt Disney Travel Company Package, online or through your travel agent (That's a full priced, non-military priced package).

This collection of hotels offers accommodations for groups of all sizes and budgets, and includes the following properties:

- Waldorf Astoria Orlando
- Hilton Orlando Bonnet Creek Resort
- Wyndham Bonnet Creek Resort

Walt Disney World Good Neighbor Hotels

Reservations may also be made at the WDW Good Neighbor Hotels, a collection of over 50 mostly national chain hotels that partner with Disney. Full packages may be reserved by calling (407) 939-5249, or room only reservation by going to: wdwgoodneighborhotels.com.

These locations offer a variety of accommodations including standard rooms, suites and villas, provide Walt Disney World Resort information, have a Guest Services desk to assist with Walt Disney World vacation planning, and offer transportation to Walt Disney World theme parks (a fee may apply).

Many of these locations also include breakfast, kitchenettes and pet-friendly rooms.

These include chains like

- Best Western
- Holiday Inn
- Comfort Inn
- Courtyard
- Fairfield Inn
- Hilton
- Radisson

Wrap Up

Well, that's it for our look at the many varied options open to you for where to stay on your Disney World vacation.

Each family's situation, needs, and preferences are different (even on different trips), I hope that I've given you the information that you will need in order to decide what the best choice is for you.

Ready for More?

Next we'll be taking a tour of Walt Disney World's four theme parks. The next chapter will give you a good overview of each and what they each have has to offer.

7. Walt Disney World's Theme Parks

What's This Chapter About?

In this chapter we will be going over the four Walt Disney World theme parks, you'll get a good overview of each park and what it has to offer.

Walt Disney World has four different theme parks, Magic Kingdom, Epcot, Disney's Hollywood Studios, and Disney's Animal Kingdom.

Each park varies in size, look, and feel, but all offer attractions (that's Disney speak for rides and shows), entertainment, parades, and nighttime firework or other type shows. You'll also find many varieties of food at various prices, plus lots of souvenirs for sale.

Attractions

Some of the more intense attractions have height restrictions. If children are shorter than the set limit they cannot experience the attraction. Disney will not bend on these restrictions as they are for safety purposes; in many cases they have to do with the attraction seating and associated restraint capability.

Attractions with height restrictions will be designated in this chapter like this: *(H33)* the H designates height restriction and the following number designates how many inches tall you must be in order to ride. In this example *(H33)* you must be 33 inches tall to ride. Cast members will measure those in question.

At all Disney World attractions you may "Rider Switch." If you have a little one who is too short or who doesn't want to ride the attraction, your family will not have to wait in line twice for each parent to ride while the other stays with the child. Simply tell the attraction cast members that you'd like to Rider Switch. Then after waiting in line, one parent will wait near the boarding area with the child while the other rides. Once the first parent to ride finishes, they will then wait with the child while the other parent rides.

I'll be describing the seating capacity and layout of the attractions in the parks. You will find all types of ride vehicles at Disney World; from small continuous feed ride systems to huge stadium seating theatres.

Many rides are of the continuous feed variety. This means that the ride vehicles are mounted one after the other on a track and while running continuously follow each other around the track through the ride. The ride is not turned off (except for handicap boarding) and you board and exit the ride from a moving beltway (like at an airport) moving at the same speed as the vehicles.

When I mention seating capacity I'll use terms like theatre seating, four across, and 2+. What I mean when I use the + sign which is usually with the number 2 is that two adults can comfortably sit in the vehicle, 3 can squeeze in or mom and dad with 2 smaller kids. You are free to try to fit all four of you in one car or split up into two.

FastPass Plus

Many WDW Attractions are part of the FastPass Plus system (or FastPass+ as Disney often puts it). FastPass Plus allows you to reserve arrival times for many attractions ahead of time via Disney World's website, the My Disney Experience smartphone app, or walk up kiosks in the theme parks. Currently WDW applies FastPass Plus to individual theme parks in two different ways. The Magic Kingdom has a single "tier" system that allows you to select three arrival times per day from the full list of that park's FastPass Plus attractions. Meanwhile the other three parks (Epcot, Hollywood Studios, & Animal Kingdom) have a two tier system, you select one arrival time from a short list of highly desired attractions and two more from the remaining attractions.

The reason for the two-tier system is to keep guests from selecting two or three of the headlining attractions for FastPass in these three parks. This causes you to select two less desired attractions instead, thus spreading out the volume. For an example at Epcot you'll have to decide if you'd rather FastPass Soarin' Around the World or Test Track and you will then have to ride the other using the standby line (or single rider at Test Track). FastPass Plus arrival times are one-hour blocks of time during which you can arrive and bypass the standby line. During slower seasons this means you can almost walk right on, in busier times you will experience some wait but much shorter than the standby lines.

In this book FastPass Plus attractions are designated like this: *(FP+)* for FastPass Plus attractions in parks with only one FP+ tier. In parks with two FastPass Plus tiers you will see *(FP+1)* for Tier 1 FastPass Plus attractions and *(FP+2)* for Tier 2 FastPass Plus attractions.

For more on the FastPass Plus system see the Walt Disney World's New Technology Chapter.

You will see some attractions and restaurants marked as "Open seasonally". What this means is that during high attendance times of the year these venues are opened to add additional crowd dissipation/dining seating capacity but are closed at other times.

Single Rider Lines

Several attractions at Walt Disney World have single rider lines. These lines are used to fill all available space on the ride vehicles. For instance a party of three will take up two rows in a ride vehicle that seats in rows of two. A rider form the single rider line will be placed in that empty seat. The single rider lines move much more quickly than the standby line, but you almost certainly will not ride (in the same row or even ride vehicle) with others in your party. Attractions with single rider lines:

- Test Track
- Rock 'n' Roller Coaster
- Expedition Everest

Disney Characters

Character meet-and-greets are locations where you and or your child get to interact one-on-one with a Disney character, get an autograph if desired, and pose for a picture(s). Disney PhotoPass photographers are almost always on hand. Some meet and greets are "open air" where people queue up at an outdoor location and take turns interacting with the character while everyone else watches, others are private meet and greets conducted for your family privately in a closed room/set.

Check your daily park schedule or My Disney Experience app for times for the open-air meet and greets. The private meet and greets are held in buildings all day long and in most cases can be FastPassed ahead of time.

For more on PhotoPass see the Walt Disney World's New Technology Chapter.

Dining

Each park offers - Counter service, grab-and-go carts, table service and some buffet restaurants. At least one table service restaurant in each park offers a character meal.

The many outdoor food carts are too plentiful and changing to list here. You'll find carts selling, popcorn, drinks, adult beverages (except in the Magic Kingdom), ice cream and frozen treats, churros, turkey legs, and fresh fruits & vegetables. These are just some of the constantly evolving offerings from Disney World Outdoor Foods.

During Character meals, designated Disney characters (different at each location) will circulate through the dining area periodically. They will stop by each table for personal interaction, autographs, and pictures.

Advance Dining Reservations may be made up to 180 days in advance for restaurants with Table Service, Buffet, and Character Meals.

For more on reservations see our Walt Disney World Dining chapter.

Online Meal Ordering - New in 2017 you may use you're my Disney Experience app to order and prepay for meals at designated Counter Service restaurants. Just complete your order and then upon arrival go to the online pickup line/window. A credit card is required.

In this chapter look for these keys to the rough cost of restaurants and the meals they offer:

- $ = Less than $15 per adult
- $$ = $15 - $30 per adult
- $$$ = $30 - $60 per adult
- $$$$ = over $60 per adult
- B = Breakfast
- L = Lunch
- D = Dinner
- S = Snack

Note: alcohol is served in the Magic Kingdom only in several table service restaurants. At the other parks adult beverages are widely served in all restaurants and at walk-up counters and carts.

Shopping

As you tour Disney World's theme parks you will find a wide variety of merchandise and souvenir options available to you.

You'll find Disney character and theme park centric items like stuffed characters, clothing, hats, and many other varied items. Some of these will be generic, others will be themed for the land or area they are being sold in, e.g. a Mickey Mouse in a space suit in Tomorrowland, Aerosmith items at Rock n' Rollercoaster, and Star Wars items at Star Tours. Other items are not at all Disney centric, e.g. Books on American history at the American Adventure, Canadian souvenirs at the Epcot's Canada Pavilion, or wines and foods from the various counties at Epcot's World showcase.

Walt Disney World makes lots of money on souvenirs (and food) that helps offset discounts like the Armed Forces Salute. They use many techniques to encourage you to make purchases such as, when you exit the parks, the merchandise shops are on the right side of the street or pathway (Americans naturally walk on the right, morning type foods are on the right as you enter) or by designing their newer attractions so the ride exits into a gift shop which sells items associated with that attraction. They will also pipe tantalizing smells, such as that of baked goods to the outdoor areas near restaurants to encourage you to enter!

Package Delivery

A great service that Disney World offers is Package Delivery. Any item that you purchase in the theme parks can be delivered to either your on property resort (Disney Resorts, Shades of Green, the Swan and Dolphin, Disney Springs Hotels, and The Four Seasons) or to the park entrance (for pickup on your way out). This way you do not have to lug your purchase around the park all day!

Bag Check... Bag Check...... Bag Check!

All guests entering Disney's parks with bags will have to pass through a bag check area prior to entering. All bags, purses, backpacks, camera bags, coolers, etc. must be opened for a visual inspection by WDW Security.

Please have all pockets on your bag open prior to reaching the Security Cast Member to speed things up and keep the line moving.

Those without bags, or cameras without a bag may bypass the bag check and walk right through the "Guests Without Bags" entrance to the side of the bag check lines. They can then wait on the other side of the bag check area if needed.

Starting in early 2016 Disney instituted a second layer of physical security. Now guests who are "randomly" selected are required to empty their pockets and walk through a metal detector. Often they also institute a scan of 100% of entering guests.

Free Wi-Fi

Wi-Fi service is available for free in all Disney World theme parks and resort hotels!

Strollers, Wheel Chairs, and Scooters

Strollers, wheel chairs, and scooters, are available for rent from Disney World at the theme parks and downtown Disney.

Strollers - Disney strollers are made from rigid plastic and they don't recline. They do offer a canopy for sun protection and seat belts. *Note: these plastic strollers really heat up in the afternoon Florida sun!*

There is a pouch on the back to hold items, but no cup holders. These strollers can only be used within the park, which means at the end of a long day, you will be stuck carrying your children back to the car, tram, bus, or monorail.

They are not available at water parks or at the resorts, which means more carrying children around. *Note: infants and children under age 2 don't do well in these strollers; they just aren't designed for them.*

There are many Orlando area companies that rent modern strollers at reasonable prices. These companies deliver to and pick up from your resort, so you'll have the use of the stroller for the entire vacation, not just in the parks.

Scooters and Wheelchairs - The same is true for Scooters and Wheelchairs, Disney rents them in the parks and at Downtown Disney but you cannot take them elsewhere and Disney's prices are high.

There are many Orlando area companies that rent Scooters and Wheelchairs at reasonable prices. These companies deliver to and pick up from your resort, so you'll have the use of the stroller for the entire vacation, not just in the parks.

For recommendations on Stroller and Scooter rental companies see the Links Section at the end of this chapter.

Lockers

Lockers are available for rent on a daily basis at the front of each theme park. Many find it convenient to stash sweatshirts for later in the evening, purchases, camera bags, or other bulky items for later retrieval. Current rates are $10 per day for a large locker and $7 per day for a small one in addition you'll be charged a $5 refundable key deposit. Your locker fee is good for locker use the entire day at any park, so save the receipt.

Theme Park Hours

The regular hours of operation of WDW's theme parks vary depending on the time of year and expected attendance. Below is a general overview, excluding Extra Magic Hours.

All of WDW's parks open at 9am except during Morning Extra Magic Hours

Magic Kingdom – The hours of operation at the Magic Kingdom vary the most closing anywhere from 6 pm to 1am.

As a general rule, about the same amount of attractions can be accomplished on a short day as can be on a long day. This is because of the much lower crowd levels and associated attraction wait times on short days.

Epcot – Epcot is usually open until 9 pm, but occasionally will stay open till 10 pm. While the Future World section opens at 9, the World Showcase doesn't open until 11 am. During the slower times of the year Future World attractions will close earlier than 9 pm.

Hollywood Studios – Closing times at the Studios vary between 7 and 10 pm.

Animal Kingdom – Animal Kingdom has recently increased their hours with a closing time usually around 9 pm.

Extra Magic Hours

Participation in Extra Magic Hours is a benefit available to those staying in a Walt Disney World Resort, Shades of Green, and the Walt Disney World Swan and Dolphin.

Extra Magic Hours, or EMH allow Disney's on property guests the ability to spend more time in specific parks on specific days, than the general public.

There are two types of Extra Magic Hours, Morning EMH and Nighttime EMH.

Morning EMH allow on property guests to enter the designated theme park one hour earlier than the regular opening time. This early start to your day gives you a big advantage, as you can get in quite a few attractions during that first hour when the specified EMH park is relatively empty.

Nighttime EMH allow on property guests to stay in the designated theme park two hours later than the regular closing time.

Nighttime EMH can be particularly effective for those who want to ride lots of rides. Off property guests, those who started the day early, and families with little kids will have mostly cleared out, freeing up the standby lines so that you can quickly ride over and over.

Theme Park Capacity Closures

Each Walt Disney World theme park and water park has a set maximum capacity, these limits are for safety. During the busiest times of the year these capacities can be reached. Disney has procedures which they will implement by stages as a park nears capacity.

The Magic Kingdom is the park most likely to experience capacity-based closures because it is the most popular. On Christmas Day the Magic Kingdom can be closed to off property guests by 10 am. Disney Hollywood Studios and Animal Kingdom have smaller capacities and next in the probability of closing. Epcot is the least likely to close due to its large size.

As people exit the closed park, bringing the number inside back down, Disney will begin allowing others to enter again.

Occasionally a theme park parking lot will reach capacity before the park does. In this event Disney will divert those trying to park to another theme park parking lot and bus you back to the park you were headed to.

Below are the different phases of Disney's park closing plan, in escalating severity.

Walt Disney World capacity closing phases

Phase 1 Park Closing - Guests with Magic Your Way base tickets or a 1-Day 1-Park Ticket, Guests without an admission ticket, and Cast Members using Main Gate & Silver Passes will be turned around at the parking lot booths.

Phase 2 Park Closing - Admission is limited to:

•Disney Resort Guests (including Shades of Green, the Walt Disney World Swan and Dolphin, the Four Seasons, and guests arriving by bus from the Hotel Plaza Boulevard hotels.

•Annual, Premier and Premium Annual Pass holders

•Guests with Hopper tickets coming from another park

•Guests re-entering the park

•Guests with dining reservations

•Magic Kingdom Guests with reservations for Bibbidi Bobbidi Boutique or The Pirates League

•Guests using Walt Disney World Resort Transportation

•Guests with pre-purchased 1 day Magic Kingdom tickets

Phase 3 Park Closing - Admission is limited to:

- Disney Resort Guests (including the Walt Disney World Swan and Dolphin, and guests arriving by bus from the Hotel Plaza Boulevard hotels)

- Annual, Premier and Premium Annual Pass holders

- Guests with dining reservations

- Magic Kingdom Guests with reservations for Bibbidi Bobbidi Boutique or The Pirates League

Phase 4 Park Closing - Closed to all guests.

As you can see the key to being admitted during closures (except Phase 4) is to be a Disney Resort guest (including Shades of Green) or to have a dining reservation in the theme park.

That's it for the basics; now let's start exploring the four Disney theme parks. We'll start with the first park opened at Disney World, the Magic Kingdom and then continue on with the other parks, in the order they opened.

Magic Kingdom

The Magic Kingdom is Walt Disney World's busiest theme park with twice the annual attendance of the other individual parks at WDW. Those going to WDW for shorter periods will make sure they go to the Magic Kingdom versus seeing all of the other parks.

The Magic Kingdom is sometimes mistakenly referred to as "Disney World" by those who are unfamiliar. This is because it was the original, single theme park when Disney World opened and also because people were familiar with Disneyland which only had a single theme park for most of its existence and is both the name of the whole California resort and the theme park.

Walt Disney World is the name of the entire Florida resort property covering over 27 thousand acres, which encompasses the four theme parks, two water parks, resort hotels and shopping and entertainment venues, as well as conservation areas and waterways. The Magic Kingdom is just one of the four theme parks.

The Magic Kingdom is divided into different areas or lands as Disney calls them. Each land is themed much as you'd expect based upon its name. The theming includes the architecture, cast member costumes, types of attractions and food, and even the background music.

Arrival

Your arrival location at the Magic Kingdom will depend upon your method of transportation.

Those traveling from a Disney-owned resort will arrive just steps from the Magic Kingdom main entrance. Right outside the Magic Kingdom entrance is the Magic Kingdom bus terminal where buses from the Disney resorts arrive, the boat docks where boats from the Disney resorts arrive, and the monorail station where both the Disney Resort and Express Monorails arrive.

Those traveling from a non-Disney resort, or those who drive their car will arrive at the Transportation and Ticket Center, or TTC for short.

The TTC is adjacent to the Magic Kingdom Parking lot and separated from the Magic Kingdom by the Seven Seas Lagoon and about three quarters of a mile in distance.

Those arriving by car will park in the Magic Kingdom parking lot and then board trams for a brief ride to the TTC or walk if they are parked close enough.

Buses from non-Disney resorts arrive at the bus terminal just to the side of the TTC.

Once at the TTC you may buy your Disney World tickets if needed and then board the Disney transportation to the Magic Kingdom.

There are two transportation methods available, the Monorail and a large ferryboat.

There are three different monorail lines, the Express, Resort, and Epcot lines.

-The Express Monorail only stops at the TTC and the Magic Kingdom. Those getting on at the TTC will whisk by (actually through) the Contemporary Resort on their non-stop trip to the Magic Kingdom.

-The Resort Monorail runs in the opposite direction and makes stops at the TTC, and the Magic Kingdom as well as all of the Disney Resorts on the monorail loop. Those getting on at the TTC will stop at the Polynesian Village Resort and then the Grand Floridian Resort for several minutes each before arriving at the Magic Kingdom.

-The Epcot Monorail is a direct line to the Epcot theme park.

The ferryboat dock is to the left as you enter the TTC. Two to three ferries will be running at any given time based upon load requirements. The ferryboat will make a direct trip to the Magic Kingdom dock

Security

Starting in 2017 Disney World decentralized their Magic Kingdom bag check area. Those traveling to the Magic Kingdom from Magic Kingdom Area Resorts via the monorail or boats will process through security at their resort before boarding. While those traveling from the TTC will go through security prior to entering the TTC.

Main Street USA

You'll enter the Magic Kingdom at the south end of Main Street USA, one of the Magic Kingdom's themed lands. This is the one and only entrance and exit to the park.

At the far (north) end of Main Street is the hub, the central area around which the rest of the lands are arranged. Cinderella Castle sits on the far side of the hub. Moving clockwise around the hub are the entrances to: Adventureland and Frontierland, Liberty Square, Fantasyland, and finally Tomorrowland.

Main Street U.S.A. is a re-creation of early 20th century small-town America. Here you can meet Mickey Mouse in person or get princess/pirate makeovers for the kids in the barbershop.

Attractions

Flag Retreat – Though not an actual attraction this is highly recommended! This awesome event is held daily at 5 p.m.

A military member or retiree is selected at random daily to participate. If you want to try to be selected, be at the Magic Kingdom well prior to opening so that you are standing against the rope used to keep people out until "Rope Drop." Wear something that is very conspicuously military related (unit or service tee shirts, Veteran ball caps, military logo backpacks, etc), you may be noticed and selected.

Town Square Theater *(FP+)* – Enjoy a private character meet-and-greet with Mickey Mouse and Tinkerbell. Disney PhotoPass photographers will take your picture with Mickey and Tink. You can take your own too or they'll use your camera for you. Each character has their own private room and separate wait queue.

Walt Disney World Railroad – Ride on a real steam train on an approximately 20-minute journey around the Magic Kingdom. Your train returns to Main Street after stops at Frontierland and Storybook Circus in

Fantasyland. The four trains that run this loop were all built around the turn of the century in the U.S. In the 70's Disney found them in Mexico and brought them home to be lovingly refurbished for the Magic Kingdom. Walt was a huge railroad fan. You can board or exit at any stop.

Sorcerers of the Magic Kingdom – This immersive, role-playing game features interaction with Disney characters who come to life in previously hidden areas throughout Magic Kingdom park. Families, friends and individuals can take on the animated Disney Villains by casting spell cards featuring Rafiki, Rapunzel, Woozles and more than 60 other characters. This is a self-paced, self-guided interactive quest.

Dining

Tony's Town Square Restaurant – LD $$ - Table Service - Pastas, salads, and Italian entrees. Italian wines by the glass and bottle as well as Italian beers by the glass.

Main Street Bakery – BS $ - Counter Service – Featuring Starbucks breakfast selections, gourmet sandwiches, desserts, and cookies.

Plaza Ice Cream Parlor – S $ - Counter Service - Ice cream, snacks and soft drinks.

The Plaza Restaurant – LD $ - Table Service - Sandwiches, fries, salad, desserts and soda fountain treats.

Casey's Corner – LDS $ - Counter Service - Hot dogs, fries, soft drinks, snacks. **Online Ordering Available.**

The Crystal Palace – BL $$ D $$$ - Buffet Service – Features an all-you-can-eat Character Buffet featuring Pooh, Tigger, Eeyore, and Piglet.

Shopping

Harmony Barber Shop - Haircuts, beard and mustache trims, princess and pirate makeovers. The Dapper Dans barbershop quartet entertains at times through the day. Call 407-939-7529 for an appointment.

The Chapeau - Hats and monogramming. Get your Mickey Mouse Ears here.

Confectionery - Gifts of candy, baked goods, and sweets.

Crystal Arts - Glass cutting, glass blowing.

Disney Clothiers - Disney character fashions for men and women.

Disney & Co. - Souvenirs, frames, children's clothing, and assorted Disney merchandise.

Emporium – A huge retail location (the whole west side of Main Street), they carry most Disney World gifts, clothes and souvenirs.

Main Street Athletic Club - Sports apparel and equipment.

The Main Street Cinema – Carries plush toys, pins, books, Disney videos, CDs, and cassettes.

Main Street Gallery - Posters, lithographs, books, and postcards.

Adventureland

Adventureland Embodies the edge of civilization, here you'll find pirates, shipwrecked survivors, the wild rivers of the world and even a Middle Eastern bazaar. Adventureland is home to Pirates of the Caribbean.

Attractions

Swiss Family Tree House - Walk through the recreated home of the Swiss Family Robinson. Based on the 1960 Disney feature film. As you follow the stairs, platforms, and bridges that guide you along you will see various "rooms" that the Robinsons have set up and the ingenious ways they've used bamboo and other basic things to make "modern" conveniences. There are a lot of stairs to climb on this self-guided tour.

Jungle Cruise *(FP+)* - Cruise down the rivers of the world: the Nile, Amazon, Congo and the Mekong Rivers. Your campy Boat Captain, who is full of jokes, will lead your 10 minute long expedition. On this ride you will board a boat that will take you on your journey along with about a dozen other people. As the ride moves along you will see lots of vegetation interspersed with audio-animatronic scenes while your Boat Captain spouts a continuous stream of corny jokes. You'll see lions, elephants, gorillas and many other "animals" on your journey.

Walt Disney's Enchanted Tiki Room – A musical show featuring audio-animatronic birds. You'll enter a theatre for this show, which is put on by 200 talking and singing audio-animatronic tropical birds and flowers. Several songs and jokes will be performed in this nine minute long performance. This is one of the attractions to skip if you are time limited.

Audio-animatronics are one of Walt Disney's big innovations, lifelike figures (human or animal) that are animated via hydraulics, pneumatics, and mechanics, with movements timed precisely to an audio track. You'll find these characters in many WDW attractions.

The Magic Carpets of Aladdin *(FP+)* – A circular flying carpet ride, you can circle the bazaar and make your carpet rise and dive. Each carpet vehicle will accommodate four individuals. Those in the front seat can control whether the carpet goes up or down on its circular journey, but watch out for spitting camels!

Pirates of the Caribbean *(FP+)* – This ride is a classic and a must see! Board a boat with about a dozen others to hit the high seas on this 10 minute long trip through pirate locales. You'll see skeletons, pirates and villagers as you float along. The audio animatronic scenes depict the sacking of a village, you will float through a cannon battle between a pirate ship and seaside fort, then float through the village as pirates loot and plunder. During the voyage you'll be regaled with the Disney pirate anthem, Yo-Ho Yo-Ho a Pirate's Life for Me. Be sure to keep a sharp eye out for Captain Jack Sparrow!

A Pirate's Adventure – Treasures of the Seven Seas – Search through Adventureland on this self-paced, self-guided interactive quest for "Treasure Finder Cards."

Pirate's League – Transform into a pirate with a makeover and new "Pirate Name." Then have your portrait made and receive your loot. Ages 3+ requires an extra fee (4-levels of makeover and loot $30-$40 plus tax) call 407-939-2739 to reserve.

Dining

Aloha Isle – S $ - Counter Service - Floats, pineapple spears, juice and beverages, and the famous Dole Whip (soft serve pineapple goodness). **Online Ordering Available.**

Sunshine Tree Terrace – S $ - Counter Service - Non-fat frozen yogurt, citrus specialties like the citrus swirl, and assorted beverages.

Tortuga Tavern – L $ - Counter Service – Ribs and Hot Dogs. Hours vary. Open Seasonally.

Jungle Navigation Co, Ltd. Skipper Canteen – LD $$ - Table Service - Asian, South American, and African influenced cuisine. Noodle Bowls, Chicken, Pork, Steak, appetizers and deserts plus novelty drinks all served with the dry, corny humor you'll find on the Jungle Cruise. Wines by the glass and bottle as well as beers by the glass.

Shopping

Agrabah Bazaar – An open-air marketplace, Aladdin souvenirs and Middle Eastern items.

Island Supply Company - Surfing gear, island apparel, leis, sunglasses, and grass skirts.

Pirates Bazaar – All the pirate gear you'll ever need, hats and hooks, shirts, rings, ships in a bottle and eye patches. Argh!

Frontierland

Frontierland depicts life in America's expanding western frontier, from the Mississippi pushing westward to the Wild West, from Tom Sawyer's Island, to Indian Territory and further West to gold prospecting camps. Frontierland is home to two of the Magic Kingdom's "Mountains", Big Thunder Mountain and Splash Mountain.

Attractions

Frontierland Shootin' Arcade – Try your best to get a bull's-eye. Grab your Buffalo Rifle and take your best shot at the various targets. There is an extra minimal charge for this attraction and it can be skipped if time is an issue.

Country Bear Jamboree - Audio-animatronic bears perform a vaudeville type show. Enter Grizzly Hall, with theatre type seating to enjoy this show. You'll see a collection of all kinds of bears singing and performing songs and jokes in their version of the Grand Ole Oprey. You'll either love it or have to Grin and Bear it…

Tom Sawyer Island – A Fort, caves, tunnels, trails, and barrel bridges are some of the fun things to explore on this island. You'll have to catch a raft across the river to get to the island where kids will love to explore. It is a great place for them to blow off some steam! The island closes at dusk.

Walt Disney World Railroad - An approximately 20-minute journey around the Magic Kingdom on a real steam train. Your train returns to Frontierland after stops at Storybook Circus in Fantasyland and Main Street USA. Located near Splash Mountain it is a great way to make the hop over to Fantasyland.

Splash Mountain *(FP+)(H40)* – A log flume ride through Brer Rabbit's Laughin' Place. One of Magic Kingdom's favorite thrill rides. Board your eight person log to float through the scenes from *Song of the South* where you will see Brer Rabbit's adventures while listening to songs from the movie. You'll progressively get higher during this calm portion of the ride. There may be a few small plunges along the way, until you come to the big final drop and splash. You will get wet! Some more than others, the left side is alleged to get less water.

Big Thunder Mountain Railroad *(FP+)(H40)* - Hold on to your hats this runaway mine train is the "Wildest Ride in the Wilderness." You will board a 15 row train, complete with locomotive in the front for this rollercoaster ride. This fun outdoor coaster zips through mining town scenery based upon Utah's Brice Canyon with lots of dips and curves. Don't miss, one of our favorites!

Dining

Golden Oak Outpost – LDS $ - Counter Service – Chicken nuggets, waffle fries, and soft drinks.

Pecos Bill's Tall Tales Cafe – LD $ - Counter Service – fajitas, burritos, tacos, burgers, salads and beverages. All with a southwest flair. One of the two all you want "fixins' bars" in the Magic Kingdom. **Online Ordering Available.**

Westward Ho – BS $ - Cart Service – Grab and Go breakfast items, corn dogs, churros, snacks.

Shopping

Briar Patch - The Splash Mountain co-located gift shop. An assortment of Winnie the Pooh, Tigger, and friends related merchandise.

Frontier Trading Post - Items from the Old West, cowboy hats, sheriff's badges, and Native American headdresses.

Liberty Square

Liberty Square will immerse you in America's colonial history, from the thirteen colonies to the Hudson River of the Gilded Age. Listen to and see our Presidents, past and present in the Hall of Presidents or hangout with hitchhiking ghosts in the Haunted Mansion.

Attractions

Liberty Square Riverboat - Ride aboard a recreated steam powered paddle wheel boat on the Rivers of America. The Liberty Belle a real functioning paddle wheel steamboat was built right on property. Enjoy the 17-minute ride along the Rivers of America where you'll see lots of scenery while listening to your tour guide Mark Twain.

The Hall of Presidents – A patriotic show featuring audio-animatronic versions of all the American Presidents. This is a 20 minute long presentation in a nicely air-conditioned theatre. The show is more patriotic than fun and youngsters may get antsy and over tired, hot adults may nod off. But I love this show (along with the American Adventure at Epcot). After a film there is a discussion of the importance of the Constitution from its framing through the space age. Then each president is introduced in order from George Washington to the present. The audio-animatronic figures behave in a life-like manner, swaying, fidgeting, whispering to each other as the show progresses and each acknowledges being introduced.

The Haunted Mansion *(FP+)* - Ride through this haunted mansion and then the graveyard outside. Kids will enjoy the interactive items in the queue area. Once you enter you will be directed into a small room with a group of others and be sealed in. Your Ghost Host will then introduce you to the mansion. **Note at the end of this sequence the lights go out momentarily and there is a medium loud scream heard on the sound track, meanwhile Haunted Mansion aficionados in the group will scream out loud themselves playing along.** *This is the scariest moment of the attraction.*

Afterwards a door will open and you'll board your Doom Buggy for a tour of the mansion and the graveyard "outside." The doom buggies will accommodate 2+ with small kids. You will see lots of unique visual illusions and audio-animatronic ghouls and ghosts. Beware of hitchhiking ghosts!

Take time to admire the Liberty Tree, a 135-year-old live oak which was transplanted from another location on Disney property that had a full-grown weight of 35 tons when moved in 1971. The tree represents the communal meeting places in many New England towns, where American Revolutionaries met. The 13 lanterns hanging in the tree represent the 13 original colonies. Look for the replica of the Liberty Bell nearby.

Dining

Liberty Tree Tavern – LD $$ - Table Service - A la carte lunch featuring entrees, soups, and sandwiches with American flavors. All-you-care-to-eat family style dinner beginning at 4 p.m. Wines by the glass and bottle as well as beers, hard ciders, and mimosas by the glass.

Columbia Harbour House – LD $ - Counter Service - Seafood, chicken potpie, and salads. **Online Ordering Available.**

Sleepy Hollow – LS $ - Counter Service – Waffle sandwiches, corn dogs, pretzel dog, funnel cakes, beverages. During breakfast they have a Breakfast Egg and Cheese Waffle.

Liberty Square Market – S $ - Cart Service - Fresh fruit and other "grab 'n' go" items, including "jacket potatoes" (baked potatoes with toppings).

The Diamond Horseshoe – LD $$$ - Table Service, All You Care to Eat – BBQ pork, turkey, smoked sausage, braised beef all with cowboy beans, corn on the cob, and mac and cheese.

Shopping

Heritage House - Historical items, early-American gifts, flags, books, and t-shirts.

Liberty Square Portrait Gallery - Silhouette drawings by artists.

Memento Mori – Haunted Mansion art, collectibles, gifts, and housewares.

Ye Olde Christmas Shoppe - Christmas gifts and decorations, Disney-themed and traditional.

Fantasyland

Fantasyland embodies all things fanciful, here castles abound. Take a flight with Peter Pan, eat lunch in the Beast's castle, or go on a ride through the Seven Dwarf's mine. With the recent "New Fantasyland" expansion, this is the biggest land in the Magic Kingdom.

Attractions

Peter Pan's Flight *(FP+)* – Ride in a pirate ship over the rooftops of London and into Neverland as you follow Peter Pan on his adventures. Board a 2+ person (with small kids) pirate ship for this airborne journey. You'll cruise over all major scenes from the movie until the crocodile catches the Captain.

"it's a small world" *(FP+)* – A Disney classic, audio-animatronic dolls from all over the world entertain you during this indoor boat ride. Your boat will seat about a dozen people in 4+ person rows. Each scene you pass through will feature children and animals of the world singing and dancing together in friendship, all to that tune many love to hate or hate to love, *"It's a small world after all."*

Mickey's PhilharMagic *(FP+)* – This is a 3D movie experience, featuring Donald Duck hijacking Mickey's Sorcerer's Hat. Grab your 3D glasses and enter the theatre where the gang is preparing for a show. During the setup Donald unwisely tries to use Mickey's hat. A whirlwind adventure through several of the best loved Disney movies ensues until Mickey saves the day. One of our family favorites.

Prince Charming Regal Carrousel - A 1917 carousel with beautifully carved horses. This beautiful carrousel was saved by Disney from the closed Olympic Park in Maplewood NJ. It was then refurbished to its current beauty.

Princess Fairytale Hall *(FP+)* –Cinderella, Rapunzel, and other princesses in one on one character meet and greets.

Seven Dwarfs Mine Train *(FP+)(H38)* - Race through the diamond mine from *Snow White and the Seven Dwarfs* on an adventurous family coaster. Board your two person to a row mine train for a new kind of coaster experience. The individual mine cars sway side to side in turns like a pendulum. This coaster is milder than Big Thunder Mountain and slows in the middle for an audio-animatronic visit with the dwarfs. The seating is quite tight in these cars and six footers like me will be jammed in. This is the newest attraction at the Magic Kingdom and is also in high demand. This is also one of the first items to be used up in FastPass Plus. A must do!

The Many Adventures of Winnie the Pooh *(FP+)* – Ride in a honey pot and relive all of Pooh's adventures. Your 4+ person honey pot will take you on a fun journey through the Hundred Acre Wood where you'll see scenes from the books and movies. Join Pooh and friends in a celebration as the ride ends.

Enchanted Tales with Belle *(FP+)* – An interactive story adventure featuring Belle, Lumiere, and you. First you'll tour Maurice's cottage and workshop and then you will pass through a magic mirror. Several guests will be chosen to help reenact Belle's story and the rest will be seated in the library (theatre) to watch.

Under the Sea - Journey of the Little Mermaid *(FP+)* – Ride in your own clamshell to follow Ariel and her friends through the scenes of the Little Mermaid. After getting into your 2+ person clamshell you'll descend under the sea in this recreation of the new classic Disney movie. You'll hear all the famous songs too. As the ride nears the end you'll surface and see Ariel.

Ariel's Grotto *(FP+)* - A character meet-and-greet with Aerial, the Little Mermaid. Since Aerial can't walk around the park with her fins you can join her where she sits in her grotto to say hello.

Casey Jr. Splash 'N' Soak Station - A water play area that is part of the new Fantasyland. This is a big splash area for the kids to run around on the rubberized surface and cool off in the water jets.

Pete's Silly Sideshow – Disney classic character meet and greet with The Astounding Donaldo, The Great Goofini, Minnie Magnifique, and Madame Daisy Fortuna.

Dumbo the Flying Elephant *(FP+)* - Ride on your favorite elephant, Dumbo. Make him fly up then down as you fly in a circle. Your 2+ person elephant can be controlled to fly up and down on this circular journey. With the New Fantasyland expansion this ride now has double the capacity with two sets of elephants. There is an interactive play area for kids to blow off steam while waiting.

The Barnstormer *(FP+)(H35)* – A kids' coaster, features Goofy as a stunt plane pilot. Fly around with Goofy on his barnstorming flight. The coaster resembles a biplane and is the Disney coaster most like the typical open-air coaster, though it is not a rough thrilling one.

Mad Tea Party *(FP+)* - Spinning oversized teacups with an *Alice in Wonderland* theme. This 2 minute long ride whizzes round and round while each group of cups also revolves and you can manually spin your own cup. This ride is not for those with weak stomachs! It is 2 minutes longer than it should be for me…

Fairytale Garden – A character meet and greet with Merida or other rotating characters.

Walt Disney World Railroad - An approximately 20-minute journey around the Magic Kingdom on a real steam train. Your train returns to Fantasyland after stops at Main Street USA and Frontierland. It is a quick ride to Main Street from here. There is also a short walking path that connects the railroad station with the Space Mountain area in Tomorrowland. This is convenient for those in Tomorrowland who want to get to Main Street or Frontier land.

Dining

Pinocchio Village Haus – LD $ - Counter Service - Sandwiches, flatbread pizzas, pasta, salads, and soft drinks. **Online Ordering Available.**

Cinderella's Royal Table – BLD $$$ - Table Service – You can dine in Cinderella Castle with the princesses during breakfast, lunch and dinner. Breakfast and lunch are Character meals. Reservations are necessary (this restaurant fills up within minutes 180 days prior!). Characters vary, but almost always include Cinderella and the Fairy Godmother and may include Belle, Jasmine and Snow White. Breakfast options are from basic to decadent, while kids dine on scrambled eggs and waffles. Lunch and dinner offerings include: Soup of the Day, salad, Seared Pork Tenderloin, Pan-seared All-Natural Chicken, and Summer Vegetable Couscous. At Lunch and dinner enjoy expensive wines by the glass and bottle.

Friar's Nook – LS $ - Counter Service - Hot dogs, mac 'n cheese, and drinks.

Be Our Guest Restaurant – BL $ D $$ - Modified Counter Service for breakfast and lunch and Table service for dinner – Dine in Beast's Castle, during breakfast and lunch order at the Quick Service registers at the end of the queue and your meal will be delivered to your table. During dinner enjoy regular table service. Breakfast includes eggs, quiche, and breakfast sandwiches. Lunch features: sandwiches, salads, and soups. While dinner offerings include: steak, seafood, pork, lamb and more. Beer and wine served with dinner.

Gaston's Tavern – S $ - Counter Service – Ham and cheese-stuffed pretzel, fruit and cheese Picnic Platter, the unique beverage LeFou's Brew, other snacks, and a extremely awesome cinnamon roll are some of the offerings.

Prince Eric's Village Market - S $ – Cart Service - Grab and go healthy options.

Storybook Treats – S $ - Counter Service – Ice cream, snacks and soft drinks.

Cheshire Cafe – S $ - Counter Service – Ice coffee, slushies, snacks, and soft drinks.

Shopping

Bibbidi Bobbidi Boutique - Salon for girls and boys, with character costumes and more. Ages 3-12 call 407-939-7895 for appointments.

Castle Couture - Mickey ears, apparel, accessories, toys & plush items.

Sir Mickey's – Here you will find snow globes, costumes, and hats.

Fantasy Faire – The Mickey's PhilharMagic co-located shop, offers plush toys and Donald Duck items.

Big Top Souvenirs - Merchandise and food items under the circus Big Top.

Bonjour Village Gifts - Beauty and the Beast merchandise.

Hundred Acre Goods – Pooh themed apparel and accessories.

Tomorrowland

Tomorrowland is a look at what the "Future That Never Was" might look like, as imagined by sci-fi writers from the 1920's and 1930's. Take a spin on the third of the Magic Kingdom's "Mountains", Space Mountain, or help Buzz Lightyear defeat Emperor Zurg.

Attractions

Tomorrowland Speedway *(FP+)(H32)(H54 to ride alone)* - Drive a mini racecar around the Tomorrowland Speedway. These little two-person gas powered cars tool around the track on a guide rail. You can steer side to side and around corners, but the rail keeps you "firmly" in your lane. The combo gas pedal/brake is quite hard to push and is mounted in the center of the floorboard so the adult can operate it while the child attempts to steer. Pre-driving kids will enjoy this, adults will be glad when the left to right jerking and bumping into stopped cars is over!

Space Mountain – *(FP+)(H44)* The Magic Kingdom's original "Mountain" ride a high-speed, indoor coaster on a dark track! Seating is two persons per car in 2 car trains. Each car has a forward and rear seat. After boarding you'll blast off into space, the coaster runs through an almost totally dark area, you will never know which way it is going to turn or when the next drop is coming. This wins the prize as the most exciting ride in the Magic Kingdom.

Tomorrowland Transit Authority – Take a tour of Tomorrowland on this elevated track. One of Walt's passions was designing and one day building cities of tomorrow, he constantly explored technologies, invented new ways of doing things and then tried them out in his parks. This ride was originally called the WEDway (for Walter Elias Disney) PeopleMover and it runs on a linear magnetic induction system. The ride vehicles have no motors they are pulled along the track by magnets activated in sequence. Ride vehicles seat 4+ per car in 2 car trains.

Astro Orbiter - Fly in a circle high above Tomorrowland, make your astro orbiter rise and fall. Another of Disney's circular up and down rides like Dumbo and the Carpets in Adventureland. This versions claim to fame is that the whole ride is elevated high over Tomorrowland rather than being at ground level like the others. The ride vehicles look like rockets and seating is 2 per rocket side by side.

Walt Disney's Carousel of Progress – Enjoy several audio-animatronics scenes depicting 100 years of progress in technology. This attraction is quintessentially Walt! Originally created for the 1964-1965 World's Fair it moved to Disney World in 1975. In this unique experience you will sit in a small theatre mounted along with others on a ring that surrounds the stages. The stages are set facing outward in a circle. After viewing each scene the ring spins to move you along to the next scene, hence the carousel in the name. During the show you will follow along with an American family through the decades and see how technology has improved and changed their lives.

Buzz Lightyear's Space Ranger Spin *(FP+)* – Shoot your laser to defeat Zurg and score points! Your 2+ person space ship is equipped with two lasers so that you can help Buzz defeat Emperor Zurgg. As you move through the various rooms in your space ship you can shoot at the plethora of targets and when you score a hit your points will accumulate on your individual score board. There is also a joystick so that you can spin your space ship from side to side to get a better angle on targets. This is a fun ride for the whole family! See who gets the highest score.

Monsters Inc. Laugh Floor *(FP+)* – Featuring Mike Wazowski from Monsters Inc. the premise of this attraction is that Monstropolis is in the midst of an energy crisis and Mike has decided to open a comedy club to gather the power of laughter. It's filled with jokes and slapstick.

Stitch's Great Escape *(H40)* – This attraction is nothing like the Disney cartoon movie! It is a dark scary theater in the round experience where Stitch transforms into something like the alien in the *Alien's* movies. Rollercoaster type restraints keep you in your seat once the show starts and there are loud noises and interactive 4D effects that will make you think the monster is right by you in the dark. This is not for young kids or those who are claustrophobic or scare easily. Open Seasonally. **Note: rumors abound that Stitch has closed permanently (after the Christmas/New Year seasonal opening) to make way for a new attraction.**

Tron – Last July Disney announced the construction of a Tron attraction like the one at Shanghai Disney. Construction is underway in a previously unused area adjacent to Space Mountain. Disney says they hope to complete construction in time for the 2021 50th year celebration.

Dining

Cosmic Ray's Starlight Cafe – LD $ - Counter Service - Chicken, cheeseburgers, soup, salad, sandwiches, beverages, and snacks. One of the two all you want "fixins' bars" in the Magic Kingdom. The audio-animatronic Sonny Eclipse plays tunes during your meal. **Online Ordering Available.** *A bit of trivia, this restaurant was originally called the Tomorrowland Terrace and was where the author worked in the Magic Kingdom.*

Auntie Gravity's Galactic Goodies – S $ - Counter Service - Iced Coffee, soft-serve ice cream, and smoothies.

The Lunching Pad – LDS $ - Counter Service - Hotdogs, pretzels, snacks and beverages. **Online Ordering Available.**

Tomorrowland Terrace – LD $ - Counter Service - Serving burgers, Pasta, and sandwiches. Open seasonally. **Online Ordering Available.** *Originally called the Plaza Pavilion.*

Shopping

Mickey's Star Traders - Souvenirs, clothing, jewelry, film, books, toys, and hats.

Merchant of Venus - Wigs, jewelry, Stitch merchandise, home decor, and futuristic toys.

Magic Kingdom Entertainment

Fireworks

Happily Ever After, a fireworks display set to narration and music captures the heart, humor and heroism of many favorite Disney animated films with a special fly-by featuring Tinker Bell in the flesh, is held in the distance behind Cinderella Castle. Held most nights usually at 9 or 10 pm, it will be omitted on some lower attendance nights.

Once Aon a Time, a nighttime projection show on Cinderella Castle. The show magically transforms Cinderella Castle with spectacular projection effects, choreographed to a music soundtrack.

Parade

Festival of Fantasy Parade; this is the infamous 3 o'clock parade (a Disney Cast Member joke that goes back to the opening day's of the park tells of the guest that asks "What time is the 3 o'clock parade?" But this has actually happened! Numerous times. WDW can be overwhelming…) Held most days, it will be omitted on some lower attendance days. Features the cast from *The Little Mermaid, Brave, and Frozen among other Disney Films.*

Move it! Shake It! Dance & Play It! Street Party - This mini-parade/show starts on Main Street, U.S.A. as favorite Disney characters, including new additions Stitch and Phineas & Ferb, parade toward Cinderella Castle as the emcee, stilt walkers, and others encourage everyone to join in. Once in the Central Plaza, hosts Mickey Mouse, Minnie Mouse, Donald Duck, and Goofy appear atop giant gift boxes, leading everyone in a medley of remixed classic party songs. Now held three times a day 11:00 am, 12:30 pm, and 5:45 pm.

Shows & Other Entertainment

At all four theme parks you will find a wide variety of entertainment venues and pop-up performances plus what Disney calls "Streetmosphere" characters. These characters are supposed to be residents of the area that you see them in, such as the Mayor of Main Street. These are larger than life characters who both have set performances with scripts (people will gather to watch these) and they will also interact with you on an individual basis when walking around and not performing. I even saw the Mayor rendering assistance with security cast members to a guest who had tripped in the trolley tracks that run down Main Street.

Captain Jack Sparrow's Pirate Tutorial - A 20-minute open air show featuring Captain Jack Sparrow and his scallywag sidekick plus some kids from the audience.

During the day various live stage shows take place on the stage in front of Cinderella Castle featuring your favorite Disney characters.

Final thoughts on the Magic Kingdom

The Magic Kingdom is the crown jewel of Walt Disney World! The original park with the closest ties to all the beloved Disney films, it has a special place in my heart as it does for many people. This is the busiest of the four parks, the must do park, and one that may take more than a day to explore during your vacation.

This is the last park that Walt had a part in designing!

I have mixed feelings over some of the changes the years have brought about. I miss some of my childhood favorite attractions that are now long gone, but change can be good and necessary, and many amazing new attractions and experiences have appeared over the years.

If you haven't been before, I'm sure your first visit to the Magic Kingdom will cause it to have a special place in your heart too!

Epcot

Epcot was the second theme park to be opened at Walt Disney World. It opened on 1 October 1982. It is a very large park and is almost twice the size of the Magic Kingdom.

Epcot is like two different theme parks in one. It is comprised of Future World and the World Showcase. The Epcot main entrance is at Future World.

In Future World you'll get to explore technologies which are shaping the future and see just what the future might look like.

While in World Showcase you'll get to experience eleven different countries, which encircle the World Showcase Lagoon. You'll be immersed in the culture of each country as you explore the shops and taste the cuisine. Each Pavilion's cast members are actually guest workers from that country!

Every evening Epcot presents IllumiNations: Reflections of Earth on the World Showcase Lagoon. IllumiNations is a nighttime spectacular combining Fireworks, lasers, fire, and water effects all to a great soundtrack.

Epcot is open daily from 9 a.m. to 9 p.m. Most of Future World remains open until 7 p.m. with just a few things remaining open until closing time. World Showcase opens at 11 a.m. and remains open usually until 9 p.m. IllumiNations is shown nightly prior to closing. On busy days and holidays (4th of July, Christmas, Easter) Epcot may remain open until 10 p.m. or later.

History and Name Changes

EPCOT stands for Experimental Prototype Community of Tomorrow, or alternately as some say: Every Person Comes Out Tired. Epcot Center was Walt's original vision for where his Florida Project would lead. After the Magic Kingdom was established he would then begin building a community of tomorrow using all of the great technological innovations used in the theme park and many new evolving ones. People would live and work in this community.

After Walt's death the Magic Kingdom and Disney World was completed, but the company floundered for direction and focused solely on theme parks and entertainment, abandoning Walt's dream of community innovation.

When EPCOT Center opened in 1982 the name was a tip of the hat to innovation and community rather than the beginnings of an actual Experimental Prototype Community of Tomorrow. Over the years the park's name was changed several times, starting out as EPCOT Center then becoming: Epcot '94, Epcot '95, then finally in 1996 it became just Epcot.

Arrival

There are two entrances to Epcot, the Main Entrance and the International Gateway.

The International Gateway is an entrance for those guests staying at Disney's Deluxe Epcot Area Resorts, those transferring from Disney's Hollywood Studios via boat, and in the near future those arriving via Disney's Skyliner gondola system. It is located towards the rear of the park in the World Showcase section between the UK and France.

Note, while the Moderate level Caribbean Beach Resort is considered an Epcot Area Resort by proximity, it is not co-located with Epcot. You will need to use Disney Transportation's bus service to get to Epcot.

Guests from the Deluxe Epcot Resorts may walk or take a water taxi to the International gateway, where they will go through a Security check and then enter the park. The water taxis run on a loop from the

International gateway, to each of the Deluxe Epcot Resorts and also to Disney's Hollywood Studios.

All other guests, no matter where they are coming from will arrive at Epcot at the Main Entrance.

Those driving will park and then board trams for a brief ride to Epcot or walk if they are parked close enough.

Both Disney and non-Disney buses arrive at the bus terminal just to the side of the Epcot entrance.

The Monorail, which runs to Epcot from the Transportation and Ticket Center, also arrives here.

After a bag check you'll enter the ticketing area, where you can buy tickets if you need to, and then on to the entrance area, which leads into Future World.

Future World

Once you enter Future World, Spaceship Earth the 'Golf Ball' looking sphere, which is one of Future World's attractions dominates your view.

To pass further into Future World you'll walk under Spaceship Earth on either the right or left. Both routes come together on the backside of the attraction on a long central plaza.

Future World is arranged in two semi-circle sections on each side of this plaza. The inner portion of the semi-circle consists of buildings which surround the plaza that contain dining and shopping options as well as Innoventions, which houses interactive games and exhibits.

The outer portion of the semi-circle behind these buildings is made up of individual themed pavilions containing attractions, restaurants and shopping venues. On the left side looking from the park entrance are

Mission: SPACE, and Test Track and on the opposite side Imagination! The Land, and The Seas with Nemo and Friends.

Straight across the plaza on the far side is the entrance to World Showcase.

Attractions

Ellen's Energy Adventure – This attraction closed in August 2017 to make way for a *Guardians of the Galaxy* thrill ride that is under construction.

Spaceship Earth *(FP+2)* – Ride through an audio-animatronic history of communications. Board your 2-person car for a ride through time. As your vehicle proceeds up the track into the geosphere (the Spaceship Earth "golf ball") you will pass many scenes of how communication has progressed from cave paintings to the printing press and on to computers. At the top you'll emerge into the top section of the sphere which is wide open and dark except for the huge planet earth projected near the top. Then your car turns around for the steep backwards journey down. While descending you can answer some questions about your preferences on your vehicle screen and then see what your future might be like.

Mission: SPACE *(FP+2) (H44 – Orange; H40 Green)* – Experience a simulated launch into space in this realistic simulator which NASA helped design. Centrifugal force is used to simulate periods of both high and low gravity for liftoff, space travel, and landing. Each rider is assigned a task to perform on the mission, which involves pushing a couple of buttons. The ride vehicles are a bit cramped and those with a bit of claustrophobia might not want to attempt this. You will enter the vehicle from the side and sit in one of the four seats and then pull down a roller coaster type torso restraint. As the vehicle closes the instrument panel will tilt towards you so that it is just a couple feet from your face and the controls can be reached without moving your arms.

The method of simulating gravity on this ride has been known to make some queasy. So much so that after opening, half of the ride vehicles were dedicated to a non-motion version (the Green Version). In 2017 the Green version was totally redesigned to add some motion, but not enough to induce motion sickness (hopefully).

Today the ride has the Orange (original, full motion) and Green versions. Prior to entering you will pick which version you would like to experience.

The orange version simulates a rocket launch from Florida during which you will experience 2.5 Gs followed by a Zero G experience. Then you on your way to Mars, with a gravity slingshot around the moon, "Hypersleep", a meteor storm, deceleration for landing, followed by a very nerve racking landing. While the Orange version ride is operating you should keep your head facing straight ahead at all times to help with any motion issues.

The Green version consists of a lift off from Florida (not as intense as the Orange version) and an orbital tour around the Earth and a landing back in Florida during a thunderstorm.

Test Track *(FP+1) (H40)* – Riders design their own custom concept vehicle then test it out on the Test Track in a six-passenger car. You will first use a computer screen to design your car balancing power versus efficiency and customize the look. Then you will move on to ride. The cars seat 6 people, three each in the front and back rows. Your car will then perform a set of "test runs" to measure performance under different conditions: climbing, swerving and braking to name a few. After each test you will see how your design performed. The grand finale is a high speed run outside the building reaching speeds over 65 mph. **A single Rider Line is available.**

Journey Into Imagination with Figment *(FP+2)* – Tour the Imagination Institute on this classic ride with Figment, the original EPCOT Center Character. This is a look at how our senses play a part in our imagination with Dr. Nigel Channing and a cute purple dragon named Figment as your guides!! Each ride vehicle has 2 rows and seats 2+ per row.

Epcot Character Spot *(FP+2)* – Meet your favorite Disney Characters. Mickey Minnie, and Goofy.

Soarin' Around the World *(FP+1) (H40)* - Fly over scenic world destinations on this hang-glider simulator. Each section of this huge simulator has three long rows of seats. You will strap into your seat and then be lifted up into the air where you will be suspended in front of a huge wide screen upon which the flyover scenes are displayed. Try to notice the scents that accompany many of the scenes! Your seat will move and sway in tune with the video to strengthen the feeling of flying.

Living With the Land *(FP+2)* – This boat ride takes you on a tour of greenhouses and other methods of food production. You will tour several greenhouses with different environments like tropical and temperate and see methods of efficiently raising crops like hydroponics and farm raised fish. You will even see some Mickey shaped produce.

The Circle of Life – Learn about conservation in this 20-minute film with the cast of *The Lion King*. Enjoy this wide-screen movie about the environment and our relationship with the land, hosted by the stars of The Lion King.

The Seas with Nemo and Friends *(FP+2)* – Ride your Clam-Mobile and have fun under the sea with the cast of *Finding Nemo*. The clam-mobiles are 2+ person continuous feed ride vehicles. After you board you will meet Mr. Ray and his class on a field trip and learn that Nemo has wandered off and you must find him. The ride deposits you in a large lofted two-story area where some of the walls are huge aquarium tanks. Explore all types of interactive exhibits all about life under the sea.

Turtle Talk with Crush *(FP+2)* – Engage in real-time questions and answers with Crush in this interactive show. This interactive show is the headliner in the Seas with Nemo and Friends. It features a computer-animated version of Crush the surfer dude turtle from *Finding Nemo*. He has 10-minute conversations with his visitors and interacts personally with the audience. Be sure to do this before you leave Nemo and Friends.

Dining

Electric Umbrella LD $ - Counter Service - Angus burgers, chicken, and salads. **Online Ordering Available.**

Fountain View - BS $ – Counter Service - Starbucks coffees, sandwiches and pastries.

The Garden Grille - D $$$ - Table Service - Chip n' Dale's Harvest Feast offers an all you care to enjoy meal served family style on platters, plus character dining with: Mickey, Chip and Dale, and Pluto. Enjoy char-grilled filet of beef, roasted turkey breast with stuffing and gravy, sustainable fish of the day. Plus garden vegetables, sweet potato fries, buttermilk mashed potatoes, rice pilaf, and home-style macaroni & cheese.

Sunshine Seasons - BLD $ - Counter Service - Seasonal soups, salads, sandwiches, and desserts. **Online Ordering Available.**

Coral Reef Restaurant - LD $$ - Table service - Seafood steaks, and more. Enjoy watching the Living Seas aquarium while dining.

Shopping

Mouse Gear – One-stop shopping for Disney character gifts and park merchandise.

The Art of Disney – Collectibles, framed artwork, and sculptures.

World Showcase

Epcot's World Showcase is a change of pace from both Future World and the other Disney theme parks. World Showcase is comprised of 11 "pavilions," each representing a different country. The pavilions are spread out on a promenade that circles the World Showcase Lagoon. In all it is about a 1.2 mile walk around the World Showcase.

Each pavilion is designed to be representative of that country and make you feel as if you are there. Each features entertainment, dining and shopping unique to their culture. Some also have attractions, short tourism movies, or street performers.

The World Showcase is much beloved by military families, as many of the countries represented are ones that we have spent time in. Enjoying the sights, foods and shopping brings back fond memories.

The countries of the World Showcase, moving clockwise around the promenade are: Mexico, Norway, China, Germany, Italy, America, Japan, Morocco, France, The United Kingdom, and Canada. Each country is staffed primarily by residents of that country who are in the US to work for a period of time as a Disney intern.

As you tour the World Showcase you'll enjoy entertainment provided by various street performers and bands in set locations. Some of the entertainers you'll see are: jugglers, mini-plays with audience participation, Japanese drummers, and a British rock show.

The World Showcase boasts some very good restaurants, which are not to be missed.

While the grownups are enjoying the sights, foods, and wines of the world, there are two great things for the kids to do too.

-Kidcot Stations – Each country around the World Showcase has a Kidcot Station. These are areas set up so kids can have fun creating free arts and crafts.

- Disney Phineas and Ferb: Agent P's World Showcase Adventure - Partner with Agent P and Major Monogram from the Disney Channel Phineas and Ferb show, to outwit evil scientist Dr. Doofenshmirtz and save the world.

Kids are given a F.O.N.E. (Field Operative Notification Equipment) at one of the kiosks in Epcot's World Showcase (located at Odyssey bridge, Norway, Italy, International Gateway). These interactive devices help the kids keep in touch with the Phineas and Ferb characters and find clues to save the day. 11:00 am - 8:15 pm daily.

The World Showcase opens each day at 11:00 am.

Every evening Epcot presents IllumiNations: Reflections of Earth. This is a presentation right on the World Showcase Lagoon, which includes fireworks, lasers and dancing fountains and flames set to a soundtrack.

Annual Special events at the World Showcase are:

- The Epcot International Festival of the Arts – January and February
- The Epcot International Flower and Garden Festival - Spring.
- The Epcot International Food and Wine Festival - Fall.

The following is a listing of the World Showcase Pavilions working your way clockwise around the lagoon.

Mexico Pavilion

Dominating the Mexican pavilion is a pre-Colombian pyramid. Inside you'll enter into a nighttime scene in a Mexican shopping plaza, the Plaza de Los Amigos, with carts and shops offering Mexican jewelry, pottery, clothing and leather goods. As you go further in you'll find a tequila bar, restaurant, and boat ride. Look across the way at the smoking volcano in the night sky.

Outside the pyramid on the promenade are two more restaurants, one table service and one counter service as well as a frozen margarita cart.

Attractions

Gran Fiesta Tour Starring the Three Caballeros – This tour features Donald Duck, Jose Carioca and Panchito from Disney's 1944 animated film *The Three Caballeros*. Search for Donald all over scenic Mexico on this slow boat ride. You and a dozen others (rarely is this ride busy, so it might be just you) will float past the volcano and through various scenes of beautiful areas of Mexico with Donald comically superimposed.

Dining

The San Angel Inn Restaurante - LD $$ - Table Service - located within the pyramid. Regional Mexican dishes featuring beef, chicken and seafood.

La Cava del Tequila - S$ - Table and Bar Service - The tequila bar within the pyramid. Authentic Mexican tequila in margaritas and tasting flights, plus appetizers.

La Hacienda de San Angel - D $$ - Table Service - located outside the pyramid. Authentic Mexican cuisine. Enjoy the view of the World Showcase Lagoon and Illuminations at the close of the evening.

La Cantina de San Angel - LD $ - Counter Service- Tacos, churros, tostados, Mexican beer and margaritas.

Choza de Margarita – S$ - Walk up Stand – Margaritas on the rocks and blended, cerveza, tacos, empanadas, and guacamole.

Shopping

The Plaza de Los Amigos - Authentic Mexican souvenirs and treasures.

Artesanias La Familia Fashions - Casual Mexican styled clothing and jewelry.

El Ranchito del Norte - Souvenirs and gifts from Northern Mexico.

Vendors' carts offer home décor gifts, silver jewelry and other Mexican souvenirs such as sombreros, piñatas, pottery and worry dolls.

Norway Pavilion

The Norway pavilion portrays a Norwegian town square complete with its cobble stone courtyard and replicas of a 14th century fortress and 13th century Stave church.

Attractions

Many fans were sorry to see Norway's Maelstrom ride close. It has been totally replaced by Frozen Ever After, a *Frozen* themed attraction. The new attraction takes guests to Arendelle via a boat ride and immerses them in many of their favorite moments and music from the film. In addition, a Frozen character meet and greet location was also added.

Meet Anna and Elsa at Royal Sommerhus – Meet the royal sisters of Arendelle in a private meet and greet.

Frozen Everafter – *(FP+1)* – Board a wooden sailing ship to ride through the world of *Frozen*. Don't worry, you'll get to hear Elsa sing *Let It Go*! This is a high demand FastPass!

Dining

Akershus Royal Banquet Hall - BLD $$$ - Table Service – Offers "Princess Storybook Dining" character buffet meals for Breakfast, Lunch and Dinner. All menus are a mix of traditional Norwegian offerings and more recognizable items. Characters: Belle, Jasmine, Snow White, Sleeping Beauty, Mary Poppins, and occasionally Ariel in her gown.

Kringla Bakeri og Kafe - S$ - Counter Service - Open-faced sandwiches, pastries, and specialty coffees.

Shopping

The Puffin's Roost: Curios and Collectibles – Books, silver jewelry, Norwegian clothing, perfumes, and colognes.

China Pavilion

The Chinese Pavilion is fronted by the triple arched ceremonial gate patterned after the Temple of Heaven in Beijing. To the right is the Hall of Prayer for Good Harvest which houses the movie Reflections of China. To the left is a side street with a commercial feel, here you find dining and shopping options.

Attractions

Reflections of China - a 360 Circle-Vision presentation filmed in Disney's movie in the round style, which features multiple screens that totally surround you, giving you a 360 degree view. The movie shows footage of China including the Great Wall, the Forbidden City of Beijing, the Gobi Desert, Inner Mongolia, the Yangtze River and the tropical rain forests of Hainan Island.

Circle-Vision is a Disney film technique invented for the theme parks in which cameras are mounted on a platform in a circle pointing outward to provide 360 degrees of coverage. The platform was then mounted on dollies, automobiles, helicopters, etc. In the attraction huge screens are mounted in a circle around the audience, who stand with hand rails for balance and are able to look all around themselves in a full circle at the scenes in the movie.

Dining

Nine Dragons Restaurant - LD $$ - Table Service – A variety of Chinese cooking, including noodles, beef, chicken, and seafood.

Lotus Blossom Cafe - LD $ - Counter Service - Orange chicken, steamed rice, egg rolls, potstickers, shrimp fried rice, and vegetarian stir fry.

Shopping

Yong Feng Shangdian Shop – A wide variety of Chinese merchandise: clothing, furniture, jade carvings, and paper fans.

The Outpost

On your way between China and Germany you will find two things, a drawbridge and the Outpost.

As you leave China the pathway begins to go uphill. At the top you'll pass over a drawbridge. At several times during the day the bridge is raised, preventing your crossing so that fireworks and other barges which are part of the Illuminations nighttime spectacular can pass from their backstage storage area into the World Showcase lagoon.

Once you cross the bridge you'll go downhill again and the path will curve to the right. On the outside of the curve is the Outpost. Here you'll find a Quick Service food location, African souvenirs, as well as face painting and hair braiding.

This area was once thought to be the precursor to a full-fledged African pavilion for the World Showcase, but Disney went all out and created Disney's Animal Kingdom instead. Nothing has ever been done with this space which could house a new pavilion.

Attractions

The Outpost has no attractions, other than some outdoor drums for the kids to bang on.

Dining

Refreshment Coolpost – S $ - Quick Service – Here you'll find drinks and snacks: hot dogs, frozen yogurt, as well as hot and cold drinks including specialty cocktails and beer. There are a few tables with umbrellas across the walkway.

Shopping

A variety of African trinkets are offered in an open-air setting.

Germany Pavilion

Enter the German platz (plaza), the surrounding architecture reflects a diverse cross section of German regions, from the replica of the medieval castle to the fairy tale Bavarian style buildings. A fountain with a statue of St. George slaying a dragon is the centerpiece of the cobblestoned platz.

Attractions

Germany has no attractions

Dining

Biergarten - L $$ D $$$ - Buffet Service - Traditional German food served in an Oktoberfest-style atmosphere. The all-you-can-eat buffet contains assorted sausages, rotisserie chicken, child's Frankfurters, assorted salads, breads, red cabbage, wine kraut, potatoes and spatzle.

Guests are seated at long communal tables.

Sommerfest - LD $ - Counter Service - Bratwurst and frankfurter sandwiches, sauerkraut, soft pretzels, and apple strudel as well as German beer.

Shopping

Karamelle-Kuche – Fresh caramel corn, caramel apples, strawberries, marshmallows, and gourmet baked goods.

Weinkeller - Homemade fudge and nut clusters, pretzels, chocolate, cookies and Haribo brand candies.

Die Weihnachtsecke - Christmas decorations of all kinds, plus the Christmas pickle.

Kunstarbeit In Kristall - Crystal jewelry and decorations.

Der Teddybar - German teddy bears, toys and gifts.

Glaskunst – Crystal, glassware, and personally engraved steins.

Italy Pavilion

The Italy Pavilion represents various areas of the original country. It features an authentic 83-foot tall replica of the Campanile Bell Tower in St. Mark's Square, a replica of the 14th century pink and white Doge's Palace, and Venice with its bridges and gondolas that are moored to striped barber shop-style poles alongside the World Showcase lagoon.

You'll also find the "Fontana de Nettuno" a fountain inspired by Bernini's Neptune fountain.

Attractions

Italy has no attractions

Dining

Tutto Italia Ristorante - LD $$ - Table Service - Authentic Italian cuisine is found at this full service restaurant that uses wall murals, dark wood booths and banquettes to make guests feel as if they've stepped out of the theme park and right into Italy. You will find a wide variety of Italian appetizers, entrees, and desserts including: Lasagna alla Bolognese, Ravioli di Ricotta, Pollo al Forno, and Cannoli.

Tutto Gusto Wine Cellar - LD $$ - Table Service - An appetizer-type menu, with various cheeses, mini panini sandwiches, pastas and seafood, plus more than 200 varieties of Italian wine.

Via Napoli Ristorante e Pizzeria - LD $$ - Table Service – A stone oven Italian pizzeria and restaurant. This restaurant features a big menu including many pizza varieties as well as build your own and a wide variety of Italian appetizers and entrees.

Shopping

La Bottega Italiana - Venetian masks, cookware, decorative items and Italian foodstuffs.

Il Bel Cristallo - Italian wares including Murano glass, porcelain, crystal, handbags, clothing and accessories.

American Pavilion

The American pavilion features a colonial-style mansion whose roots are found in the architecture of Independence Hall, Boston's Old State House, Monticello and Colonial Williamsburg. Within you will find the American Adventure attraction.

Across the World Showcase promenade on the lagoon is the outdoor stage and amphitheater known as the America Gardens Theatre. Live shows such as the Candlelight Processional, Eat to the Beat and Flower Power concerts are held here.

Attractions

American Adventure - The American Adventure is an attraction that takes audio-animatronics to the next level, coordinating them with scenes and footage, which takes place on the 72-foot wide projection behind them.

The show is narrated by the figures of Benjamin Franklin and Mark Twain, each chosen to represent their century of American progress.

The pair takes us through various scenes in the development of America. The scenes are presented both in still images, animations, movies, and 35 other audio-animatronic figures.

Scenes include: the Mayflower and the Pilgrims; the Boston Tea Party; the writing of the Declaration of Independence; Valley Forge and the Revolutionary War; slavery and the Civil War; the suffering of Native

Americans; the Philadelphia Centennial Exposition; the founding of Yosemite National Park; and both World Wars.

While waiting for the next showing, listen to the Voices of Liberty, an a cappella singing group, who perform American folk songs in the lobby. I love the patriotism!

Dining

Liberty Inn - LD $ - Counter Service - American fare such as hamburgers, BBQ, steak, salads, fruit plates and desserts. **Online Ordering Available.**

Fife & Drum - LD $ - Counter Service - Turkey Legs, popcorn, ice cream, smoothies, and adult beverages. No seating.

The Funnel Cake Stand – S$ - Counter Service - Funnel cakes with various toppings.

Block and Hans - $ - A wide range of bottled beer.

Shopping

Heritage Manor Gifts – Books, apparel, bags, and souvenirs all with a patriotic American theme.

Japan Pavilion

Japan pavilion is overlooked by a towering blue-roofed pagoda, which is a replica of a 7th century Horyuji Temple. Enjoy the spectacular Japanese garden with water lilies and colorful koi fish.

Don't miss the Japanese Taiko Drumming, which is performed several times a day. This energetic performance can be heard around the World Showcase during showtimes.

Attractions

Japan has no attractions.

Dining

Teppan Edo - LD $$ - Table Service - A Benihana type restaurant, guests are seated around a large grill where chefs chop, prepare and cook your meal. If there are less than 8 in your party, be prepared to sit with other guests. Entrees include chicken, beef, and seafood cooked alone or in combinations with crisp vegetables served with tasty sauces, steamed rice and salad. Sushi appetizers are also available.

Tokyo Dining - LD $$ - Table Service - Traditional Japanese cuisine and ingredients with modern innovative presentations. Entrees include sushi and sashimi, steak, chicken, and shrimp, as well as beverages such as hot sake, green tea and Kirin beer.

Katsura Grill - LD $ - Counter Service - Japanese curry, teriyaki, sushi, udon noodles, miso soup, and Japanese beers, wines, or sake.

Shopping

Mitsukoshi Department Store. - A very large variety of Japanese gifts and souvenirs. From Hello Kitty and Tamagotchis to traditional Japanese footwear and clothing.

Morocco Pavilion

The Moroccan pavilion features a reproduction of the Koutoubia Minaret of Marrakesh, the prayer tower of the 12th century mosque. Explore the winding alleys with stucco archways and the ever-changing exhibits of Moroccan arts, artifacts and costumes.

Attractions

Morocco has no attractions.

Dining

Spice Road Table - LD $ - Table Service – Mediterranean small plates and specialty entrées—spicy garlic shrimp, fried calamari, beef and chicken skewers, and coriander-crusted rack of lamb

Restaurant Marrakesh - LD $$ - Table Service – An assortment of hearty meats, Moroccan pastries and more.

Tangierine Cafe - LD $ - Counter Service - Mediterranean specialties, salads and desserts.

Shopping

Tangier Traders - Moroccan fine jewelry, traditional clothing and shoes, Camel bone mirrors, and handmade daggers.

Brass Bazaar - features brass or silver decorative plates and mirrors. This shop also has an Outdoor Bazaar where ceramic tiles, native instruments, and handmade baskets can be found.

Medina Arts - Moroccan crafts and ceramic plates.

Casablanca Carpets - Hand knotted carpets and rugs.

France Pavilion

Overlooking the France Pavilion is a $1/10^{th}$ scale reproduction of the Eiffel Tower. It is placed in a way that makes it look as if it is the actual size, but off in the distance behind the alley that goes deeper into the pavilion.

Attractions

Impressions de France – An 18-minute trip through France, giving guests a glimpse into the beauty of both the French countryside and the densely-populated cities. See the palace of Versailles, winemakers, hot air balloons and the celebration of Bastille Day, all set to a beautiful soundtrack of French composers.

Under Construction – Disney Pixar's "Ratatouille" inspired attraction will be added to the France Pavilion. Similar to the 4-D attraction "Ratatouille: The Adventure" that opened at the Walt Disney Studios Park in Paris in 2014, guests will be able to shrink to Remy's size and scurry to safety in a dazzling chase across a kitchen with the sights, sounds and smells of Gusteau's legendary Parisian restaurant.

Dining

Les Chefs de France - LD $$ - Table Service – Celebrating fresh and simple ingredients, the menu changes seasonally but may include such delicacies as beef tenderloin, classic onion soup and roasted duck with cherries.

Monsieur Paul - LD $$$ - Table Service – Inventive twists on traditional French dinner. Enjoy items like: black truffle soup, lobster, herb-crusted rack of lamb, mussel soup, and Grand Marnier soufflé.

Les Halles Boulangerie Patisserie - S$ - Counter Service – A traditional French bakery. Offerings include: soups and salads, fresh baguette sandwiches and pastries. Wine, champagne, beer and gourmet coffees are also available.

L'Artisan des Glaces, - S$ - Counter Service – There are 16 flavors of handcrafted frozen treats, including ice cream and sorbet.

Shopping

La Signature - French cosmetics, fragrances, and makeup.

Plume et Palette - Designer French fragrances from Chanel, Escada, Givenchy, Lacoste and more.

La Maison du Vin – French wines can be sampled and purchased. Wine accessories, chocolates, cookies, kitchen linens, and cookware.

Souvenirs de France - French souvenirs, berets, miniature Eiffel Towers, and t-shirts.

International Gateway

Located between France and the United Kingdom is the International Gateway, this is the "back entrance" to Epcot. Guests staying at the Deluxe Epcot Resort area can stroll or take the boat from their hotels to the International Gateway to enter Epcot.

Non- Epcot Resort area guests are welcome to exit here to check out the resorts, great restaurants and BoardWalk area that this resort area has to offer.

Construction is underway here for the Disney's Skyliner gondola station that will connect the Art of Animation, Pop Century, Caribbean Beach, and Riviera Resorts with Epcot and Disney Hollywood Studios.

United Kingdom Pavilion

Enter the UK and stroll by red phone booths, a neighborhood pub and a quaint tea shop. Turn down the cobbled side street with shops, which leads to a park where you can listen to a British Rock concert.

The architecture represents the Tudor, Georgian, and Victorian influences that the United Kingdom is noted for.

Attractions

The UK has no attractions.

Dining

Yorkshire County Fish Shop - LD $ - Counter Service – Fish and chips, English cookies, soft drinks and "draught" beer, including Bass and Harp Lager.

Rose and Crown Dining Room - LD $$ - Table Service – English favorites like cottage pie, fish and chips, bangers and mash, plus variety of beers and ales and scotch. Food service is available at the bar.

Shopping

Crown & Crest - Beatles and Rose & Crown merchandise, get your family coat of arms on a plaque.

The Tea Caddy - Twinings tea and tea accessories.

The Queen's Table – Irish Belleek fine Parian china, native music and books from Scotland, Ireland and Wales. Scottish or Welsh tartans and ties.

The Sportsmans' Shop - Offers all things rugby and soccer - Clothing, balls, hats, and books.

Canada Pavilion

The Hotel du Canada overlooks the pavilion, it was inspired by the Chateau Laurier, a historic hotel found in Ottawa. Below you'll find log cabin trading posts, landscaped grounds, and even totem poles.

Attractions

O Canada!" - This is a Circle-Vision show featuring Canadian native Martin Short. This 14 minute film shows off the diverse country inhabited by our neighbors to the north. You will see the country end to end with scenes of Calgary, Montreal, Toronto, Vancouver and Niagara Falls among other sights.

Dining

Le Cellier Steakhouse -LD $$$ - Table Service - One of Disney's most popular restaurants, reservations go fast. Enjoy Canadian Cheddar Cheese Soup, steaks, prime rib and salmon.

Shopping

Northwest Mercantile - Kitras Art Glass, Hatley clothing, Roots fragrances and athletic wear, Deauville perfume, Ice Wines, body care items, and Canadian hockey gear.

The Trading Post - Maple products like syrup, candies, tea, and cookies. Handmade native jewelry, Maplefoot Babies stuffed animals, Anne of Green Gables books, BOMA totem poles, and faux raccoon and skunk skin caps.

Epcot Entertainment

Fireworks

Epcot's nighttime show, Illuminations *(FP+1)* – Reflections of Earth, has fireworks (1,105 shells from 34 firing positions), but it also has so much more! A great 13 minute-long musical score, four fountain barges which can pump 4,000 gallons per minute, an inferno barge which uses 37 nozzles to shoot propane flames skyward, a battery of full color spectrum of lasers, and the star of the show the 350 ton barge with an Earth Globe which is the world's first spherical video display system, wrapped in 15,000 LEDs.

Parades

There currently are no parades at Epcot.

There hasn't been one for many years. The last parade to run at Epcot was the Tapestry of Nations/Tapestry of Dreams parade, which ran from 1999 to 2001 as part of the millennial celebration. The parade had a unity and world peace theme and featured a variety of large puppets and massive rotating drum units. My family loved it!

Shows & Other Entertainment

One of the great impromptu performances that you might catch in Future World Is the Jaminators. These janitorial percussionists entertain crowds with their infectious beats on trash cans. You'll find them near Innoventions.

You will find lots of cultural specific entertainment as you tour the countries of the World Showcase. Here are a few:

In Mexico, see a Mariachi band play inside the pyramid.

In China, see the Jeweled Dragon Acrobats perform amazing feats.

In Germany, enjoy Oktoberfest Musikanten, the "oompah" band inside the Biergarten restaurant.

In the American Adventure, see the Voices of Liberty, an a capella ensemble with a full repertoire of traditional American folk songs.

In Japan, see Matsuriza the traditional Taiko Drummers. When they are playing you can hear these huge drums all across the World Showcase Lagoon.

In France, see Serveur Amusant a comical waiter and wine steward duo that among other things perform a stacked chair routine.

In the United Kingdom see the Paul McKenna Band and the British Revolution. The Paul McKenna Band plays traditional Scottish and folk music, while the British Revolution plays a chronological journey through the decades of popular British music.

Final thoughts on Epcot

Epcot had historically been a favorite of adults, while definitely not on the top of kid's lists. Mom and Dad enjoyed the World Showcase, "touring" other countries while enjoying adult beverages; at the time it opened and for many years Epcot was the only one of the two parks where you could have a drink. While at the same time most kids were bored.

But in recent years with the addition of a few new big "E Ticket" rides like, Test Track, Soarin Around the World, and Mission Space, plus the Phineas and Ferb adventure, and Frozen Ever After Disney has made Epcot a draw for the younger crowd too.

Military families will really enjoy Epcot's World Showcase, I certainly do as the represented countries are many that we've traveled to or been stationed in. Recently a group of other military aviators and I got together on a special occasion for a day at Epcot. There we were on a cool November day, the seven of us sitting around two tables in the sunny German platz drinking German beer, eating brats, and telling flying stories! A good day, one of the best!

Disney's Hollywood Studios

Disney's Hollywood Studios was the third theme park to be opened at Walt Disney World. It opened on 1 May 1989.

When the theme park first opened it was called Disney MGM Studios. In 2008 the name was changed to the current Disney Hollywood Studios. Some people get confused by the similarly named theme park run by another company in the Orlando Area (Universal Studios, Orlando).

Disney's Hollywood Studios departs from the traditional Disney park arrangement of a series of lands arranged around a central area, Disneyland, the Magic Kingdom, Epcot's Future World, and Animal Kingdom all follow this template.

Disney's Hollywood Studios, however is laid out as a series of "Streets" running off in different directions. Some connect with the central area, while others do not and connect two areas together.

Currently large portions of Hollywood Studios are under construction for the additions of the Star Wars and Toy Story Lands. The Star Wars construction has closed the rear area of the park, while the Toy Story construction is taking place in a new expansion of the park and does not impact touring. Toy Story Land is due to open on 30 June 2018.

After entering the park you'll proceed up Hollywood Boulevard, which is a short street with shopping venues on both sides, towards what serves as the Hollywood Studio's plaza.

Off to the right, prior to getting to the plaza is Sunset Boulevard, a long street which dead ends at the entrances for Rock n' Rollercoaster, the Hollywood Tower of Terror, and Fantasmic.

Opposite Sunset Boulevard a path loops around Echo Lake and rejoins on the left side of the plaza.

To the right side of the plaza is the Animation Courtyard.

From the plaza and Animation Courtyard two streets head off at diverging angles, these form two sides of a big triangle. From Animation Courtyard Pixar Place heads to the rear of the park and the new Toy Story Land. Commissary Lane heads off at a ninety-degree angle from the plaza. These two streets are the 2 sides of the triangle. Currently the third side is missing due to Star Wars construction.

And finally there is also another courtyard, Muppets Courtyard which angles off from the Echo Lake loop and Commissary Lane.

Confused? You should be! Disney's Hollywood Studios is the most confusing park to navigate. It took me years to become comfortable finding my way around without a map. And believe me; I had a hard time just describing it here.

As noted above a good-sized portion of Hollywood Studios has been closed for a complete makeover into the new Star Wars and Toy Story Lands. This has thrown the arrangement of the park off and made how to describe it even more difficult than it used to be. This construction could take well more than a year to complete! Star Wars Land is not due to open until sometime in 2019.

Arrival

Disney's Hollywood Studios has a single entrance. All guests, no matter where they are coming from will arrive at the main entrance.

Those driving will park and then board trams for a brief ride to Hollywood Studios or walk if they are parked close enough.

Both Disney and non-Disney buses arrive at two bus terminals near the front of the Hollywood Studios entrance.

Guests from the Epcot Deluxe Resorts may walk (.75 miles from the end of the Boardwalk plus the distance to your hotel) or take a water taxi to the Studios. The water taxis run on a loop from the Epcot's International gateway, then to each of the Epcot Deluxe Resorts on their way to Disney's Hollywood Studios.

After a security check you'll enter the ticketing area, where you can buy tickets if you need to, and then on to the entrance, which leads into Hollywood Boulevard.

Hollywood Boulevard

Hollywood Boulevard is the "Main Street" of Hollywood Studios. Along the sides of the street, you will see classic Hollywood landmark stores representing a bygone era of Hollywood with its glitz and glamour.

As you begin to walk up Hollywood Boulevard look up to the right on top of the buildings, you'll see a cool billboard for the "Hollywood Canteen, Servicemen's Entertainment, Games and Refreshments" with the image of a 40's GI and girl dancing.

There is a large open area at the far end of Hollywood Boulevard, where you'll find a reproduction of Grauman's Chinese Theatre. All other areas of the park branch out from this area.

Attractions

The Great Movie Ride – This opening day attraction closed in August 2017 to make way for a Mickey and Minnie Low Key Thrill Ride.

Dining

Hollywood Brown Derby - LD $$ - Table Service - Try the famous Brown Derby Cobb Salad, or steak, seafood, and chicken.

Hollywood Brown Derby Lounge - LD $$ - Table Service - Brown Derby light items served on the patio under shading umbrellas. This is a hidden gem, walk right in and pick your seat, there are usually open tables. It's shady and a great place to take a break.

Trolley Care Café – S$ - Starbucks drinks and pastries as well as breakfast sandwiches.

Shopping

Mickey's of Hollywood – Disney character gifts and park souvenirs.

Keystone Clothiers – Men's and women's clothing and accessories.

Celebrity 5 & 10 - Standard souvenirs and Disney Studios merchandise.

Cover Story - Get your picture on the cover of a magazine.

The Darkroom - Camera sales, developing, film and supplies.

Edith & Adrian's Head to Toe - Personalized character merchandise.

L.A. Prop Cinema Storage - Children's clothing.

Sweet Success - Chocolates and other candies.

Sunset Boulevard

Sunset Boulevard is a side street off of Hollywood Boulevard, Sunset Boulevard represents the theater district of Hollywood. The theaters you'll see as you proceed down the street are actual reproductions of several theatres in California, including the Carthay Circle, where Snow White and the Seven Dwarfs premiered.

Attractions

Rock n' Roller Coaster – Starring Aerosmith *(FP+1) (H48)* – Ride your stretch limo coaster through the dark "streets" of L.A. This is the fastest take-off of any coaster on Disney World property. It features loops, inversions, and Aerosmith music in your own private speakers. Riders sit two by two in these long "stretch limos." You will see the band in a brief preshow video where they will invite you to their concert. Then it's time to board your limo for the fast trip to the show. **A single Rider Line is available.**

The Twilight Zone Tower of Terror *(FP+2) (H40)* – Thrill to multiple, randomly generated drops in the haunted elevator. First you'll see a brief pre-show featuring Rod Serling, from the *Twilight Zone* television series. Then head to the Hotel's boiler room, where you board your "elevator" to the 13th floor. The elevator will first rise and then move horizontally through the haunted corridors of the Hotel arriving at another elevator shaft. The elevator alternately launches guests skyward and then plunges them in randomly computer generated patterns. Sparks will shower and at one point the doors of the elevator open to reveal the Disney's Hollywood Studios below you!

Beauty and the Beast – Live on Stage *(FP+1)* – Enjoy this Broadway style retelling of the classic story. A mini-version of Disney's 30th animated classic, Beauty and the Beast, Live on Stage, features the popular characters and songs from the film in a lavish, Broadway-caliber production. Theatre seating for the 20 minute long production.

Dining

Sunshine Day Café - S $ - Counter Service – Gourmet Hot Dogs, beer, and snacks (open seasonally).

Anaheim Produce - S $ - Counter Service – Fresh fruit, pretzels, frozen lemonade and margaritas.

Rosie's All-American Cafe - LD $ - Counter Service – Burgers, vegie burgers, and chicken nuggets. **Online Ordering Available.**

Cantina Eddie's - LD $ - Counter Service – Caesar salads, pizzas, and deli sandwiches. **Online Ordering Available.**

Fairfax Fare - BLD $ - Counter Service – Smoked Chicken and ribs, hot dogs, and salads. **Online Ordering Available.**

Hollywood Scoops - S $ - Counter Service – Sundays and hand dipped ice-cream.

KRNR The Rock Station – S$ - Hot dogs, ice cream, frozen beverages, and beer

Shopping

Carthay Circle Theater – Disney themed items for your home, as well as gifts and holiday items.

Legends of Hollywood - Character figurines, apparel & souvenirs.

Mouse about Town - Disney clothing and house wares.

Planet Hollywood Super Store - Planet Hollywood logo items.

Rock Around the Shop – Offering Rock n' Roller Coaster and Aerosmith mementos.

Sunset Club Couture - Jewelry, watches and character sketches. Watches can be personalized by an in-store artist.

Sunset Ranch Pins and Souvenirs – Sells trading pins and other related merchandise

Tower Hotel Gifts - "The Twilight Zone Tower of Terror" gifts

Villains in Vogue – Disney villain-themed merchandise, along with a few Fantasmic items.

Echo Lake

Off to the opposite side of Hollywood Boulevard from Sunset, is Echo Lake. Echo Lake is the central lake around which are placed restaurants and attractions. Check out the dinosaur in the middle of the lake!

Attractions

For the First Time in Forever - A Frozen Sing-Along Celebration *(FP+2)* – Join Elsa, Anna, and the newly appointed Royal Historians of Arendelle for your favorite songs.

Indiana Jones Stunt Spectacular *(FP+2)* – See how stunts are performed for features like the Indiana Jones movies in this 30-minute action show. This show is presented in a huge covered outdoor theatre with stadium seating and runs on a set schedule. Some helpers from the audience will be selected to help out during one of the scenes, all of which demonstrate just how stunts are performed.

Star Tours – The Adventure Continues *(FP+2) (H40)* – Ride this thrilling combo of a full motion flight simulator combined with a 3D forward view screen presentation. Grab your 3D glasses and board your StarSpeeder 1000 with about 40 other people. There are multiple long rows to sit in. Your StarSpeeder will take you randomly to one of several different planets in the Star Wars universe, there you will get to experience one of several different adventures. With more than 50 different combinations, you can have a new experience with every flight.

Dining

Hollywood and Vine - B $$ LD $$$ - Buffet Service (BL Character Dining) – Featuring American Cuisine and the Disney Junior Play n' Dine for the breakfast and lunch buffets. The characters featured are Doc McStuffins, Sofia the First, Handy Manny, and Jake of the Neverland Pirates.

50's Prime Time Cafe - LD $$ - Table Service –Comfort food, pot roast, meatloaf, fried chicken and all the fixins.

Tune In Lounge - LD $$ - Table and Bar Service - Enjoy the Prime Time Café's menu at the bar next to the waiting area. (Sometimes referred to as Dad's Lounge, because Mom is your host in the 50's Prime Time Café)

Min and Bill's Dockside Diner - LD $ - Counter Service – Makes specialty sandwiches

Back Lot Express - LD $ - Counter Service - Burgers, salads, sandwiches, and chicken nuggets. **Online Ordering Available.**

Shopping

Tatooine Star Traders – Star Wars toys, apparel, and gifts.

Golden Age Souvenirs - Selected character souvenirs.

Indiana Jones™ Adventure Outpost - Items themed to Indiana Jones such as hats, t-shirts, and other items.

Frozen Fractal Gifts – Apparel, costumes,, and toys inspired by Elsa Anna and friends.

Animation Courtyard

The large mock movie studio buildings around Animation Courtyard are home to shows and attractions that are all about animation. Disney movies of course!

Attractions

Voyage of the Little Mermaid *(FP+2)* - Enjoy the highlights of the movie in this 17-minute live show. Scenes from the movie are interspersed with live action featuring puppets of your favorite *Little Mermaid* characters as they tell the story of the Little Mermaid. The theater is quite dark and some children may find the scenes with Ursula, the Sea Witch, a bit scary or intense.

Disney Junior – Live Onstage *(FP+2)* – Sing, dance and play in this 24-minute stage show with your Disney Junior friends. Stars of the Disney Channel's popular *Disney Junior* take to the stage in this fun-filled show, with sing-along and dance activities. In addition to the fun special effects (bubbles and confetti rain down on you at various points of the show), youngsters in the audience can join the gang in singing along with catchy tunes and dancing.

Star Wars Launch Bay – View movie props, screen videos, and shop for collectables from the movies.

Walt Disney Presents – This is a multi-media tour through Walt's life and career. It features both a walk through exhibit and a 15-minute movie about Walt's life featuring lots of clips of the innovator himself. At times, upcoming Disney films are previewed instead of the movie about Walt.

Dining

Animation Courtyard has no dining of note.

Shopping

Animation Gallery - Features animation cells to purchase as collectors items.

Disney Studios Store - Features items and souvenirs from a current Disney animated release (theme changes frequently).

In Character - Children's costumes and accessories.

Walt Disney: One Man's Dream's exit leads to a gift shop.

Pixar Place

Pixar Place is the newest addition to Disney's Hollywood Studios. It is the home of all the Pixar characters and features the great Toy Story Midway Mania attraction. The new Toy Story Land is being constructed behind this area in a former backstage area.

Attractions

Toy Story Mania *(FP+1)* – Try to get the most points on this 4D shootin' arcade ride. The fairly recent addition of a third track helped to alleviate severe throughput problems. The issues of long wait times and no FastPasses available have been greatly reduced.

Dining

Pixar Place has no dining of note.

Shopping

Toy Story Midway Mania Shop - Toy Story Mania and Toy Story films toys and gifts.

Toy Story Land

Pixar Place will be melded into Toy Story Land, with the entrance to Toy Story Mania being reconfigured. Opens 30 June 2018.

Attractions

Toy Story Mania *(FP+1)* – Try to get the most points on this 4D shootin' arcade ride. The fairly recent addition of a third track helped to alleviate severe throughput problems. The issues of long wait times and no FastPasses available have been greatly reduced.

Slinky Dog Dash – *(FP+1) assumed* – Take the entire family for a toy-filled ride on Slinky Dog as his coils twist around curves, hills, and dips.

Alien Swirling Saucers – *(FP+2) assumed* – Hang on tight for an interstellar romp in a toy rocket, set to an out of this world beat.

Dining

Woody's Lunch Box – BLD$$ - Counter Service – Breakfast offerings: Breakfase bowls and sandwiches. For lunch and diner, sandwiches, grilled cheese,

Shopping

Toy Story Midway Mania Shop - Toy Story Mania and Toy Story films toys and gifts.

Commissary Lane

Running between Hollywood Boulevard and the Streets of America is Commissary Lane, which is home to a couple of restaurants.

Attractions

Mickey and Minnie Starring in Red Carpet Dreams – A private meet and greet with Mickey and Minnie.

Dining

Sci-Fi Dine-In Theater Restaurant - LD $$ - Table Service – Burgers, sandwiches, seafood, pasta, steaks, and chicken. Dine in your "car" at a simulated drive-in-theater showing 50s and 60s Sci-Fi movies.

ABC Commissary - LD $ - Counter Service – Burgers, fried seafood, chicken sandwiches, and salads. **Online Ordering Available.**

BaseLine Tap House - California craft ales, lagers (19 beers on tap) and cider are the stars of the drink menu. California wines on tap along with specialty cocktails. A gourmet non-alcoholic lemonade and soda on tap round out the drink selection. As far as bar snacks they currently offer: a Bavarian Pretzel, California cheese charcuterie, and spiced almonds.

Shopping

Commissary Lane has no shopping of note.

Muppets Courtyard

Muppets Courtyard currently just houses Muppet Vision 3D and a couple of restaurants. The exits to the rear sections of the park where the Star Wars Land construction is taking place have been walled for the time being.

Attractions

Muppet Vision 3D *(FP+2)* – Enjoy this 25-minute 3D movie featuring the Muppets. The preshow area features videos and is filled with visual gags such as a net suspended from the ceiling holding Jell-O squares (A net full of jello = Annette Funicello, from the original Mickey Mouse Club). Once in the theatre and donning your 3D glasses you'll get a tour through Muppet Laboratories. This show also contains Disney's 4D effects where you'll be blasted with bursts of air, squirted with water, and see a shower of soap bubbles at various times throughout the show.

Dining

Studio Catering Company - LD $ - Counter Service – Sandwiches, wraps, and salads.

Momma Melrose's Ristorante Italiana - LD $$ - Table Service – Brick oven pizzas, pasta, chicken, seafood, and steak.

PizzeRizzo - LD $ - Counter Service – Opening late Fall 2016 -Pizza, salads, meatball subs. Rizzo is the rat from the Muppets. **Online Ordering Available.**

Shopping

It's a Wonderful Shop - Just what you need to get you into the Christmas spirit...even in July! Lots of ornaments and holiday items.

Stage One Company Store - Muppets merchandise, toys and Children's wear.

Studio Wardrobe Dept - merchandise themed with Lights, Motors, Action! Extreme Stunt Show.

Hollywood Studios Entertainment

Fireworks

Fantasmic – *(FP+1)* The nighttime show at Hollywood Studios is called Fantasmic. It is a 25 minute long presentation where the audience sees a dream that Mickey Mouse is having. There are several different acts featuring many of your favorite Disney characters.

The show of course has a musical score and during the show you'll see: dancing water, water projection screens, the front rows splashed by Monstro the Whale, cannons, pyrotechnics, battle scenes, villains and evil spells, a 40-foot fire breathing dragon, and Mickey prevailing. Then all the good characters celebrate on a steamboat that floats by.

Fantasmic is usually presented almost nightly with times varying based on park hours. During the holidays and peak season, the show is often performed twice. If possible, take advantage of the second showing of Fantasmic! It's typically much easier to get a seat. Many people arrive as much as an hour early.

Star Wars a Galactic Spectacular - Projection effects, dynamic lighting, lasers, and pyrotechnics light up the night, all set to the music of Star Wars. This projection show in the main Hollywood Studios courtyard is a collection of clips from all the movies in no particular order. There is no overall story or progression, such as good defeating evil, to bring all the shots together.

Parades

There is currently no permanent parade at Disney Hollywood Studios.

Shows & Other Entertainment

Jedi Training: Trials of the Temple is a 30-minute session that takes place near Star Tours. The Jedi Master and his/her assistants work with participants in a light saber training exercise -- robes and plastic light sabers are provided. Those who successfully complete the training are proclaimed to be Padawans, and receive a certificate.

Sign up for the Jedi Training start as soon as the park's turnstiles are opened (this includes Extra Magic Hour mornings). If your child wants to participate, this should be your first stop once you enter the park. The earlier you sign up, the earlier the show you will participate in. Spots fill up very quickly and it is not uncommon for all spots to be filled by 10 or 10:30 a.m. The participating child must be there for the sign up. The sign up location is outside the ABC Sound Studio.

Final thoughts on Hollywood Studios

Disney Hollywood Studios has some of the biggest thrill rides on Disney World property and some of the most unique table service theme park restaurants; it is well worth a full day's touring!

The disorganized layout can take some getting used to but if you are having trouble finding your way, just ask a cast member to point you in the right direction.

Disney's Animal Kingdom

Disney's Animal Kingdom is the newest of Walt Disney World's theme park. It opened on 22 April 1998. It is a very large, sprawling park.

Disney's Animal Kingdom sticks to the traditional Disney park arrangement, which is a single entry corridor that leads to a central area with a series of lands arranged around it.

In Disney's Animal Kingdom the main entry corridor is called the Oasis, this area connects the ticket and entry area to the central area called Discovery Island.

Discovery Island is indeed an island, it is totally surrounded by water. Bridges connect it with the Oasis and the other areas of the park.

Arranged around Discovery Island are four areas, which are: Pandora, Africa, Asia, and Dinoland USA.

Arrival

Disney's Animal Kingdom has a single entrance. All guests, no matter where they are coming from will arrive at the main entrance.

Those driving will park and then board trams for a brief ride to the main entrance or walk if they are parked close enough.

Both Disney and non-Disney buses arrive at separate bus terminals near the Animal Kingdom entrance.

After a Security check you'll enter the ticketing area, where you can buy tickets if you need to, and then on to the entrance, which leads into the Oasis.

Dining

Rainforest Cafe Table Service - BLD $$ - Omelets, waffles, French toast, burgers, ribs, and pasta. The Rainforest Café is located outside of the Animal Kingdom to the left of the entry.

There is a second entrance to the Animal Kingdom from the Rainforest Café. If there are long lines at the main entrance, you can enter the Rainforest Café, go through their gift shop, exit to the rear and the park entrance will be just in front of you. Note, you cannot activate your et Disney Armed Forces Salutes here.

The Oasis

The Oasis is your transition into Disney's Animal Kingdom. There are two main paths (left and right) through the Oasis, both lead to the same place. The pathways are lined with lush tropical plants, trees and flowers as well as animal viewing areas where you can discover some unusual live animals.

Attractions

There are no attractions in the Oasis, but there are plenty of animals which you can spend lots of time observing or photographing.

Dining

There is no dining in the Oasis.

Shopping

There is no shopping in the Oasis.

Discovery Island

Discovery Island is the central hub of Disney's Animal Kingdom. The other lands are arranged around it. Clockwise they are: Pandora, Africa, Asia, and Dinoland USA.

Attractions

The Tree of Life - Standing 14 stories tall, this massive icon contains carvings of over 325 animals. See how many you can find!

It's Tough to Be a Bug *(FP+2)* – Located under the Tree of Life. This is a 4D experience, that is a 3D movie coordinated with other "real world" effects. Grab your 3D glasses and learn how tough it is to be a bug with Flick from *A Bug's Life*. **There are some creepy crawly moments in the dark on this attraction that might frighten the little ones or even you if you don't like spiders.** You always hear several kids crying during the show!

Discovery Island Trails – You'll find trails around the base of the Tree of Life where you can view many small exotic animals. This is a great way to get away from the crowds and kids love seeing the tree's carved animals and the real animals too.

Dining

Flame Tree Barbeque – LD $ - Counter Service - Smoked chicken, beef and pork, tossed salads and kid's meals. There are lots of shaded areas to sit and dine. **Online Ordering Available.**

Pizzafari – BLD $ - Counter Service - Breakfast platters, Pizza, pasta and sandwiches are offered. Be sure to spend time exploring the detail and theme of the various rooms. **Online Ordering Available.**

Tiffins – LD $$$ - Table Service – Seasonally inspired world cuisine. Features African, Asian, Latin Cuisine such as Chermoula-rubbed

Chicken, Berkshire Pork Tenderloin, and Wagyu Strip Loin and Braised Short Rib. Appetizers, desserts, and specialty drinks.

Nomad Lounge S $$ - Located right next to Tiffins, enjoy beers, wines, and specialty drinks plus appetizers from the Tiffins menu, like Indian Butter Chicken Wings, Vegetarian Summer Roll with Ponzu, and Honey-glazed Coriander-spiced Pork Ribs.

Shopping

Beastly Bazaar - Island Clothing and Souvenirs.

Creature Comforts - Focused on children's items, clothes, toys, etc.

Island Mercantile - Themed merchandise from around the park

Pandora – The World of Avatar

In this new land journey into the magnificent world of Pandora which includes spectacular floating mountains, a bioluminescent jungle and the winged creatures known as Banshees.

This area of the park is well worth seeing both during the day for the spectacular floating mountains and other interesting scenery as well as after dark when the bio-luminosity of the flora is beautiful.

Attractions

Both new attractions in Pandora are in **very high demand!** Online FastPasses for Flight of Passage will all be taken 60 days prior (some are reserved for same day kiosk use). Wait times are exceedingly high for both attractions, but weighted more towards Flight of Passage.

Avatar Flight of Passage *(FP+1)* - Fly on the back of a mountain banshee during an exhilarating, 3D ride above this vast moon. Get a banshee's-eye view of the beauty and grandeur of Pandora on a rite of passage you won't soon forget!

This ride is simply spectacular! The visuals are stunning!

The stationary ride vehicle is similar to a motorcycle body. You sit astride it leaning forward wearing your 3D glasses. Braces are moved into place behind your lower back and calves to keep you in the proper position. The cover over the screen in front of you opens and you are presented with the most spectacular 3D ride imagery that I've seen. Your "banshee" dives, climbs, twists, and turns over the Pandoran landscape. Your ride vehicle will be tilting back and forth and to the sides, but not moving. You will also feel your banshee breathing between your legs in time to hearing it on the soundtrack (so keep your legs squeezed lightly around your banshee.

Na'vi River Journey *(FP+1)* Your adventure begins as you set out in a boat to venture down a mysterious, sacred river hidden within the bioluminescent rainforest. The full beauty of Pandora reveals itself as the boat passes by exotic glowing plants and amazing creatures. The journey culminates in an encounter with a Na'vi shaman, who has a deep connection to the life force of Pandora and sends positive energy out into the forest through her music.

Dining

Satu'li Canteen – LD$ - Counter Service – Features pick your own content bowls. Pick a main item, base, and sauce. Mains include: beef, chicken, fish, and tofu. Bases are: Quinoa and Vegetable Salad, Red & Sweet Potato Hash, Mixed Whole Grain & Rice, and Romaine & Kale Salad. And the sauces: Charred Onion Chimichurri, Black Bean Vinaigrette, and Creamy Herb Dressing. "Steamed Pods" which are Bao Buns stuffed with a cheeseburger or curry filling. Deserts and assorted beverages. **Online Ordering Available.**

Pongu Pongu – S$ - Counter Service – Alcoholic and non-alcoholic specialty drinks with a Pandoran flair and a Pineapple Cream Cheese Spring Roll.

Shopping

Windtraders – Offering all things Pandora including pet banshees, build your own Avatar, and other items.

Africa

You'll enter Africa by walking across the bridges from Discovery Island or Pandora into the "village" of Harambe. Harambe is a Disney version of the central area of an African village. Dining and shopping are centrally located here, with attractions towards the rear.

Attractions

Festival of the Lion King *(FP+2)* – A Broadway style show featuring song, dance, and large puppetry. This is a 30 minute long show. The show is staged in an enclosed (air conditioned) octagonal timber theater. The theater is sectioned into four parts labeled as either elephant, giraffe, warthog or lion. This is an awesome presentation with a large energetic cast and four large moving stages. FastPass or get there really early (1hr) for each scheduled performance.

Kilimanjaro Safari *(FP+2)* - Ride into the African Savannah and find animals all around you on this marque must see attraction! You will board a large truck fitted with multiple 4+ person rows on the truck bed. As you drive along your driver/tour guide will point out all of the animals that are viewable. You will see a very wide variety of animals! Here are a few:

- Bongo
- Black Rhino
- Okapi
- Savanna Flamingo
- Hippos
- Giraffes
- Sable

- Antelope
- Ostriches
- Mandrill Baboon
- Elephants
- Pink Flamingoes
- White Rhinos
- Kudu
- Scimitar-Horned Oryx
- Long-Horned
- Cheetahs
- Lions
- Warthogs

Gorilla Falls Exploration Trail - Walk at your own pace on this self-guided adventure where you will see exhibits and lots of animals such as hippos, okapi, meercats, gorillas, birds, and more. Guides are stationed at intervals to answer any question that you might have about the animals. Your walk along the trail should take you about 20 to 30 minutes depending on how long you pause at each station and it is a quiet and shady reprieve from the park.

Maharajah Jungle Trek - a self-guided walking tour of Southeast Asia—home to tigers, dozens of bird species, a flying fox and a Komodo dragon. Some of the animals you may come across include:

- Asian tiger
- Gibbons
- Elds deer
- Blackbuck
- Komodo dragon
- Malayan flying fox
- Water buffalo
- Over 50 species of birds

Wildlife Express Train to Rafiki's Planet Watch - Take a train ride to Conservation Station - Rafiki's Planet Watch which is focused on the environment, conservation and animal well-being. Here you will find animal viewing areas, exhibits, and an animal petting area. There are several other areas to explore including the Sounds of the Rainforest, and the Veterinary and Training Exhibits. Trains run about every 10 minutes and there is a five to seven minute walk to Conservation Station - Rafiki's Planet Watch after getting off the train.

Dining

Tusker House - BLD $$ - Table Service –Breakfast is a buffet character meal with Donald, Daisy, Mickey and Goofy. Lunch and dinner are served buffet style, featuring regular buffet fare with a few African-inspired dishes in the selection.

Harambe Market – LD$ - This collection of walk up windows features four serving stations: Chef Mwanga's Ribs Shop, Famous Sausages (serving sausages fried in curried corn batter), Kitamu Grill, and Wanjohi Refreshment (which focuses on cocktails and cold beverages). **Online Ordering Available.**

Dawa Bar - S$ - Bar and Table Service - Adult beverages – The totally outdoor seating tends to get crowded with folks who are waiting to eat at Tusker House next door (especially for the Character Breakfast).

Harambe Fruit Market - S$ - Cart Service - Fruit, snacks, and beverages.

Kusafiri Coffee & Bakery - B $ - Counter Service - Coffee and bakery items offered from an outside window just past the Tusker House entrance.

Tamu Tamu Refreshments – BLD $ - Counter Service – Ice cream, smoothies and sodas.

Shopping

Mombasa Marketplace/Ziwani Traders - Safari clothing, African gifts, and unique items.

Daka La Filimu – Film, batteries, and memory cards.

Asia

Moving clockwise around Discovery Island from Africa, you'll come to Asia. There you'll find the mythical Kingdom of Anandapur (place of delight) complete with the crumbling ruins of an ancient village, temples, and a Maharajah's palace.

Asia, Animal Kingdom's newest land, opened in 1999 and features a water raft ride, walking animal trail, bird show, and roller coaster.

Attractions

Expedition Everest *(FP+2)(H44)* – This is Disney World's newest coaster. It is a high speed coaster that climbs, plummets, turns, and even backs up! After walking through the queue area which contains tons of items gathered by Disney from Nepal you'll board your train to go in search of the fabled Yeti. As your train heads into the mountains you will see signs of the Yeti until you come to a section of ripped up train track. Your train halts, pauses, and then rushes backwards to reverse course. When you are clear the train switches tracks and you race down the mountain to get away! Riders sit two by two in the long coaster trains. There is an extra wait for the front row option. **A single Rider Line is available.**

Kali River Rapids *(FP+2)(H38)* – A white water raft ride. There are no steep drops but you will get wet. Twelve riders sit facing inward in a circle in the rafts. There is a water proofish bag in front of your seat for valuables. I recommend bringing your own big zip lock! You'll board your raft from a constantly moving turntable as the rafts move along the perimeter. Once the ride starts you will float along and go up hill on belts which is followed by cruising down the river. There are dips, turns, and plunges as well as rapids. Large amounts of water can come into the raft!!! There is an elevated foot rail to keep your feet off the floor. Count on someone in the raft (not everyone) getting very, very wet!

Maharajah Jungle Trek- This is another self-guided walking adventure. You will wander through the ancient ruins of India while getting to view native animals like Asian tigers, gibbons, fruit bats, flying foxes, and many more.

Flights of Wonder - An exotic bird show featuring a trainer showcasing the natural abilities of a number of different birds, including macaws, a crowned crane, and different types of hawks as they do tricks and stunts. Closed as of 31 December 2017. This show will be replaces by one featuring Russell and Dug from Pixar's *Up* as they discover bird species from around the world. Opening TBD (Spring?), but in time for the 2018 20th anniversary.

Dining

Yak & Yeti - LD $$ - Table service - Pan-Asian cuisine dishes such as Dim Sum, Lo Mein, Egg Rolls and Maple Tamarind Chicken.

Yak & Yeti Local Cafes - LD $ - Counter Service - This is the Yak & Yeti walk up counter. Serves honey chicken, orange beef, mandarin chicken salad, and sweet-and-sour chicken.

Shopping

Serka Zong Bazaar - Expedition Everest gift shop, souvenirs, apparel, and Yeti toys.

Dinoland USA

Continuing clockwise from Asia you'll enter DinoLand U.S.A. where you can explore dinosaurs both real and imagined.

Attractions

The Boneyard – An interactive playground for the kids. Your kids will love climbing, sliding, and exploring. The flooring is soft and spongy in case someone falls while blowing off steam.

Dinosaur *(FP+2)(H40)* – Enter the Dino Institute, home to this thrilling attraction. You'll first pass through the outer queue area with lots of dinosaur skeletons and information to read. Then you will see a pre-show movie explaining your upcoming tour to the past in your time rover. Unfortunately your tour is about to be hijacked by a researcher trying to bring a dinosaur back with you. He changes the date of your arrival in the past too close to the extinction meteor event and things go awry. Fortunately it's Disney and you make it out just fine, but not until after a rough ride. This is a fast, very bumpy dark ride, with scary looking lunging dinosaurs! If young ones scare easily or someone doesn't like herky-jerky rides, this might not be for you. Your time rover seats four to a row with three rows. There is a pouch in front of you to hold items.

Finding Nemo - The Musical - Find Nemo during this 30-minute show featuring music and large scale puppetry. This is a retelling of the Disney-Pixar movie set to music especially for the theme park. The show features a combination of puppets, dancers, acrobats, and animated backdrops. Stadium seating in a huge indoor location.

TriceraTop Spin - A circular flying dinosaur ride. You can make your dinosaur rise and dive if you are sitting in the front row of the two-row dinosaur. Each row seats 2+. This is another in Disney's non-innovative, cheap to produce Dumbo the Flying Elephant copies.

Primeval Whirl – *(FP+)(H48)* – Spin and slide on this "time machine" coaster. This is a rather tame coaster that seats 4+ on a curved bench in a circular shaped car. The difference about this coaster is that the car will also spin around while cruising along the tracks.

Fossil Fun Games - A dinosaur-themed midway featuring carnival type games of chance. These include Dino-Whamma, a classic mallet strength game; Mammoth Marathon, a racing derby; Comet Crasher, a goblet toss game; Fossil Fueler, a water-squirt game themed to a prehistoric gas station; and Bronto-Score, a basketball game.

Dining

Restaurantosaurus – Table Service – LD $ - Burgers, sandwiches, hotdogs, and tossed salads. **Online Ordering Available.**

Shopping

Chester and Hester's Dinosaur Treasures – Disney toys and souvenirs.

Animal Kingdom Entertainment

Fireworks

Due to all of the animals living in the park there is not a fireworks or fireworks type show at the Animal Kingdom.

Rivers of Light *(FP+2)* - Celebrate the kinship of all living things during a nighttime water and light show awash with breathtaking special effects all on floating rafts and boats.

Tree of Life Awakenings - Watch in wonder when the animal spirits within the great tree awaken during a mesmerizing showcase of color and light. Approximately every 10 minutes, flickering fireflies magically appear and stir to life the wondrous animals spirits carved into the tree's towering trunk—bringing to light a stunning visual swarming with vivid color and animated imagery.

Parades

Animal Kingdom currently has no daily parade.

Shows & Other Entertainment

Wilderness Explorers – Become a Wilderness Explores and win badges as you make your way around the park. This is a self-paced interactive adventure.

The Animal Kingdom features a variety of live performers who entertain periodically throughout the day at various locations. Check the park Times Guide for details!

African percussion and dancers – Various bands can be seen throughout the day in various spots in Africa.

Final thoughts on the Animal Kingdom

Since its opening, many people considered the Animal Kingdom to be a "Half Day Park." They'd hit the big attractions in the morning and then move on to another park. While this was certainly one touring technique, for those kids (and big kids) who enjoy nature and animals it is possible to spend the whole day there slowly enjoying the wonders of nature that others are just whizzing by.

Since mid 2016 park hours have been extended to 9 or even later with the addition of nighttime shows and safari rides.

The addition of Pandora has created a huge draw and has increased Animal Kingdom attendance and put an end to the idea of AK being a half-day park.

Touring Disney World's Parks

With the addition of the 5-day Salute ticket in 2017 (in addition to the original 4-day), military families now have the option to spend a 5th day at one or more of the four parks to finish up any touring they might have left.

FastPass Plus has changed the way people tour the parks. They used to get there prior to the park opening and get as much done as possible as early as possible while utilizing the old paper FastPasses where you had to physically go to the attraction to get your FastPass and you could only hold one FastPass at a time.

Now there are two schools of thought:

If you plan to stay at one park you can make your FastPasses for the morning and then continue to do other attractions between and after your fastpasses in order to get as much as possible accomplished. After your initial passes check with a FastPass kiosk or you're my Disney Experience app to see if any attractions that are still available are ones you want to do. If so get your +1 FastPasses. Then keep repeating.

If you plan to park hop make your FastPasses for the second park of the day in the afternoon. In the morning go to the first park as early as you can and get as much done as you can. Then park hop and enjoy your FastPasses.

+1 FastPasses are additional single passes you may obtain after using your initial three. See more on FastPasses in the next chapter Disney's New Tech.

Wrap Up

You can see that Disney World's theme parks have a lot to offer. You will find things that interest every member of the family both young and not so young. It is important to have a good idea what you'd like to accomplish prior to starting each day so that you don't lose time floundering and backtracking your steps across the park.

Ready for More?

I hope that you have enjoyed our whirlwind tour of the Walt Disney World theme parks. There is so much to see and do at Disney World, plus they are always changing things that it is almost impossible to get it all down on paper or experience it in a single vacation!

Our next chapter covers the new and exciting technologies that Disney World has put into play to help you plan and manage your vacation.

8. Walt Disney World's New Technology

What's This Chapter About?

Over the last few years, Disney World has implemented quite a few new high tech enhancements for their guests to use. Collectively Disney calls this technology My Magic Plus. There are multiple types of technologies involved, from hardware and software to websites and smartphone apps.

For the guest these enhancements help improve the customer experience by allowing better preplanning, on the fly (re)scheduling, crowd disbursement, and generally making for easier guest transactions.

For Disney this technology builds brand loyalty and is a huge data collection tool. Guests opt in to using this technology (just like they opt into using Facebook or grocery store cards) and Disney then gains more insight into guests' vacation planning and trip execution habits.

Some examples of how Disney can use this info are:

Guests make resort, dining, and attraction reservations well ahead of time online. This allows Disney to schedule cast members when and where they are needed. Thus saving costs by not scheduling unneeded cast members and improving the guest experience by having enough cast members where needed.

Controlling how many and for what attractions guests may make advance reservations, aids in distributing crowds, therefore improving the guest experience.

Disney can detect where everyone is in each park, what Disney resort they are staying at or if they are a non-Disney resort guest. This can be (but isn't yet) used for things like at park closing to proactively schedule how many buses, to what resorts, at what times they arrive to pick up guests, or how many parking lot trams they need to have in service, thus improving the guest experience.

What Makes up My Magic Plus?
Disney's RFID Technology

The key to My Magic Plus is Radio Frequency Identification (RFID) technology.

RFID chips are very small circuitry chips that can be imbedded into items such as a plastic credit card like ticket or wrist band. These chips have a small battery to power them and transmit an identification number over a limited range.

The military uses these chips in our access badges, which we hold up to scanners for entry.

No identifying information is stored on these chips, they only transmit an ID number. Radio frequency receivers that interact with the chip will then look up the chip's ID number on various computer systems that are located behind Disney's firewall to determine the chip's status for that particular system.

I'm sure you've heard the scam advertisements on the radio for ID protection wallets etc. These are to protect RFID credit/debit cards from remote theft. Unfortunately most banks never even used this technology they went straight from the old tape (swipe) cards to the new very secure chip cards. These ads unfortunately make some people wary of RFID technology.

Relax, all of your personal data is stored behind a firewall on Disney's regular secure systems, not on the chip itself. No one with a scanner can get any of your personal data by being near you!

Systems that Disney is using these chips for (and how they are used):

- Ticketing (is this chip associated with a valid ticket? Does the fingerprint data match the stored data? If so admit the bearer and deduct a day if required)
- FastPass Plus reservations (is this chip associated with a FastPass Plus reservation for this attraction at this time?)
- Disney Dining Plan (is this chip associated with a DDP account? If so deduct this meal)
- Room/parking/pool access (is this chip associated with a guest in this room/at this resort?)
- Charging to your room (is this chip associated with a room with charging privileges? Is the pin input by hand correct? Then charge this amount to that room)
- Connecting to your PhotoPass/Memory Maker account (this picture should be associated with the PhotoPass/Memory Maker account associated with this chip).
- Displaying personal messages as surprises in unlikely (theme park) situations. For example you may see "Welcome Steve" (insert your name in place of mine) on a digital sign at a ride.

Pretty Cool Stuff!!!

Disney has incorporated RFID chips into all of their theme park tickets and their Magic Bands.

RFID Tickets

With the switch to RFID technology Walt Disney World began using plastic tickets, which have an embedded RFID chip. This includes the Disney Armed Forces Salute tickets and all other types of military and civilian tickets.

Those who are staying at a Disney Resort will also be given Magic Bands to use as their primary RFID device. Those with military tickets may have the plastic tickets as a backup.

Those who are not staying at a Disney Resort will only be given the RFID tickets. They may purchase their own Magic Bands and use both in a limited manner.

The RFID interactions allowed for a non-Disney resort guest's plastic ticket or purchased Magic Band are limited to only being used as your theme/water park ticket, PhotoPass/Memory Maker ID, and for FastPass Plus admittance. You cannot at this time preload the chip with funds for charging.

Magic Bands

A Magic Band is a RFID device that takes the place of your plastic RFID ticket.

Wearing your band on your wrist is so much more convenient than having to get your ticket out of your pocket every time that you need to use it.

If you are staying at a Disney World Resort, your Magic Band will be used as your room key, theme/water park ticket, room charge device, resort access (parking, pool, etc.), PhotoPass/Memory Maker ID, and FastPass Plus ticket.

Using your My Disney Experience account, you'll be allowed to customize your band's color and add your name on the back as well. Disney will mail you your Magic Band prior to your trip. If you are making a short notice trip your personalized band will be waiting for you at check in, very short notice trips will receive generic grey bands at check in.

If you are not staying at a Disney Resort, you can buy Magic Bands once you arrive at Disney World for about $13 each at most Disney gift shops. You can then link them to your My Disney Experience account and use them for FastPass Plus, PhotoPass/Memory Maker, and have your park ticket linked to them as well. You can purchase Bands ahead online through the Disney Store.

My Disney Experience

My Disney Experience – is a section of the Disney World website. It is your area to manage your Disney tech and all areas of your Disney World vacation, from planning to reservations.

You'll link your Disney resort reservations and theme park tickets to your account (if Disney hasn't done it for you), you'll make your FastPass Plus reservations here, and you can make dining reservations as well. Non-military tickets may also be purchased using your account.

My Disney Experience can be accessed by your computer via the Disney World website or by using a free smart phone app.

You will first need to register for a free Disney.com account to use My Disney Experience.

Reservations - My Disney Experience has the ability to:

- Make and store your Disney World Resort Reservations **(you cannot make military resort reservations using it).**
- Make and store your Disney World Advance Dining Reservations.
- Purchase general public priced Disney World tickets.
- Link and manage your Disney World Tickets or Passes (this is required to use FastPass Plus).
- Link and manage your Disney World Magic Bands.
- Link to your Disney PhotoPass/Memory Maker Account.
- Pre-Order/Pre-Purchase meals at select counter service restaurants
- Monitor the use of your Disney Dining Plan Credits
- Monitor charges to your Disney Resort Room

- Open your Disney Resort Room using the smart phone app (Coming soon, first to the Wilderness Lodge, then other resorts over time)

Planning – My Disney Experience has convenient links to all other parts of the Disney World site where you can:

- Find things to do – Learn about and explore Walt Disney World.
- Plan your vacation – Suggestions with links on things you'll want to plan for each day of your vacation. Like FastPass Plus, Dining, Shows, and Character Greetings.
- Once you link your tickets and reservations to your account, your Disney Resort hotel and dining reservations will appear in your plans. You'll even be able to add your own reminder notes.

On the Go – While in the parks you can:

- Check attraction wait times
- Get directions to any location (theme park or otherwise)
- Make and store your FastPass Plus Reservations.
- Make adjustments to your FastPass Plus or Dining reservations on the fly.
- Order and prepay for meals at select Counter Service Restaurants
- Track Disney Dining Plan credit usage
- Track charges to your WDW Resort room

FastPass Plus

FastPass Plus (Often shortened to FastPass+ or just FP+) is a free service at Walt Disney World which allows those who have valid tickets linked to their My Disney Experience account to make reservations ahead of time for many of WDW's attractions, shows, and experiences.

You do so by logging into your My Disney Experience account. You are allowed to make reservations a set number of days in advance depending on where you are staying for your vacation.

Those staying at Disney World owned Resorts, Shades of Green, the Swan and Dolphin, and Disney Springs Hotels can make their FastPass Plus reservations **60 days prior to their check in date.** They may make reservations for the entire length of their stay through the checkout date, up to a maximum of 10 days, whichever is less.

Note: if you have fewer days on your ticket(s) than the length of your stay, while each day of your trip (up to 10 days) will be available for making FastPass Plus reservations, you will only be allowed to make reservations for the number of days available on your ticket(s).

So – If I'm staying for seven nights and eight days, but only have a 4-day ticket, I'd be able to make reservations on any of those eight days, but once I'd made the 4th day of reservations, no more days would be available.

All others - Non-Disney resort guests, Passholders, Day guests, etc. can make their FastPass Plus reservations **30 days prior to the day they would like to use those reservations.**

Note: For all valid tickets linked to your My Disney Experience account the next 30 days are always available for FastPass Plus reservations. As each day passes the 30-day window moves forward one day.

Non-Disney guests simply wait until their rolling 30-day window rolls to the day they would like to make their reservations for and then do so. The system will only allow you to make FastPass Plus reservations for the number of days available on your ticket.

So if I log into My Disney Experience without a Disney resort reservation and I have a 4-day ticket linked to my account, I could make FastPass Plus reservations on any four of the next 30 days.

Disney Resort Guests will also open the 30-day FastPass Plus window as described above when they link their tickets.

Linking your Disney Resort Reservation (Disney owned Resorts Shades of Green, the Walt Disney World Swan and Dolphin, and the Disney Springs Hotels) is what will eventually open up your 60-Day FastPass Plus window.

If you are more than 60 days from your check in date all you will see is the 30-Day Window as described above. This is normal!

You will not see any change until the 60th day prior to your check in date. On that day your 60-Day FastPass Plus window will open. Your window will be the shorter of: all the days of your trip including check in and out days or 10 days (this only affects those on 11+ day vacations).

You will be allowed to make FastPass reservations at that time for any of the days within your 60-Day Window, up to the number of days on your ticket.

There will be a gap of non-selectable days between your 30-day window and your 60- window.

How Many FastPass Plus reservations can I make?

At press time the WDW FastPass Plus system is working as follows (and has been for some since inception). But Disney can make "permanent" or temporary changes at any time.

Initially you can make 3 FastPass Plus reservations per day. They must all be for the same theme park. Multi-park, same-day FP+ reservations are not possible ahead of time.

Once you have used your initial three FastPass Plus reservations during a day you will be able to get additional FastPass Plus reservations one at a time via you're my Disney Experience App or the in park kiosks. Once you use the 4th you may make a 5th, etc. You may do this at the same or a different park from where you made your initial three reservations.

Disney World can cut your initial allotment back to 2 during higher attendance periods on a park-by-park basis. There are only so many slots available per day on each attraction based on hourly FastPass Plus ride capacity and the number of hours the park is open. When very high attendance is projected Disney can cut back the number allowed so more people have the opportunity to get at least some FastPasses. To my knowledge they have never done this.

FastPass Plus Attractions

Currently you may select 3 from the full list of FP+ attractions/experiences at the Magic Kingdom. While Epcot, Animal Kingdom, and Hollywood Studios have a two-tiered system. You may select **one** from tier 1 and **two** from tier 2

Magic Kingdom (Choose 3):

- The Barnstormer
- Big Thunder Mountain Railroad
- Buzz Lightyear's Space Ranger Spin
- Dumbo the Flying Elephant
- Enchanted Tales with Belle
- The Haunted Mansion
- It's a small world
- Jungle Cruise
- Mad Tea Party
- The Magic Carpets of Aladdin
- The Many Adventures of Winnie the Pooh
- Meet Ariel at Her Grotto
- Meet Cinderella and Elena at Princess Fairytale Hall
- Meet Mickey Mouse at Town Square Theatre
- Meet Rapunzel and Tiana at Princess Fairytale Hall
- Meet Tinker Bell at Town Square Theatre
- Mickey's PhilharMagic
- Monsters, Inc. Laugh Floor

- Peter Pan's Flight
- Pirates of the Caribbean
- Seven Dwarfs Mine Train
- Space Mountain
- Splash Mountain
- Tomorrowland Speedway
- Town Square Theater and Greet
- Under the Sea: Journey of the Little Mermaid

Epcot

FastPass+ Tier 1 (Choose 1):

- Frozen Ever After
- Illuminations – Reflections of Earth - Special viewing area
- Soarin'
- Test Track

FastPass+ Tier 2 (Choose 2)

- Disney/Pixar Short Film Festival
- Journey Into Imagination With Figment
- Living with the Land
- Meet Disney Pals at the Epcot Character Spot
- Mission: SPACE Green
- Mission: SPACE Orange
- The Seas with Nemo & Friends
- Spaceship Earth
- Turtle Talk with Crush

Hollywood Studios

FastPass+ Tier 1 (Choose 1)

- Beauty and the Beast - Live on Stage
- Fantasmic!
- Rock 'n' Roller Coaster Starring Aerosmith

- Toy Story Midway Mania!

FastPass Tier 2+ (Choose 2)

- Disney Junior - Live on Stage!
- For the First Time in Forever - A Frozen Sing-Along Celebration
- Indiana Jones Epic Stunt Spectacular!
- Muppet Vision 3D
- Star Tours 2: The Adventures Continue
- The Twilight Zone Tower of Terror
- Voyage of the Little Mermaid

Disney's Animal Kingdom

FastPass+ Tier 1 (Choose 1):

- Avatar Flight of Passage
- Na'vi River Journey

FastPass+ Tier 2 (Choose 2)

- DINOSAUR
- Expedition Everest
- Festival of the Lion King
- Finding Nemo - The Musical
- It's Tough to Be a Bug!
- Kali River Rapids
- Kilimanjaro Safaris
- Meet Favorite Disney Pals at Adventurers Outpost
- Primeval Whirl
- Rivers of Light - Special viewing area

Where Can I Make In Park Reservations and Changes?

A percentage of all FastPasses are reserved for same-day bookings for every attraction. This is for those who have not purchased their tickets ahead of time or do not care to plan ahead.

You may make or adjust FastPass+ reservations online using your computer or pad, on your smart phone app, or at the following in park locations. *Note these do tend to change and migrate around. Sometimes impromptu ones will spring up.*

Magic Kingdom FastPass Plus Kiosks

- Guest Relations at City Hall
- The walkway between Adventureland and Liberty Square, near The Diamond Horseshoe Saloon in Liberty Square
- Outside Mickey's PhilharMagic in Fantasyland
- At the entrance to Jungle Cruise in Adventureland
- Near Stitch's Great Escape in Tomorrowland

Epcot FastPass Plus Kiosks

- In the Future World West walkway, on the way to Mission:SPACE
- At the digital "tip board" in the middle of Future World Plaza (behind Spaceship Earth and the Future World fountain)
- At the International Gateway entrance to the park
- In the Future World West walkway, on the way to The Land pavilion

Disney's Hollywood Studios FastPass Plus Kiosks

- At the "wait times" board on the corner of Hollywood and Sunset boulevards
- Outside Toy Story Midway Mania

- Outside the Twilight Zone Tower of Terror entrance
- Near MuppetVision 3D in Muppet Courtyard

Animal Kingdom FastPass Plus Kiosks

- At the Discovery Trading Company on Discovery Island
- Near Kali River Rapids
- Kiosk at Island Mercantile on Discovery Island
- Kiosk near Harambe Market

Steps For Using My Disney Experience

1. Create a My Disney Experience Account at disneyworld.go.com/plan.

2. Make your Disney resort reservation. This step is optional but remember if you want to have 60-day vs. 30-day advance FastPass Plus reservation ability you'll need to stay at a Disney Resort.

3. Link your Disney resort reservation to your MDE Account using the confirmation number (you will then see everyone on your reservation in your account). This step N/A for non-Disney resort guests.

4. Personalize Your Magic Bands in My Disney Experience, you may select the color and edit the name printed on each before they are mailed to you. This step N/A for non-Disney resort guests.

5. Purchase your Disney tickets, Armed Forces Salute or other type from your local base Ticket Office.

6. Link your tickets or vouchers to your My Disney Experience account for each individual person (mark each ticket with the person's name).

7. Make your FastPass Plus Selections, individually (if you'll split up) or as a group 60 or 30 days out as appropriate.

8. Upon arrival, check in to your Disney Resort Hotel, they will activate your Magic Bands to be used as your room key, for charging (if desired), and resort access (pool, parking, etc.). Again only for Disney resort guests.

9. Activate your Disney Armed Forces Salute Tickets. Disney Armed Forces Salute tickets need to be activated before they can be used for entry into the parks. This can be done at any park ticket booth, any park Guest Relations, or Guest Relations at Disney Springs.

10. You are now all set. Enjoy your trip!

Disney's PhotoPass and Memory Maker

PhotoPass and Memory Maker are Disney's two programs for having their professional photographers document your Disney World Vacation.

Almost everywhere you go in the Disney theme parks, you'll see Disney PhotoPass Photographers. They are stationed at all of the best, most scenic locations to have your picture taken, for example in front of Cinderella Castle or with France and the Eifel Tower in the background at Epcot's World Showcase.

They are also at some of the character meals (Chef Mickey's, Hoop-Dee-Doo Revue, Tusker House breakfast, 'Ohana breakfast, 1900 Park Fare, and Spirit of Aloha dinner show), at Character Meet and Greets, and many thrill rides also have automatic cameras to capture your reactions to the most thrilling part of the ride.

Taking the photos is a free service, you can decide later if you want to purchase the photos. Just have your Magic Band or park ticket scanned to identify who you are and get your picture taken.

You can then review your photos online using your My Disney Experience account or the PhotoPass/Memory Maker sites.

Many Disney theme park rides snap photos of you at exciting moments, such as plunging down a hill. You can also scan your Magic Band or ticket to "claim" these as yours.

How purchasing pictures works

The two systems work exactly the same when you are on vacation, the difference is that Memory Maker is a prepaid package, while PhotoPass is an a la carte, pay by the picture after the fact system.

Memory Maker, which replaced PhotoPass+ costs $149 for the package if you order at least 3 days before your vacation ($169 within 3 days). You can do this through your My Disney Experience account or the Memory Maker site. For this price you'll receive unlimited digital downloads of all the pictures you had taken on your vacation for up to 45 days afterwards, a CD backup can be purchased for an extra fee.

With PhotoPass you can download any of the pictures that you select, which were taken of you on your vacation. You'll pay $14.95 each photo though.

With these prices, if you think you'll want to buy more than 11 pictures you will be better off going with the Memory Maker.

Memory Maker Military Discount

As part of the Disney Armed Forces Salute you can purchase Memory Maker for the discounted price of $98.00 from January 1, 2018 through December 19, 2018.

The discounted Memory Maker can only be purchased at Walt Disney World theme park ticket windows by Eligible Service Members or their spouses.

Mobile Food & Beverage Ordering

You may use you're my Disney Experience app to order for meals at designated Counter Service restaurants. You must pre-pay when doing so. Just complete your order, enter a form of payment (Credit/Debit card or Disney Dining Plan). Upon arrival at the restaurant, open your app, tap on the image of your character and press the "I'm Here, Prepare My Order" button. This lets them know you're here, so they can start your order.

When your food is ready to enjoy, you will receive a notification from the app and you'll pick up your meal at the area with the "Mobile Order Pick Up" sign.

Participating restaurants:

- ABC Commissary
- Aloha Isle
- Backlot Express
- Casey's Corner
- Catalina Eddie's
- Columbia Harbour House
- Cosmic Ray's Starlight Café
- D-Luxe Burger (Disney Springs)
- Electric Umbrella
- Fairfax Fare
- Flame Tree Barbecue
- Harambe Market
- Liberty Inn
- Pecos Bill Tall Tale Inn and Cafe
- Pinocchio Village Haus
- Pizzafari
- PizzeRizzo
- Restaurantosaurus
- Rosie's All-American Café
- Satu'li Canteen

- The Lunching Pad
- Tomorrowland Terrace Restaurant

Wrap up

That's it for right now, but you can count on Disney to keep innovating and creating new tech to improve our vacations.

Ready for More?

Our next chapter is the General dining chapter, where we'll do an overview of your dining options at Walt Disney World and then talk about ways that you can save some on this pricey vacation item.

9. Walt Disney World Dining

What's This Chapter About?

This is our general dining chapter where you'll get an overview of the types of dining options at Walt Disney World, the discounts that are available for dining, and some ways to economize on your food costs.

You'll find the listings of specific restaurants within the chapters pertaining to where they are located, those being the Theme Park, Resorts, and Other Entertainment chapters.

The range of dining options at Disney World is absolutely fantastic! There is everything available from grab and go locations, to Starbucks, counter service, sit down dining, and even signature dining. You can even dine with your favorite Disney character.

There is something for every taste and budget!

Dining Terms at Disney World

Any discussion of dining at Disney World requires the use a few Disney specific terms that Disney uses in regards to dining.

Disney classifies their restaurants by how the food is served, here are the Disney terms and what they mean.

- Quick Service – These are dining locations at which you wait in line to order your food at a counter, window, or freestanding cash register. You then wait for your food and carry it to the table of your choice.

- Table Service - These are dining locations at which you are seated at a table by a host or hostess and a waitress or waiter takes your order and delivers your food.
- Family Style - These are dining locations at which you are seated at a table by a host or hostess and a waitress or waiter takes your order and delivers your food. These locations may have one set menu or a variety that you can choose from. In either case, your food will be delivered to the table on platters and in serving bowls. Your family will then fix their own plates from the serving dishes. These locations are usually "All You Care to Eat."
- Buffet Service - These are dining locations at which you are seated at a table by a host or hostess and a waitress or waiter takes your drink order. You'll then go to the buffet area to fill your own plates, these meals are "All You Care to Eat."
- All You Care to Eat – Disney for "All You Can Eat", used in conjunction with Family Style and Buffet Meals.

In this chapter look for these keys to the rough cost of restaurants and the meals they offer:

- $ = Less than $15 per adult
- $$ = $15 - $30 per adult
- $$$ = $30 - $60 per adult
- $$$$ = Over $60 per adult
- B = Breakfast
- L = Lunch
- D = Dinner
- S = Snack

Disney Dining Overview

Reservations

Most Disney World Table Service restaurants accept Advance Dining Reservations or ADRs. ADRs are slightly different from the reservations you are used to in the non-Disney World.

An Advance Dining Reservation time, is a time at which you should be present at the restaurant (Disney recommends arriving 15 minutes prior to that time). When you arrive you'll check in and then be placed in the queue for the next available table. There may be others both with and without ADRs in this queue ahead of you.

Advance Dining Reservations are recommended even in the slower times of the year, especially for popular restaurants!

A credit card is required at the time you make your ADR and there is a fee that will be charged for same day cancellations. You may only make one ADR per meal. The single ADR requirement and cancellation fee are due to the fact that in the past there were those who made multiple ADRs per meal at different locations to "cover their bases" no matter where they wound up they'd have a place to eat.

Advance Dining Reservations may be made 180 days in advance. Those staying at a Disney resort may make ADRs for their entire trip (up to 10 days) on the 180th day prior to their arrival date. Non-Disney guests must make their ADRs day by day 180 days out from the desired ADR date.

Reserve online or by calling (407) WDW-DINE (939-3463).

Character Meals

At Disney World you have the ability to meet and greet various Disney Characters during your meal at certain locations. Different restaurants feature different characters.

Character meals are served several different ways depending on which restaurant you choose.

- Traditional buffet-style -- available at most of the participating restaurants.
- Family-style -- the server brings large bowls/plates/skillets of food that you serve yourself and pass around the table.
- Pre-plated meals -- These meals are served to each guest and each plate includes the same meal.

As a rule, you need to make Advance Reservations for character meals. However, during slow seasons it is sometimes possible to attend a Character Meal without an Advance Reservation. Advance Reservations are available for all character meals and can be arranged by calling 407-WDW-DINE (939-3463).

Theme park admission is required for theme park meals!

Character Meals by Location:

Magic Kingdom

Cinderella's Royal Table – BL$$$ D$$$$ - Cinderella and other classic Disney Princesses - When you arrive for your reservation, a photographer will be on hand to take pictures of your group in the lobby, before you are seated in the dining room.

Breakfast includes American favorites like: stuffed French toast, steak and eggs, baked quiche, and pastries. Lunch and dinner offer items like pork tenderloin, steak and shrimp, pan seared chicken, and summer vegetable couscous.

Advance Reservations are a must. This is the hardest Character Meal to get a reservation for!

Crystal Palace – BL$$ D$$$ - Pooh, Tigger, Eeyore and Piglet - Meals are served buffet-style with a separate buffet for kids called "Pooh Corner."

Breakfast items include eggs, pancakes, breakfast meats, breads, fruit and more. Lunch offers a variety of hot and cold entrees and sides along with a dessert bar. At dinner carved meats and peel-and-eat shrimp are added. Advance Reservations strongly recommended!

Epcot

The Garden Grill – B$$ LD$$$ - Mickey, Chip and Dale, and Pluto - Chip and Dale's Harvest Feast - Located in the Land Pavilion in the Future World section of Epcot. Kids' Breakfast includes Sticky buns, scrambled eggs, Mickey waffles, bacon and sausage, and hash browns. The lunch and dinner menu includes chicken tenders, mac and cheese. Reservations are recommended.

Akershus Royal Banquet Hall in the Norway Pavilion – B$$ LD$$$ - Snow White, Cinderella, Belle, Princess Aurora, and Ariel. A family style American breakfast is served while lunch and dinner are Norwegian style dining.

Disney's Hollywood Studios

Hollywood & Vine – BLD$$ - Meet Disney Junior characters during breakfast and Mickey, Minnie, Donald, Daisy, and Goofy during lunch and dinner. The buffet breakfast features pancakes and waffles, an omelet station, breakfast meats and potatoes, and fresh fruits and pastries. Among the lunch and dinner buffet selections are pastas, roast meats, seafood, salads, as well as a dessert and sundae station.

Disney's Animal Kingdom

Tusker House – BL$$$ - Donald, Daisy, Goofy, Mickey - The Animal Kingdom features a character breakfast, called Donald's Safari Breakfast, as well as a Character Lunch. All you can eat buffet. (Same day reservations may be available).

Disney Resorts

1900 Park Fare - Grand Floridian – B$$ D$$$ - Breakfast - Mary Poppins, Alice in Wonderland, and the Mad Hatter. Supercalifragilistic Breakfast items include omelet bar, pancakes, fruit, breads, meats, etc. Dinner - Cinderella and Prince Charming, Lady Tremaine, Anastasia, Drizella, and the Fairy Godmother (some characters may only be in the lobby for photos). Cinderella's Happily Ever After Dinner price includes dessert and a non-alcoholic beverage.

Cape May Cafe - Beach Club – B$$ - Goofy, Minnie, and Donald - Buffet breakfast offerings include eggs, pancakes, meats, breads, fresh fruit and more.

Chef Mickey's - Contemporary Resort - BD$$$ - The breakfast buffet offers the usual items - eggs, breads, meats, fresh fruit, etc. At dinner there is a salad bar, peel and eat shrimp, soups, hot entrees, breads, carved meats, vegetables, desserts and an ice cream bar with a great variety of toppings. Advance Reservations strongly recommended.

Polynesian - 'Ohana – B$$ - Lilo and Stitch, Pluto and Mickey. The meal is served family-style and features eggs, waffles, meats, breads, fruit and more. Advance Reservations are strongly recommended.

Trattoria al Forno – B$ - Ariel, Prince Eric, Rapunzel, and Flynn Rider – Plated breakfast includes items like pastries, fruit salad and yogurt, breakfast calzone, steak and egg torte, a frittata, scrambled eggs, and pancakes.

Walt Disney World Dining Discounts

No Military Dining Discounts

Unfortunately, while Disney offers great military discounts on their resort rooms and theme park tickets, they do not offer any military discounts on dining!

But don't worry, there are other discounts and options that you can take advantage of.

WDW Passholders

Walt Disney World Pass Holders receive Disney World dining discounts at many WDW restaurants. The list is long and ever changing, so be sure to ask before ordering!

Save 10% on regularly priced food and non-alcoholic beverages during various meal periods at select Walt Disney World Resort Table-Service locations

See disneyworld.disney.go.com/passholder-program/passholder-benefits-and-discounts/ for a current a list of participating restaurants.

Tables in Wonderland

Tables in Wonderland is a Walt Disney World discount dining program open to Annual Pass Holders, Disney Vacation Club members, and Florida Residents. The membership provides a 20% discount on food and beverages (including alcohol) at many restaurants and lounges in Walt Disney World's parks and hotels. The discount is good for up to 10 guests in your party.

There is an annual membership fee. Below is the fee and then in parenthesis the amount you'd have to spend on food and drink at qualifying restaurants to earn back your fee before you'll realize any savings.

-- Florida Residents: $175.00 ($875.00)
-- Disney Vacation Club members and Annual/Seasonal Pass Holders: $150.00 ($750.00)
-- Add a second membership for your spouse or partner for $50 more ($250.00)

See tablesinwonderland.com for the current list of participating restaurants.

Disney Springs Restaurant's Military Discounts

There are several non-Disney owned restaurants at Walt Disney World's Disney Springs that do offer military discounts!

Note, all of these are not owned by Disney. Here are the restaurants and their discounts.

Ghirardelli Soda Fountain and Chocolate Shop – 20% Military Discount

AMC Fork and Screen Theatres – 4 Dollars off for military member after 4pm

Cooke's of Dublin – 20% Military Discount

Paradiso 37, Taste of the Americas – Cuisine from North, South and Central America (15% Military Discount

Raglan Road – 20% Military Discount

Crossroads at House of Blues – 25% Military Discount

Don't just ask for a military discount at these locations, ask wherever you go! At locations where they do not offer one, cast members have been known to give you their employee discount just to say thanks. They do this without mentioning it, but you can see they did by checking the receipt for Cast Discount.

Note: these military discount locations and amounts are subject to change.

The Disney Dining Plan

The Disney Dining Plan is offered to Disney Resort Guests (not Shades of Green or other non-Disney guests). The Dining Plan is added on to your Disney room reservation.

The Disney Dining Plan essentially allows you to pre-pay for your meals while at Disney. There are several different levels of the plan from the basic to the Cadillac version.

There are three basic dining plans. By basic I mean they just cover meals and snacks, there are other Premium Dining Plans which are very expensive and also cover bottle(s) of wine per day, fireworks cruises, and Spa treatments.

The three basic plans and what they cover are:

Quick Service Dining Plan - Two quick service meals (entrée or combo meal, dessert at lunch and dinner and a non-alcoholic beverage (soda, coffee, or tea)) and two snacks per night on your package. New for 2018 with each meal guests under 21 receive a beverage including specialty beverages (milk shakes, smoothies, premium hot chocolates where offered) instead and guests 21 and receive a beverage including specialty beverages or one serving of a mixed cocktail, beer, or wine (where offered). Plus one Resort refillable drink mug per person. Cost : 2018 prices - $52.49 adult/$21.75 kids.

Standard Dining Plan - One table service entrée or buffet meal, dessert (lunch and dinner only), and non-alcoholic beverage; One quick service meal, including entrée or combo meal, and non-alcoholic beverage; and two snacks per day. New for 2018 with each meal guests under 21 receive a beverage including specialty beverages (milk shakes, smoothies, premium hot chocolates where offered) instead and guests 21 and receive a beverage including specialty beverages or one serving of a mixed cocktail, beer, or wine (where offered). Plus one Resort refillable drink mug per person. Cost: 2018 prices - $75.40 adult/$25.80 kids.

Deluxe Dining Plan - Three table service or quick service meals: (table service includes appetizer, entrée, and dessert (lunch and dinner), OR full buffet, plus non-alcoholic beverage); (quick service includes entrée plus non-alcoholic beverage, OR combo meal plus non-alcoholic beverage; and two snacks per day. New for 2018 with each meal guests under 21 receive a beverage including specialty beverages (milk shakes, smoothies, premium hot chocolates where offered) instead and guests 21 and receive a beverage including specialty beverages or one serving of a mixed cocktail, beer, or wine (where offered). Plus one Resort refillable drink mug per person. Cost: 2018 prices - $116.24 adult/$39.90 kids.

The Disney Dining Plan has those who love it and those who do not!

On the plus side you'll be including the cost of most of your dining needs into your room bill. You can even work on pre-paying this prior to arrival to ease your mind.

On the Quick Service Plan you'll generally break even, you'll get what you pay for. As you move up into the more expensive plans it becomes harder to get your money's worth, you generally have to order the most expensive items on the menus to avoid losing money.

Also with the more expensive plans, especially the Deluxe Plan contain a lot of food and you will have to spend time (3 plus hours a day) in table service restaurants, you'll need to plan ahead and have Advance Dining Reservations set up based on your park touring plans.

Free Dining

Disney World occasionally offers "Free Dining" usually in the fall to increase guest volume during lower projected attendance periods. During Free Dining, the Disney Dining Plan can be added for free to reservations at select resorts on certain dates.

The offer requires that you pay full price for your room. You may not use the Armed Forces Salute room discount and all guests in the room are required to buy a full price Magic Your Way tickets for a minimum number of days (usually 2-day tickets).

Deciding if this offer is better than the Disney Armed Forces Salute room and ticket offer requires a lot of calculation. You'll need to sit down and price out your vacation both ways to decide if Free Dining is right for you or not.

The Disney Armed Forces Salute is usually a better deal for: shorter stays (4-5 days), smaller groups, light eaters or non-foodies.

Deciding on the Dining Plan

Whether trying to decide on Free Dining or the paid Disney Dining Plan some calculation is required!

Free Dining - You'll need to compare the full package, that's full price room, required tickets, and any additional tickets plus your expected food extras to using the Disney Armed Forces Salute room and ticket rates plus what you think you would actually spend on food.

Paid Disney Dining Plan – You'll need to compare the cost of the Disney Dining Plan plus any food extras to what you think you would actually spend on food.

How to figure what you'd normally pay for food. I use the menus at AllEars.net, which include prices. Decide the restaurants that you'd like to eat at during your trip. If you are not sure at least pick one of the type/price range you think you'd use and then price out every meal and snack for everyone in your party to use to compare to the Dining Plan price.

Keep in mind, Disney would not offer this if they weren't making significant money doing it. Most people end up losing money for the convenience. You really have to plan ahead and work at it to break even or come out ahead. For a point of reference, with all of my many, many trips to WDW, I've only used it once!

Other Ways to Save

Bring and eat your own food. The Disney resorts and Shades of Green have mini-fridges in their rooms. You can keep some basic items for breakfast and snacks, or even lunch in the parks.

There are several ways that you can stock your room stash:

- Bring your food with you (if driving)
- Coordinate a grocery stop with your limo service (if flying)
- Have food pre-delivered to your resort by Amazon or GardenGrocer.com
- Make a supply run to Shades of Green's AAFES Store
- Buy items at your resort's sundries shop (more expensive and very limited choices)

Disney allows you to bring food and drinks into the parks. You can do so in backpacks or soft coolers, no hard coolers or glass items are allowed.

During a bag check at Epcot I was behind a family of four where both the mom and dad had full sized backpacks almost busting open they were so full. When they opened them up for security tons of food and plastic ware came spilling out, there was a whole cooked, very big chicken in one! It looked like they could have fed three or four families with all that they had…

That was a little overboard, but some snacks, sandwiches and drinks will get you through your theme park day.

Stop by Shades of Green for a meal in one of their restaurants. Prices at Shades are cheaper than Disney restaurants.

More Tips

Share meals. Disney portions are often very large. Share entrees and appetizers rather that getting one for everyone to reduce costs.

Kid's meals. Order the cheaper Kid's Meal at quick Service restaurant (if they appeal).

Quick service meals often are presented only as combo meals on the menus. But you can get the sandwich without the fries for less.

Free Soda, coffee, and tea refills. You will find that very few Quick Service restaurants at Walt Disney World offer free refills. But there are a few in the theme parks and at Disney Springs that do. Consider dining at these if you want a big volume of Coke products (there are no Pepsi products on property).

Magic Kingdom

- Be Our Guest

Epcot

- Sunshine Seasons
- Electric Umbrella

Hollywood Studios

- Backlot Express

Animal Kingdom

- Restaurantosaurus

Disney Springs

- Earl of Sandwich
- Wolfgang Puck Express
- Cooks of Dublin

Cups of water/ice. All Disney Quick Service restaurants will give you a cup of ice or cup of water (tap water vs a water bottle) for free. You can just get the water for everyone (It will help with your hydration!) or you can get one large soda and cups of ice to split up the soda. In Table Service locations opt for tap water.

Fixings bars. Several Disney Quick Service restaurants have extensive fixings bars to add to your burgers, sandwiches, and tacos.

Eat off Disney property

The Lake Buena Vista/Kissimmee area has a huge amount of restaurants. There is something for every taste and budget. There is even a McDonalds on WDW property. Shades of Green sells discounted tickets for many Orlando area Dinner Shows.

Restaurant.com

You can save at some Disney World/Disney area restaurants by purchasing discounted gift certificates from Restaurant.com ahead of time. Most certificates are for a specific amount (usually $25) and you get them at a discounted price (usually $10 or less). Most often you'll find these for the restaurants at the Swan and Dolphin hotels.

Wrap Up

As you can see there are more than a few ways to save on dining while on a Disney World vacation. This particular area takes quite a bit of calculation to determine ahead of time what it will actually cost you. If the cost for your dining is a concern for you, spend some time pricing out what you think you'll spend using the menus at AllEars.net and the various ways of saving mentioned in this chapter..

Ready for More?

We've hit all the major areas, now it's time to see what else there is to do at Walt Disney World. In the next chapter we'll cover other shows and entertainment, water parks, recreation, and even some special parties.

10. Other Things to Do at Walt Disney World

What's This Chapter About?

So far we've discussed Walt Disney World's theme parks, the tickets needed to enter them, dining at WDW, and where to stay while you're there.

Now we'll discuss everything else that there is to do at Walt Disney World and the military discounts that are available for some of them. Some of these things are even free!

We'll also touch on the discounts that are available for Orlando's other theme parks and entertainment venues.

The Electrical Water Pageant

The Electrical Water Pageant is a show that takes place every evening (weather permitting) on Walt Disney World's Seven Seas Lagoon and Bay Lake. It features 14 floats with lights that depict images of sea creatures. Think of it as a light parade on the water set to music.

The pageant consists of two strings of seven barges, each carrying a 25-foot-tall light wall. The pageant features King Neptune and sea creatures such as turtles, whales, and seahorses displayed in colored lights.

The pageant concludes with a salute to America, with Flags and Stars set to a patriotic musical medley of You're a Grand Old Flag, Yankee Doodle, and America the beautiful.

The Pageant makes a loop around the lakes passing by each resort on a loose schedule and can be viewed from the beach/shore at each resort:

Polynesian Village Resort - 9 p.m.

Grand Floridian - 9:15 p.m.

Wilderness Lodge - 9:35 p.m.

Fort Wilderness - 9:45 p.m.

Contemporary Resort - 10:05 p.m.

Magic Kingdom Entry Area (near the ferry boat dock) - 10:20 p.m. (only during extended MK park hours)

Note that when the Magic Kingdom Fireworks are scheduled for 10 p.m., the Electrical Water Pageant runs about 7-20 minutes after the fireworks end.

Disney World's Water Parks

There are two outstanding Disney water parks at Walt Disney World, Typhoon Lagoon and Blizzard Beach.

Both are themed out to the max in typical Disney fashion.

Typhoon Lagoon is themed in a tropical island setting. The park contains all of the types of activities you would expect to find at a water park: slides, pools, a lazy river, plus things that you won't find anywhere else like a surf pool and a saltwater artificial coral reef, which is home to tropical fish that you can snorkel with.

Blizzard Beach, the larger of the two is themed as a ski resort, complete with chair lifts to the water slides. This park has water slides, one of which is the tallest in the world, a family raft ride, a lazy river, and a gentle wave pool. *Note, some slides at Blizzard Beach have height restrictions.*

Both parks have beach and relaxation areas as well as plenty of snack and fast food options. Parking is free.

Water Park Tickets

There are three ways to gain entrance to Disney's water parks: Buying a separate ticket (the most costly); purchasing or adding the Park Hopper Plus option to your multi-day Disney World ticket (Disney Armed Forces Salute or Magic Your Way tickets); or by purchasing a Shades of Green Stars and Stripes length of stay pass.

Disney Armed Forces Salute Tickets come in two types: Park Hopper and Park Hopper Plus. The Plus Option will get you into the water parks.

The Park Hopper Plus Option can be added to any Magic Your Way ticket, whether purchased at full price from Disney or at a military discount from Base Ticket Offices or Shades of Green.

Shades of Green Stars and Stripes length of stay pass includes the same options (except mini golf) as the Park Hopper Plus Option.

Single day water park tickets are available at a military discount from Shades of Green's Ticket Office.

Note: if you are using Disney Armed Forces Salute Tickets, buying/adding the Plus Option costs less than buying a single day water park ticket and includes 4 or 5 water park visits!

Disney Springs

Disney Springs is Walt Disney World's shopping and entertainment complex. You'll find great dining options, merchandise stores (Disney and others), as well as many entertainment venues here.

Disney Springs is divided into four distinct areas, the Marketplace, the Landing, the West Side, and the Town Center. The Marketplace was the original section and then over the years Downtown Disney (the name prior to Disney Springs) expanded to the west, first with Pleasure Island (now the Landing), then the West Side, and now the newest section Town Center (once part of the parking lots).

The merchants at Disney Springs are a mix of Disney and non-Disney owned locations. While Disney does not offer any military discounts on food or merchandise, some of the non-Disney locations do!

Disney Springs recently finished a multi-year expansion and makeover. And in the process lost, I think, some of its "Disneyness." In the beginning Downtown Disney was primarily for and used by Disney guests, but as both it and Orlando grew so did the crowds.

Disney springs draws a lot of locals for shopping and nighttime entertainment. The addition of the new Town Center area has made this even worse. The Town Center contains no locations with a special Disney flair, it is just another outdoor Florida Mall with typical retail locations and a few new restaurants.

Below you'll find an overview of what Disney Springs has to offer. Any locations with military discounts are noted. Not all retail locations are listed as there are now over 126 total locations in Disney Springs, and as I said many of the new ones are stores you can find in your local mall. I'll highlight the ones with known military discounts and some of the best.

Note if you are told one of the locations I mention has no military discount, be sure to speak to a manager to check. The availability of military discounts has been known to change over time and also servers have been known to be wrong. Also feel free to ask about a discount at locations that are not listed as having a military discount, it never hurts to try!

Also Note: All military discounts mentioned are subject to change!

Crowds will be lowest earlier in the day. Disney Springs is quite busy in the evening!

Disney Springs Dining

Marketplace

Rainforest Café – Table Service - The national chain offers a unique dining experience that puts you in the middle of an Amazon rainforest. **(10% Military Discount, food & non-alcoholic drinks)**

T-Rex – Table Service - This restaurant features dinosaurs, waterfalls, bubbling geysers and a fossil dig site. **(10% Military Discount, food & non-alcoholic drinks)**

Earl of Sandwich - Assorted sandwiches, salads, and baked goods.

Ghirardelli Soda Fountain and Chocolate Shop – Ice Cream, Sundaes, and candy. **(20% Military Discount)**

Starbucks at Disney Springs Marketplace – The usual Starbucks stuff.

Wolfgang Puck Express - Serving grab and go pizzas, focaccia sandwiches, soups and fresh salads.

Walk Up Kiosks and Carts – Italian Ice, Aristocrepes, B.B Wolf's Sausage Co., Wetzel's Pretzels, Joffrey's Handcrafted Smoothies, Dockside Margaritas.

The Landing

Chef Art Smith's Homecomin' – Table Service - Dig into farm-to-fork cuisine showcasing Florida's fresh flavors—all crafted from recipes by an award-winning celebrity chef. A take away window is also available.

The Boathouse – Table Service - Most seats in our new favorite Disney Springs restaurant offer a view of the water. Enjoy great seafood and drinks while listening to live guitar music.

The Edison – Table Service – This lavish Industrial Gothic style restaurant, bar and nighttime destination is themed to a 1920s-period power plant. It features classic American food, craft cocktails, and live entertainment including cabaret, music, and palm reading. At 10 pm the tables are moved to create a dance floor for 21+ year olds (Dress code after 10).

Enzo's Hideaway Tunnel Bar – Table Service – Inspired by Florida's secretive "rum-running" past, this watering hole specializes in barrel-aged cocktails and has the largest selection of rums and scotches than any other restaurant at Disney Springs.

Jock Lindsay's Hangar Bar – Table Service - The aviation-themed lounge bears the namesake of Indiana Jones' trusted pilot, who appeared in the opening of Raiders of the Lost Ark. The venue features unique cocktails and small plates.

Maria and Enzo's Ristorante – Table Service - Enter the golden age of air travel while dining on authentic Italian fare.

Morimoto Asia – Table Service - The Japanese master chef's first pan-Asian dining experience will showcase flavors from across the Asian continent, all with Morimoto's creative touch. Creative Asian dishes and sushi bar.

Paddlefish – Table Service - Board an iconic paddleboat anchored on Lake Buena Vista to feast on fresh seafood and savory steaks.

Paradiso 37, Taste of the Americas – Table Service - Cuisine from North, South and Central America **(15% Military Discount)**

Raglan Road – Table Service - Traditional Irish fare prepared with a "modern flair." **(20% Military Discount)**

STK – Table Service - Retreat to this chic hideaway for an ultra-modern steakhouse experience—featuring an innovative menu, in-house DJ and a stunning outdoor patio.

Terralina Crafted Italian – Table Service - Opening Soon in the former location of Portobello Country Italian Trattoria.

Wine Bar George – Table Service - Make yourself at home in an estate-style wine bar offering shareable small plates and more than 100 wine selections from acclaimed wineries and up-and-coming regions. **Opening Spring 2018.**

Cooke's of Dublin – Carryout fish and chips, meat pies and more. Part of and around the corned from Raglan Road. **(20% Military Discount).**

Erin McKenna's Bakery NYC – The country's leading Gluten Free, Vegan, Kosher bakery.

Morimoto Street Food – Pan-Asian street foods—prepared with a twist, such as spicy Morimoto Baby Ribs, pork and cabbage egg rolls, and octopus fritters.

Pizza Pointe – Menu highlights include made-to-order sandwiches, an assortment of house-baked Italian pastries and Sicilian-style pizza by the slice. A selection of Italian beer and wine is also available.

Tea Traders Café – Delight in both the old and new traditions of tea preparation with a unique tea drinking experience.

Vivolo il Gelato – Experience the hand-crafted goodness of Italian gelati, sorbetti, espresso drinks and more.

Walk Up Kiosks and Carts – Florida Snow COmpany

West Side

AMC Fork and Screen Theatres - Table-top dining, and a personal notification button that can be used to quietly call your server at any time during the movie **($4 off for military member after 4pm).**

Bongos Cuban Cafe – Table Service - Cuban cuisine offering an express lunch and full dinner. A take away window is also available.

Crossroads at House of Blues – Table Service - Southern cooking, live music, special folk art display, and a Sunday Gospel Brunch. **(25% Military Discount)**

Planet Hollywood – Table Service - Dine amidst famous movie memorabilia. **(10% Military Discount)**

Splitsville Luxury Lanes – Table Service - 50,000-square-foot upscale entertainment center that combines bowling with billiards, dining, music and nightlife.

Coke a Cola Rooftop Bar – Specialty drinks mixed with Coke products and a great view. Take away is also available.

Food Trucks Exposition Park – A collection of Food Trucks offering Theme park and Epcot Food and Wine favorites.

The Smokehouse – Outside the Crossroads at House of Blues, offers quick-service restaurant offering an assortment of barbecue classics. **(25% Military Discount)**

Starbucks - The usual Starbucks stuff.

Walk Up Kiosks and Carts – Haagen-Dazs, Italian Ice, Joffery's Coffee and Tea, Wetzel's Pretzels, YeSake.

Town Center

Frontera Cocina – Table Service - Items include bacon guacamole, red chili chicken enchiladas and the coconut lime quattro leches cake. A take away window is also available.

Amorette's Patisserie – Pastry shop offering éclairs, New York-style cheesecake, cookies, gluten-free macarons, and signature cakes.

Blaze Fast Fired Pizza – Customize your own fast-fired 11" artisanal pie by choosing from over 40 delicious toppings and sauces. Freshly made salads, and s'mores dessert pies. A to go window is available.

D-Luxe Burger – Gourmet burgers, fries, and dipping sauces. Artisanal gelato shakes and freshly cut fries with house-made dipping sauces fully complement the savory scene that has something for every burger aficionado. **Online is Ordering available,** *see the Disney Tech Chapter.*

Polite Pig – Modern barbecue outpost featuring Florida-inspired cuisine and an array of libations on tap.

Sprinkles - gourmet cupcakes baked fresh daily with unique flavors and high-quality ingredients. You can also succumb to late-night cravings with a visit to the perky, pink Cupcake ATM nestled outside.

Walk Up Kiosks and Carts – The Daily Poutine, Gourmet Fries

Disney Springs Shopping

Marketplace

Arribas Brothers – Crystal and glass shop

Art of Disney – Disney art and collectables

Basin – Soaps and toiletries. **(10% Military Discount)**

Build-A-Dino Store -- located in T-Rex featuring dinosaur themed educational displays and merchandise.

Disney's Days of Christmas - Enjoy holiday shopping year 'round Disney style.

Disney's Pin Traders - The ultimate pin-purchasing-and-trading location.

Disney's Wonderful World of Memories - Capture your memories in photo albums and stationery.

Goofy's Candy Company – Loads of candy! Baked goods, fudge, chocolate covered fruit and pretzels, Carmel Apples (My families favorite treat!).

LEGO Imagination Center – A huge Lego store.

Little MissMatched - Sells colorful mismatched socks, gloves, pajamas, other clothing, bedding, and more.

Marketplace Fun Finds - Offers guests unique Disney gifts at great prices.

Mickey's Pantry - Featuring an assortment of Disney home and kitchen products.

Once Upon A Toy – A huge Disney toy store.

Marketplace Co-op - A store featuring six shops under one roof

- Cherry Tree Lane - Accessories for the sophisticated woman with a passion for scarves, shoes, bags and jewelry.
- D-Tech on Demand - A place to personalize and customize your own electronic accessories.
- Twenty Eight & Main – Art & Collectables, apparel & accessories.
- Disney Centerpiece - Home product for Guests that want a splash of Disney in their room furnishings, textiles and everyday wares.
- Wonderground - Art & Collectables.
- Disney Tag - Apparel & travel accessories.

TrenD - A stylish boutique with designer flair and eclectic offerings.

World of Disney – A super huge Disney character merchandise store. Clothing, jewelry, home goods, toys, tech needs, etc.

The Landing

Raglan Road's Shop for Ireland - Authentic Irish collectibles, clothing and more.

Chapel Hats - Fashionable hats and headwear for guests of all ages. The location carries just about any style of hat including fedoras, sun hats, floppy hats, outdoors hats, kid's hats and more.

Erin Mckenna's Bakery NYC - Offer the same unsurpassed core vegan, gluten-free menu as its flagship bakery in New York City, and its sister bakery in Los Angeles.

West Side

Bongo's Cuban Café Souvenir and Gift Shop - Latin inspired merchandise including clothing, music and more.

Cirque du Soleil® Store - Cirque collections and show related products. Cirque closes 31 December 2017.

Crossroads at House of Blues – House of Blues Souvenirs. **(15% Military Discount)**

Curl by Sammy Duvall – High-end Surf Shop featuring trendy Surf Wear clothing and accessories **(10% Military Discount on apparel, not sunglasses)**

D Street - Cutting edge apparel, pop culture novelties, Vinylmation figurines and other collectibles.

House of Blues Company Store - Merchandise including clothing, housewares and more.

Orlando Harley Davidson – Clothing and Accessories. **(10% Military Discount)**

Pop Gallery - Original, artist-signed limited sculptures and paintings, high-end gift items.

Planet Hollywood - Planet Hollywood Souvenirs. **(10% Military Discount)**

Sosa Family Cigars - Premium cigar store features the art of hand-rolling cigars.

Town Center

Florida Mall Type Shopping – Coca-Cola Store, Tommy Bahamma, LACOSTE, Alex & Annie, UNDER ARMOR, etc.

Disney Springs Entertainment

AMC 24 Theatres - 24 separate theaters of which 18 have stadium seating. **($2.50 off for military member after 4pm)**

Characters In Flight – Tethered Hot Air Balloon Ride. **(Military Discount $3 off adult, $2 off Kids)**

Cirque Du Solei – La Nouba - Cirque Du Solei has closed – the last show was on 31 December 2017

In Mid-December Cirque du Soleil announced the first details about the show that will eventually replace the long-running (since 1998) La Nouba.

The new show will "draw its inspiration from Disney's heritage of animation," according to Monday's announcement. "It will celebrate Disney's legacy of storytelling in Cirque du Soleil's signature way, with a tribute to the one-of a kind craftsmanship that makes Disney so extraordinary." It is being created by Cirque du Soleil Entertainment Group in collaboration with Walt Disney Parks and Resorts.

No opening date, title or specific details on which Disney characters or movies might be highlighted in the new show have yet been announced.

Military discounts had been available for La Nouba. We hope this continues for the new show.

Disney Quest -Disney Quest was an indoor virtual interactive theme park that combined Disney's magic with cutting-edge immersive technologies, such as virtual reality, to provide adventures for guests of all ages. Disney Quest has closed and is being transformed into the NBA Experience.

The NBA Experience at Walt Disney World Resort is going to be a one-of-a-kind destination featuring hands-on activities that put families and guests of all ages right in the middle of NBA game action. You'll be able to explore inside the world of professional basketball with numerous interactive experiences and enjoy a restaurant and retail store.

Splitsville Luxury Lanes - 50,000-square-foot upscale entertainment center that combines bowling with billiards, dining, music and nightlife.

Amphicars – Take a guided tour around the Disney Springs Lake in an Amphicar, a type of vintage car/boat that were manufactured in Germany in the mid-1960s. Buy your ticket at the Boathouse restaurant.

Disney's BoardWalk

Disney's BoardWalk is an entertainment, dining, and shopping complex located behind the BoardWalk Resort in the Epcot Resort Area.

The BoardWalk offers great restaurants, clubs, shopping and nighttime impromptu outdoor entertainment. It is a great place to spend a few hours or an evening.

There is no admission fee to Disney's BoardWalk itself, but certain venues may have cover charges. Self-parking is free for Disney guests,

Valet Parking is $20 (valet parking is free to Tables in Wonderland members with a valid receipt for dining reservations).

BoardWalk Dining:

Flying Fish Cafe specializes in seafood, but also features game and vegetarian dishes.

Trattoria al Forno spotlights Italian cuisine at breakfast and dinner. Enjoy lasagna, seasonal risotto, or a T-Bone steak Florentine.

ESPN Club's menu includes typical American fare, including pasta, sandwiches, salads and hamburgers.

Big River Grille & Brewing Works, a restaurant and brewpub that produces its own beers.

BoardWalk Bakery has pastries, cakes, baked goods, and sandwiches.

BoardWalk Pizza Window, grab a slice and sit at the nearby tables and chairs overlooking Crescent Lake.

AbracadaBAR – Between Trattoria and Flying Fish, a great place to wait for your table! "Curious Cocktails," "Worldly Wines" and "Baffling Beers." Travel back in time to the golden age of magic as you step inside this curious cocktail lounge.

BoardWalk Shopping:

Screen Door General Store, with a variety of Disney merchandise, as well as sundries and some grocery items.

Disney's Character Carnival features adult and golf apparel, accessories, plus Disney character merchandise.

Thimbles & Threads has ladies, children's and infant apparel, plus Disney character plush, toys and accessories.

Wyland Galleries, located near the entrance of the BoardWalk Inn, is a classic gallery of marine life artwork, featuring internationally renowned artist Wyland and others.

The Yard, next to the ESPN Club, has authentic ESPN merchandise.

Walt Disney World Golf

Walt Disney World features four 18-hole golf courses, some of which has hosted PGA Tour events for more than 30 years. In addition, there is a 9-hole, par 36, walking course.

The courses and some basic stats about them are:

Palm - Designed by Joe Lee, par for this course is 72. It has been rated a 4-star course by Golf Digest magazine. Its number one challenge is **water**.

Magnolia - Also designed by Joe Lee, this is also par 72 and has been rated a 4-star course by Golf Digest. Its number one challenge is **sand**, with 14 bunkers on Hole 4 alone.

Lake Buena Vista - Also designed by Joe Lee, this is also par 72 and has been rated a 4-star course by Golf Digest. Its number one challenge is **narrow fairways.**

Osprey Ridge - Designed by Tom Fazio, this par 72 course is rated 4.5 stars by Golf Digest. Its number one challenge is **large rolling greens.**

Oak Trail - Designed by Ron Garl, 9-hole, par 36, villain-free walking course for juniors and beginners.

Disney World Golf Facts:

- Disney's Osprey Ridge Golf Course has been recognized as one of the best courses in Florida by Golf Digests Places to Play.

- The 18th hole at Disney's Palm Golf Course is considered one of the most challenging holes on the PGA Tour.
- Disney's Lake Buena Vista Golf Course is one of the few courses that have hosted a PGA Tour event, an LPGA Tour event and a USGA event.
- Disney's courses are situated in a natural habitat that makes it a truly unique environment. Each of Disney's 4 championship courses is certified by Audubon International as a Cooperative Wildlife Sanctuary.
- Transportation is provided at no charge (via taxi) to and from select Walt Disney World Resort hotels for Guests playing at one of the Disney courses.
- The number for Disney Golf is (407) WDW-GOLF (939-4653).
- Playing Disney's 9-Hole Course is one of the items available through the Water Park Fun and More option available on theme park tickets.

Available Features Include:

- Three full-service pro shops
- Private golf instruction by PGA Pro Staff available by appointment
- Rental equipment available
- Four driving ranges, four putting greens.
- Clubhouses with on-course beverage service.

On the Green Snack Bar is located right next to the Magnolia and Palm course's clubhouse. It is very convenient to stop by prior to starting or after the ninth hole. Great sandwiches, cold beer, and ice for your golf cart cooler.

The 9-Hole Oak Trail course is one of the venues where you can use your Water Park Fun and More ticket option for entrance rather than paying for your entrance.

Military Discounted Golf Rates are offered for military members at all of Disney World's Golf Courses. These are the absolute lowest rates available to anyone. Rates vary by course and time and may be made 1 month out from your desired date either Online or by calling 407-939-4653 - (407) WDW-GOLF.

Online military rates and reservation: WDWformilitary.com/golf

Miniature Golf

Walt Disney World has two mini-golf courses, Fantasia Gardens and Winter Summerland.

Fantasia Gardens is located near the Disney Swan and Dolphin resorts and features a *Fantasia* theme. Course features include pirouetting gators, tutu-clad hippos and dancing water fountains.

Winter Summerland is located near the entrance to Blizzard Beach and is themed as Santa's permanent off-season retreat. There are two 18-hole experiences. One course carries the snow-clad Florida look reminiscent of Blizzard Beach, and the other has a more tropical holiday theme, with ornaments hanging from palm trees.

Your Water Park Fun and More ticket option can be used for a round of mini golf prior to 4pm at Fantasia Gardens Miniature & Disney's Winter Summerland.

Backstage Tours

Walt Disney World offers many different backstage tours. These special tours explore the unseen parts of the happiest place on earth. Tours do change over time and new tours are added as others are retired.

Tours all have fees ranging from $20 to $250 plus tax. Most require that you have separate theme park admission for the day of the tour and some include a meal or snack.

Call 407-WDW-TOUR (939-8687) for details, pricing, and reservations (which are recommended).

Animal Kingdom Tours

Backstage Tales - Go behind-the-scenes at Animal Kingdom. You'll get an insider's look at the innovative ways that Disney is meeting challenges in areas such as conservation, animal nutrition and medicine, animal care and behavioral studies.

Caring For Giants - During this 60-minute experience, you'll meet with dedicated animal specialists who provide for the care and wellness of our African elephant herd. They'll give you a glimpse into their day-to-day responsibilities as they provide fascinating facts about the elephants.

Wild Africa Trek, is a three-hour, expert-led wildlife experience. Participants can explore the most remote reaches of Disney's Animal Kingdom.

Savor the Savanna: Evening Safari Experience - Immerse your senses during a privately guided journey and explore the sights and sounds—and tastes—of Africa. Welcome to Savor The Savanna: Evening Safari Experience, an all-new premium tour where you can discover the wonders of the continent's most amazing creatures… and so much more!

Animal Kingdom Lodge Tour

Starlight Safari at Disney's Animal Kingdom Lodge - Set out on an immersive safari adventure reminiscent of a nighttime drive through an African game reserve. Witness the wild as it comes to life on an after-dark safari tour of Disney's African savannas and wildlife! This popular, nighttime expedition is now open to all Guests at Walt Disney World Resort.

Epcot Tours

Behind the Seeds - Take a one-hour walking tour of the LAND greenhouses and labs.

Epcot Seas Adventures - Aqua Tour - The 2.5-hour experience includes a 30-minute dive in the Living Seas aquarium.

Epcot Seas Adventures - DiveQuest - Allows certified scuba divers the ultimate diving experience. Experience a 30-minute dive adventure in The Living Seas aquarium.

Gardens of the World - (only during the Epcot Flower & Garden Festival) Learn about the basic design concepts, theming, and practices used in creating the beautiful Epcot landscapes. This 3-hour tour is hosted by a horticulture expert.

Undiscovered Future World - Learn about the history and creation of Epcot and the legacy Walt set forth for the Walt Disney World Resort. See how each pavilion in Future World celebrates human accomplishment and presents the challenge of the future.

World Showcase: DestiNations Discovered - Travel the world on a fascinating 5-hour walking tour at Epcot and experience the architecture, culture and people of 11 countries and 4,000 years of history, culture and food. From the streets of Paris to the Bavarian countryside, Guests can immerse themselves in the architecture, landscapes, streetscapes, attractions, shops and restaurants of 11 themed pavilions—each staffed by actual citizens from these countries

Magic Kingdom Tours

Walt Disney: Marceline to Magic Kingdom - Uses the Magic Kingdom as a "walking timeline" to help guests discover how the events in Walt's life helped develop his understanding and view of the world around him.

Family Magic - A tour the whole family can enjoy is offered at the Magic Kingdom. Family Magic Tour takes you on a one-of-a-kind interactive tour through Main St, Liberty Square, Tomorrowland and Fantasyland. During the 2 hours, you are taken through the park's themed lands in search of clues (like a treasure hunt).

Keys to the Kingdom - Offered daily, this four-and-a-half hour to five-hour tour celebrates Disney Magic! Learn about the Magic Kingdom's history and backstage secrets. I've done this one and loved it!

The Magic Behind Our Steam Trains - Explores Walt Disney's passion for steam trains, while giving Guests the opportunity to join the opening crew as they prepare for the daily railroad operation at the MAGIC KINGDOM. This tour also offers the rare opportunity to visit the backstage "roundhouse".

Multi-Park Tours

Backstage Magic - This seven-hour program visits backstage! Travel to the Magic Kingdom to see the Utilidors, examine backstage computer controlled attractions at Epcot, see behind the scenes at the Seas, have a special lunch at Disney's Hollywood Studios, plus other surprises.

Water Craft Rentals and Cruises

Fireworks/IllumiNations Cruises – Charter a private pontoon boat to watch the Happily Ever After Fireworks Show at the Magic Kingdom or Illuminations at Epcot up close with your guests.

Celebration and Private Dining Cruises - Celebration Cruises deliver an extra dash of pixie dust with colorful balloons and banners guaranteed to set the mood. Enhance any affair with the Private Dining menu—including personalized cakes, champagne, hors d'oeuvres, miniature desserts, chocolate-covered strawberries, fruit and cheese platters or even a full meal.

Cruise locations and numbers:

- Contemporary: 407-824-2955
- Wilderness Lodge: 407-824-1043
- Grand Floridian: 407-824-2473
- Polynesian: 407-824-2165
- Yacht and Beach Club: 407-939-3160

Pickups also available at Fort Wilderness

See: disneyworld.disney.go.com/recreation/specialty-cruises/ for more information. Reservations for cruises can be obtained by calling 407-WDW-PLAY up to 180 (90 for specialty cruises) days in advance. Prices range from $299 to $399 per hour.

Sports Related Activities

Fishing at Walt Disney World

Enjoy a private catch-and-release fishing excursion (fishing for large-mouth bass) on the lakes of the Walt Disney World Resort for up to five people that includes:

- A guide
- Rod and reel
- Tackle
- Artificial/live bait
- Beverages

- One-year membership in BASS, the world's largest fishing organization (membership includes 11 issues of Bassmaster Magazine; a membership pack with a personalized membership card, members-only decal, an embroidered patch and member handbook; free Gear Giveaways; a Boat Theft Reward; information on local BASS chapters; eligibility to compete in national events; and other special discounts and benefits)

Most trips are on a pontoon boat, which accommodates up to five people. A Nitro Bass Boat is available for more experienced anglers (no live bait is available on the Nitro Bass Boat excursions). The Nitro Bass Boat accommodates only two guests.

Fishing excursions are available from the following WDW marinas:

- BoardWalk Resort
- Caribbean Beach Resort
- Contemporary Resort
- Coronado Springs Resort
- Fort Wilderness Resort & Campground
- Grand Floridian Resort & Spa
- Old Key West
- Polynesian Resort
- Port Orleans Resort
- Saratoga Springs Resort and Spa
- Yacht Club Resort
- Disney Springs Marketplace

Sammy Duvall's Watersports Centre - Parasailing and Watersports

Sammy Duvall's offers Parasailing, Water Skiing, Wake Boarding, and Family Tubing. Personal Watercraft available for rent or guided tours of Bay Lake and Seven Seas Lagoon from the Contemporary Resort Marina. Make your reservation 407-939-0754

Surfing at Typhoon Lagoon – Craig Carroll's Cocoa Beach Surfing School - Three hours of surfing instruction, which includes a half hour of landside instruction first.

Horse-Drawn Carriage Rides and Excursions

Horse drawn wagon and carriage rides are offered at Fort Wilderness Campground and at Port Orleans Riverside Resort.

Fort Wilderness

Horse-Drawn Wagon Ride - Take an old-fashioned, horse-drawn wagon ride, which offers a 25-minute scenic tour around Disney's Fort Wilderness Resort & Campground. Wagon Rides depart at 6:00pm and 8:30pm nightly from the front of Pioneer Hall (weather permitting). These 25-minute wagon rides cost $12 for Guests ages 10 and up, and $8 for Guests 3 to 9 years of age. Reservations are recommended and can be made up to 180 days in advance by calling (407) WDW-PLAY or (407) 939-7529.

Group wagon rides (for 30 to 35 Guests) cost $300 per 45 minutes and are available with 24-hour notice by calling (407) 824-2832.

Wagon Ride Prices: $8.00 Adult; $5.00 Child (ages 3-9) Children under 3 are complimentary. Children ages 3-9 must be accompanied by an adult. Reservations: Not accepted; Wagon Rides are on a first-come, first-served basis only.

Carriage Rides - Take a relaxing and intimate 25-minute carriage ride through Disney's Fort Wilderness Resort & Campground. Carriages hold 4 adults or 2 adults and 3 small children.

Reservations - Advance reservations can be made by calling WDW-PLAY up to 180 days in advance. First ride 6pm - Last ride departs 9:30pm. Pick up in front of Crockett's Tavern at Pioneer Hall

Price: 25-minute ride for $55 (tax included), Tickets are sold by the carriage drivers, cash and Disney Resort guest room charge accepted. Credit cards cannot be accepted

Port Orleans Resort Riverside

Carriage Rides - A 25-minute carriage ride through Disney's Port Orleans Resort. Carriage holds up to 4 adults or 2 adults and three small children. Board your horse-drawn carriage for a 25-minute ride at the Riverside Levee Marina at Disney's Port Orleans Resort – Riverside.

First ride 6pm -Last ride departs 9:30pm. Pick up at Port Orleans Riverside in front of Boatwright's Dining Hall.

The 25-minute ride is $55 (tax included), tickets are sold by the carriage drivers, cash and Disney Resort guest room charge accepted, credit cards cannot be accepted.

Reservations - Advance reservations can be made by calling WDW-PLAY up to 180 days in advance. Same day reservations may be available at the Riverside Marina, carriage rides may be cancelled due to inclement weather. There is a $55 fee for no-shows or cancellations with less than 24 hours' notice.

ESPN Wide World of Sports

ESPN Wide World of Sports is a state-of-the-art 200-acre sports complex.

Disney has arrangements with major sporting organizations including the NFL, NBA, NCAA and PGA, who host annual events at the complex. The Amateur Athletic Union (AAU) has its headquarters here.

Spectator Admission gives you access to most amateur events at ESPN Wide World of Sports Complex. If you are not an athlete or coach participating in an event, tickets may be purchased at the Complex Box Office.

Note if you have a Magic Your Way Ticket with Water Park Fun & More plus options, you can use one option for admission to the Wide World of Sports.

Walt Disney World's Special Ticketed Holiday Parties

Each year Walt Disney World hosts two special Holiday events, Mickey's Not-So-Scary Halloween Party and Mickey's Very Merry Christmas Party. These events are held in the Magic Kingdom on select nights from September through December after the regular park hours and require a separate entrance ticket.

Your Disney Armed Forces Salute or regular Magic Your Way tickets will not get you into either of these parties, the purchase of an additional event admission ticket is required to attend.

Disney offers a military discount on admission during the first month of each party.

These special tickets must be purchased in person (with proper military ID) from Walt Disney World ticket or Guest Relations locations as well as at Shades of Green. They cannot be pre-purchased over the phone or via the internet.

Special procedures for sold out nights - These events are very popular and often sell out via general public advance ticket sales prior to the event. Because of the requirement that military members buy their tickets in person with proper ID, Disney World allows military members to purchase their tickets even if an event is sold out. This can be done for dates with or without the military discount except Halloween Night. **You must purchase tickets for sold out nights only at the Magic Kingdom Guest Relations location** (to the right after going through bag check before entering the park). You cannot do this at Shades of Green.

Mickey's Not-So-Scary Halloween Party

Mickey's Not-So-Scary Halloween Party is a Halloween themed special after-hours event held on select dates in Disney World's Magic Kingdom theme park.

The event is held on select nights in September and October.

During Mickey's Not-So-Scary Halloween Party, Guests of all ages are encouraged to dress up in their favorite Halloween costumes. Even better, you can collect delicious candy as you trick-or-treat around Magic Kingdom theme park.

In addition to many favorite Disney attractions, Mickey's Not-So-Scary Halloween Party is filled with special entertainment, including: Mickey's "Boo-to-You" Halloween Parade—including Disney Characters and the stars of the Haunted Mansion attraction.

The parade begins with a spook-tacular ride by the Headless Horseman. Happy HalloWishes – a spectacular firework show where the Disney Villains go trick-or-treating in the sky. See many of your favorite Disney Characters and Disney Villains in special Halloween costumes.

Special lighting, music and theming effects transforms special areas of Magic Kingdom theme park into happy haunted hollows. The tone of the event is, well, "Not-So-Scary", and is appropriate for children of all ages.

Active and Retired U.S. Military, including members of the U.S. Coast Guard and active members of the National Guard and Reserve, may purchase discounted Mickey's Not So Scary Halloween Party Tickets for special military priced event nights. They may also purchase additional tickets for up to five (5) family members and/or friends. **The military discount is only offered for September dates.** *See the links section at the end of this chapter for current pricing.*

Mickey's Very Merry Christmas Party

Mickey's Very Merry Christmas Party is a special event held each winter on select nights at Disney World's Magic Kingdom theme park.

The event is held on select nights in November and December.

Celebrate the magic of the season in the holiday wonderland of Magic Kingdom theme park. Gather with loved ones for a festive sight and sound filled special event that is sure to make you merry! This festive celebration is filled with live entertainment, spectacular fireworks and an oh-so-jolly holiday parade.

In addition to many favorite Disney attractions, Mickey's Very Merry Christmas Party is filled with special entertainment, including: Mickey's Once Upon a Christmas Parade - staring Disney Characters and Jolly Old Saint Nick.

See it snow on Main Street and enjoy Christmas cookies and cocoa. Castle Dream Lights – See the castle transformed into a beautiful display of holiday lights right before your eyes! See the special Christmas fireworks display!

Active and Retired U.S. Military, including members of the U.S. Coast Guard and active members of the National Guard or Reservists, may purchase discounted Mickey's Very Merry Christmas Party Tickets for special military priced event nights. They may also purchase additional tickets for up to five (5) family members and/or friends. **The military** discount is only offered for November dates. *See the links section at the end of this chapter for current pricing.*

Other Non-Disney Theme Parks and Activities

There is a wide range of vacation activities that are available in the Orlando/Central Florida area. There is something for everyone and many offer military discounts.

SeaWorld Orlando and Busch Gardens Tampa

The SeaWorld Parks have been offering the Waves of Honor (previously the Anheuser-Busch Here's to the Heroes) program since 2005. This fantastic offer allows a free one-day admission to one of their nationwide parks per year to current military members and up to 3 direct dependents.

There have also occasionally been seasonal discounts or free offers for retirees and veterans (usually November through December in conjunction with Veteran's Day).

Discounts are also available for Aquatica in Orlando and Adventure Island Water Park in Tampa.

See your Base or Shades of Green Ticket Offices.

LEGOLAND Florida

LEGOLAND Florida offers a **free one-time single day admission to all current military personnel** including the Army, Navy, Air Force,

Marines, Coast Guard, National Guard and Reservists. This ticket can only be purchased at the LEGOLAND Florida ticket window.

Military members and Retirees may also purchase discounted tickets for their family and friends, but they must do this **ahead of time at their Base Ticket Office**. These tickets can be purchased on base at **up to 45% off** depending on how much of the savings your base ticket office passes on to you.

LEGOLAND also offers regular military discounts. **A slight (10%) discount is offered at the gate.**

See your Base or Shades of Green Ticket Offices.

Universal Studios Florida

Universal Studios doesn't have quite the track record that Disney and SeaWorld Parks do. While they do offer slight discounts through Base Ticket Offices, they rarely offer a great discount like the other parks.

The last three years they have offered a 3-day (now 4-day for 2017) 2 – par ticket, through Base Ticket Offices. At press time this offer had not been extended for 2018, they usually do not announce until early January.

They do also offer an all-inclusive, set length military package (room and tickets), which will save you a little off of the regular individual prices.

Other Attractions

There are many other local attractions that offer military discounts through the Shades of Green Ticket Office.

Here is the current list, which is subject to change:

Gatorland (the original Orlando attraction)
Kennedy Space Center
Florida Aquarium Tampa
Fun Spot Orlando/America
Ripley's Believe It or Not
Titanic Experience
Wonder Works
Blue Man Group (at Universal)
Cirque du Solei (at Disney Springs)
Medieval Times Dinner Theatre
Sleuth's Mystery Dinner

Wrap Up

Well, that sure was a lot to take in! But you can now see that there is way more to do at Walt Disney World than just the theme parks.

You could fill a whole trip and never go to one of the parks. Here's a great idea, using the Disney Armed Forces Salute tickets and room discounts, plan two trips during the year. Use the 4-day tickets half on one vacation, and half on the other. Then fill the other days with some relaxation and other fun activities from this chapter.

Ready for More?

Well, now you know everything that there is to do at Disney World, now you just need to know how to get there. Next we'll cover all the different transportation options for WDW, both how to get there, and then getting around once you are there.

11. Transportation for your Walt Disney World Vacation

What's This Chapter About?

This chapter is all about getting to and getting around Walt Disney World. The options available to you will vary based upon where you are staying, whether it's at a Disney Resort, Shades of Green, or other accommodations. We'll cover them all.

Before we close the chapter we'll talk about getting to the other Orlando theme parks and transporting the little ones around on your vacation (strollers).

But first you've got to get to Disney World. There are two main ways that you'll travel to WDW, driving or flying. We'll cover both, plus even mention the Amtrak auto train in the driving section.

Getting to Walt Disney World

Driving

Many people elect to drive their privately owned vehicle or a rental to Walt Disney World. There are pluses and minuses to doing so.

Some of the pluses are:

- The freedom of your own transportation to get around Disney World.
- The ability to drive to other local area attractions.

- Not having to obtain transportation from the airport to some resorts.
- Being able to make trips for groceries and supplies.
- The ability to dine off property.
- Bringing more stuff.
- Potentially cheaper than flying,

Some of the minuses are:

- Potentially adding extra days to your vacation.
- Parking costs at resorts and theme parks depending on where you stay.

The Cost of Parking Your POV

Parking Fees - Depending on where you stay, you might be required to pay parking fees.

Disney Resort Guests – Parking is free all Disney theme parks. But for all reservations made after 21 March 2018 there is a parking fee at your Disney Resort: $13 at Values, $19 at Moderates, and $24 at Deluxes.

Shades of Green Guests – There is a nightly resort parking fee of $7 at Shades of Green and you'll pay $22 per day to park at Disney's theme parks.

Swan and Dolphin - There is a nightly resort-parking fee of $20 at the Swan and Dolphin.

Note: Valet parking is always extra! ($33 at Disney Resorts, $28 at the Swan and Dolphin)

Amtrak Auto Train

Amtrak's Auto Train provides service between Lorton, Virginia (just south of Washington DC) and Sanford, Florida, about an hour north of Disney World. If getting to Lorton is convenient it will save you 800 miles of driving. You can relax, dine, and sleep on the trip south while your car rides along.

You'll arrive mid-day at Lorton to check in and board and arrive in Sanford about 9:30 am the next day. You'll wait an hour or so to get your car and then you can hit the road (I-4 West) for the hour plus drive to WDW.

Flying to Orlando and Walt Disney World

How you'll get to Walt Disney World from the airport and how much it will cost depends largely on where you stay.

Walt Disney World Resort Guests are eligible for the free Disney's Magical Express bus transportation from the Orlando International Airport right to your Disney resort.

Non-Disney guests including Shades of Green and the Swan and Dolphin are responsible for obtaining and paying for their own transportation.

Disney Resort Guests

Disney's Magical Express

Disney's Magical Express is a service that Disney provides exclusively to those staying in Disney Owned Hotels.

You can set this service up when making your resort reservation through Disney or your Travel Agent.

Be aware that Disney's Magical Express service is **only** available from the Orlando International Airport. There is another airport, which identifies itself as the "Orlando Sanford International Airport" but it is not in Orlando, it is well to the north in the town of Sanford, a good 50-minute drive from WDW. The Magical Express does not service Sanford.

If you will be checking luggage on your flight to Orlando you should advise Disney or your Travel Agent how many bags that you will be checking when making your resort reservation.

Prior to your travel date Disney or your Travel Agent will send you special luggage tags in the mail. When you place these on your bags it identifies them as bags destined for Walt Disney World and they will bypass the regular baggage claim area at the Orlando airport and will go directly to the Magical Express.

Your bags will be loaded for you onto a truck heading for your hotel and will be placed in your room. You will not have access to your bags during this period, so hand-carry anything that you might need before your bags get to your room.

In short, you'll check your bags at your departure airport and the next time that you see them, they will have magically appeared in your resort room (2 or 3 hours after your plane lands).

Note if you arrive after 10 PM (either by schedule or delay) Magical Express luggage service will not be available. You will need to claim your luggage yourself and then take it with you to the Welcome Center for Disney's Magical Express.

Your Arrival in Orlando

When your flight arrives in Orlando, walk from your arrival gate and follow the signs towards baggage claim.

You'll board a monorail train, which will take you to the main terminal. Once you pass out of the security area you'll enter a large atrium. Look for the signs for Baggage Claim B (this is on one side of the airport, A is the other side), The signs will also say DIsney's Magical Express, follow the signs down the escalator and then go down one more level to the Transportation level (or take the elevator all the way).

Once on the Transportation level follow the signs Disney's Magical Express.

When you arrive at the Magical Express check-in the Disney cast members there will quickly look up your reservation, and direct you to one of several numbered lines. They will look you up via your magic band or you can use the paperwork that accompanied your luggage tags.

Each line is for a specific bus that is destined for a different set of hotels. These buses make several hotel stops and your hotel might not be first. Wait times for the bus could be up to 20 minutes and travel time will be 35 to 75 minutes depending on which stop you are on.

While you are enroute to your hotel there will be introductory videos for Disney World playing in the bus and there is a restroom available.

Once the bus arrives at your hotel just hop off and check in.

Leaving Disney World

On your departure day the service works essentially the same.

The day prior to check out you'll receive an envelope on your room door containing a letter with when and where to catch your bus to the airport (about 3 hours prior to your plane's departure time). Your luggage will ride with you this time.

You or a bellhop will bring your luggage to your pickup location. Once at the airport you'll then take your bags to the airline check-in area yourself.

It is possible on domestic flights to both check in for your airline and check your bags to your destination right at your Disney hotel for participating Air Carriers. Check with the Bellhop Staff.

- Alaska Airlines
- American Airlines
- Delta Air Lines (U.S. Domestic Flights Only)
- JetBlue Airways
- Southwest Airlines
- United Air Lines

Note Disney's Magical Express must be booked at least 10 days prior through disneyworld.com, the Disney Reservations Center by calling 407-W-DISNEY or your travel agent.

Non-Disney Resort Guests

Non-Disney Resort guests are on their own for securing transportation from the Orlando International Airport to their resort whether on or off Disney property.

Your options are:

- Taxi
- Limo Service
- Bus Service
- Rent a Car
- Uber

Taxi – Taxis at the airport are about $75 each way for Walt Disney World.

Limo Service – There are numerous limo services available to take you to WDW. Prices start near $100 one-way. Many will make a food stop for room supplies.

Bus Service – A company called Mears Transport runs regular buses vans and limos from the airport to all WDW and local area resorts. They are about $80-100 one-way.

Car Rental - You might be able to find a good military rate. I'm a USAA member and they have discounts negotiated with all the major car rental companies.

A $15 Military Discount is available for readers of this book from Orlando Shuttle Service on round trip shuttle rides. Just go to orlandoshuttleservice.com and use the MDT15 discount code. You may use this discount on all your transportation needs, whether, airport, other theme parks, other local destinations, or even to the east or west coasts (Disney Cruise Line, Kennedy Space Center, Busch Gardens).

Uber – Another cheaper way to get to your non-Disney resort is Uber. New members get a Free ride up to $15 using this promo code: steveb14703ue. This promo is for your first ride only, any value not used expires so this is not good for a quick hop across WDW property, but it is perfect for a ride from Orlando International to WDW. This code is for new members so if you have an account; have someone else in your party who doesn't have one sign up. Fares are currently starting at around $25 one way to WDW on Uber-x.

Deciding to Drive or Fly

Make sure that when you are comparing the cost of flying to driving, that you include all of the associated costs of each.

For Driving – Hotel, gas, and food costs enroute as well as all tolls and parking fees at WDW.

For Flying – Airfare, baggage fees, airport parking or shuttle fees, and meals enroute. Plus any costs for getting to and around WDW if any.

Getting Around Walt Disney World

Driving

If you'll be driving around Walt Disney World, whether it is your own car or a rental from the airport there are some things to be aware of.

First the road system on Disney property is first class and the roadways are well maintained and clearly marked. Most locations are just a 5 to 10 minute drive away. The exception to this is the area around Disney Springs, traffic is always backed up here.

Parking Fees

Guests who are not staying at a Disney owned resort, are required to pay a daily fee for theme park parking. Those who must pay for parking include guests at Shades of Green and the Disney World Swan and Dolphin resorts.

- Standard parking: car or motorcycle – $22 per day
- Preferred parking: car or motorcycle – $45 per day
- Shuttle, Limo, Camper, Trailer or RV – $27 per day
- Bus or Tractor Trailer – $27 per day

This is a daily rate, so if you pay to park at Animal Kingdom in the morning and plan to visit Epcot later in the day, keep your receipt to show at the Epcot parking tollbooth.

Disney Resort Guests – who park their car at their resort will pay $13 at Values, $19 at Moderates, and $24 at Deluxes.

Shades of Green guests who park their car at Shades of Green will pay $7 per day for parking.

Disney World Swan and Dolphin guests pay $20 per day to park at their hotels.

Disney's deluxe resorts offer optional Valet Parking for $33 per day. You might opt for this when having dinner at a resort, checking out the BoardWalk, or doing a monorail hotel tour. This is a daily fee so should you desire to valet again during the same day there is no additional charge (tipping is suggested though) keep your receipt.

Complimentary Transportation

Both Walt Disney World and Shades of Green offer complimentary transportation around Walt Disney World for their guests.

Shades of Green guests may use both, while Disney Resort guests would have little need to use Shades transport as it only offers single leg routes between Shades and several locations on property.

Disney Transportation

Walt Disney World operates a huge fleet of buses, watercraft, monorails, and parking lot trams, the use of which is free to everyone on WDW property. The buses, watercraft, and monorail are all handicap accessible.

Buses – Disney World maintains a fleet of approximately 325 buses, which transport both guests and cast members around property. The bus fleet runs on a hub and spoke system, meaning that not all locations on property have a direct bus route between each other. Wait times are typically 20 minutes between buses.

The Hubs are:

- The four theme parks
- Disney Springs (partial hub)
- ESPN Wide World of Sports (mini hub)

Resort Service

At each Disney Resort (with some exceptions) you will find bus service to each of the four theme parks. Buses travel back and forth between the two points along the "spoke" part of the system. Some routes also stop at Blizzard Beach Water Park enroute.

Resorts that do not have bus service to select parks have other forms of transportation, those being:

- Magic Kingdom Monorail Resorts and Fort Wilderness Campground do not have bus service to the Magic Kingdom as they have the monorail and or watercraft service.

- The Deluxe Epcot Area Resorts do not have bus service to Epcot or Hollywood Studios as they have watercraft service instead.

At each Disney Resort you will find bus service to Disney Springs. Some routes also stop at the Typhoon Lagoon Water Park.

Generally you cannot take Disney's buses between the resorts. You must take a bus to one of the theme parks or Disney Springs to catch a bus to another Disney Resort.

While they are very limited, there are one-way exceptions, which do travel between Disney Resorts, but there are easier methods to get between the resorts in question as they are all in close proximity. The Deluxe Epcot Area Resorts are an example, while there is one way flow around the loop on three bus lines and a connection between two hotels in the opposite direction on another route, it is much easier and quicker to walk or take the watercraft service between all of them.

Theme Park Service

At each theme Park you will find bus routes servicing all Disney Resorts, the other three theme parks, Disney Springs, and the water parks via theme park or resort routes.

Disney Springs - Typhoon Lagoon Service

At each Disney Resort you will a find bus route that runs to Disney Springs. In the morning buses stop at Typhoon Lagoon prior to Disney Springs. Between 11 am and 2 pm buses stop at Typhoon Lagoon after stopping at Disney Springs. After 2 pm the only bus route for Typhoon Lagoon runs from Epcot.

You will not find buses to the theme parks at Disney Springs! This is because people were parking for free at Disney Springs and then using the bus service to the theme parks to avoid paying for theme park parking.

ESPN Wide World of Sports

There is bus service between ESPN Wide World of Sports and the following resorts: all three All-Star Resorts, Pop Century, and the Caribbean Beach Resorts. This is because these are the hotels at which young athletes and their families stay at when competing at ESPN. *Note the Art of Animation is within walking distance of Pop Century.*

Local Resort Service

Some of the bigger spread out resorts offer bus service within the resort making stops at locations spread around the resort and the resort's main building.

Resorts with internal routes:

- Fort Wilderness Campground
- Caribbean Beach Resort
- Coronado Springs Resort
- Port Orleans Riverside

Watercraft – Walt Disney World has a large fleet of water launches, water taxis, and ferry boats which offer alternate or at times the sole transportation method for Disney guests.

Disney's watercraft operate mainly on four bodies of water and their attached waterways:

- The Seven Seas Lagoon
- Bay lake
- Crescent Lake
- Village Lake

Seven Seas Lagoon – The western Magic Kingdom Resort area. Water Launches run on a circular route that encompasses the Grand Floridian Resort and Spa, the Polynesian Village Resort, and the Magic Kingdom.

Bay Lake - The eastern Magic Kingdom Resort area. Water Launches ferry passengers between Fort Wilderness Campground, the Wilderness Lodge, the Contemporary Resort, and the Magic Kingdom.

Crescent Lake and attached waterway – Deluxe Epcot Area Resorts. Water Taxis ferry guests on a route that includes Epcot's International Gateway, the BoardWalk Resort, the Beach and Yacht Club Resorts, the Disney Swan and Dolphin Resorts, and Disney Hollywood Studios.

Village Lake and attached waterway – Disney Springs Resort Area. Water Taxis ferry guests on a route that include Port Orleans Riverside, Port Orleans French Quarter, Saratoga Springs Resort (a Disney Vacation Club Resort), Old Key West Resort (a Disney Vacation Club Resort), and Disney Springs.

Theme Park Transportation

Guests traveling from the Transportation and Ticket Center have the option of taking giant ferry boats or the monorail for the journey of a little over a half mile to the Magic Kingdom.

Monorails – Walt Disney World's monorail system was a look at the future of transportation when it was first built in 1971, many airports now use similar systems to move travelers between terminals.

WDW's monorail system consists of 12 electric monorail trains, which ride on elevated concrete loops. There are three passenger loops: the two Magic Kingdom loops (the Express and the Resort) and the Epcot loop.

The Express Loop runs counter clockwise around the Seven Seas Lagoon from the Transportation and Ticket Center to the Magic Kingdom and back, with no stops in between. This loop's primary users are guests who have parked in the Magic Kingdom's parking lot, who have arrived at the TTC on non-Disney buses (such as Shades of Green's buses), or are transferring from the Epcot Monorail loop. Excluding any wait time, this is the fastest way between these two monorail stations.

The Magic Kingdom Resort Loop runs clockwise around the Seven Seas Lagoon from the Transportation and Ticket Center with stops at the Polynesian Village Resort. The Grand Floridian Resort and Spa, the Magic Kingdom, and the Contemporary Resort before arriving back at the TTC. This route takes longer to travel between the TTC and the Magic Kingdom with the stops at the resorts on the way and is designed mainly for the use of Disney Monorail Resort guests.

The Epcot Monorail Loop runs from the Transportation and Ticket Center to the Epcot station which is approximately three and a half miles away. The Main users of this line are Disney Monorail Resort guests, Shades of Green guests (there is no Shades bus to Epcot), and those wishing to park hop between the two parks.

At Epcot, Water Taxis run on two routes across the World Showcase Lagoon, both routes run from points just east and west of the entrance to the World Showcase from Future World to Morocco and Germany respectively.

Trams – Disney also has a fleet of trams, which are used in each of the theme park parking lots. These parking lots are huge so you could be parking a long way from the entrance to the park. These trams will pick you up at the end of your parking row and deliver you to the park entrance. When you are on your way out they will drop you at one central location per parking lot or pair of lots.

Disney Skyliner Gondola System

Construction has begun on this new transportation system for parts of Walt Disney World. No completion date has been announced, but it conceivably could be in late 2018.

This new transportation system will connect Disney's Art of Animation, Pop Century, Caribbean Beach, and the upcoming Riviera Resort resorts with Disney's Hollywood Studios and Epcot's International Gateway.

There will be five stations (Caribbean, Animation/Pop, Riviera, Hollywood Studios, & Epcot) with three lines (Caribbean-Riviera-Epcot, Caribbean-Studios, & Caribbean-Animation/Pop). Each gondola would hold 10 guests.

The north end of the Caribbean Beach Resort is the site of construction of the new Riviera Disney Vacation Club Resort.

Expect prices at these existing resorts to increase (perhaps significantly) the when gondola service begins.

Shades of Green Transportation

Shades of Green operates a small fleet of buses which run throughout the day to limited locations on WDW property.

ADA options include ramps and lifts on all routes.

The bus loading area is located in the front of the resort on the lower level. In order to get to the bus stop you need to exit the hotel lobby through the front doors.

As you exit you'll see a large central area with a stairway leading down through a beautiful rocky waterfall area. If you would like to use the elevator rather than the stairs it's located on the left wall when exiting the lobby.

At the bottom of the stairs is the entrance to the Express Cafe, a great place to grab a quick breakfast or lunch on the way to the theme parks. Also at the bottom of the stairs to the left is an ATM machine.

In order to get to the bus stop, walk straight through the Express Cafe. The bus stop is just outside the opposite door.

Note *All adults using Shades of Green fleet of buses will have to show their Shades of Green resort ID and either a military ID or a photo ID card (for sponsored non-military).*

Shades of Green runs 4 bus lines to:

- Transportation and Ticket Center (Magic Kingdom and Epcot)
- Animal Kingdom & Blizzard Beach
- Hollywood Studios
- Disney Springs & Typhoon Lagoon

Shades of Green's Bus Schedule

Animal Kingdom/Blizzard Beach: Once per hour

- Leaves Shades of Green on the half hour a half hour before the Park opens
- Leaves Animal Kingdom at 10 minutes before the hour (Space #7 in charter bus area starting at 0850)
- Leaves Blizzard Beach on the hour (Space #1 in bus area starting at 1000)
- Last Animal Kingdom pick up 1 hour and 50 minutes after park close
- Last Blizzard Beach pick up 1 hour after park close

Hollywood Studios: Once per hour

- Leave Shades of Green on the half hour a half hour before the Park opens
- Leaves Hollywood Studios on the hour (Space C6 in the Charter Area)
- Last pick up 1 hour and 30 minutes after park close

Disney Springs/Typhoon Lagoon: Once per hour

- Leaves Shades of Green on the half hour a half hour before the Park opens
- Leaves Typhoon Lagoon at 10 till the hour (Space #9)
- Leaves Disney Springs on the hour (Marketplace Bus Stop Space 1)
- Last Disney Springs pick up 10 minutes prior to closing

- Last Typhoon Lagoon pick up 1 hour after park close

Transportation and Ticket Center (Magic Kingdom/Epcot): Every 20 minutes

- First bus leaves Shades of Green starting a half hour before the Park opens (30, 50, & 10 minutes past the hour)
- Bus leaves Transportation and Ticket Center on the hour and 20 & 40 minutes past the hour (Space C10)
- Last pick up 1 hour and 40 minutes after park close

From the Transportation and Ticket Center you can take a monorail to the Magic Kingdom or EPCOT, or another option for the Magic Kingdom is to take the ferryboat.

At the Magic Kingdom you can board Disney World transportation buses for destinations all over the WDW resort.

Shades of Green guests have access to the Walt Disney Transportation System, which includes: monorail, ferry boat and bus transportation to destinations all over Disney World property.

Note: this schedule subject to change based upon operating hours. Extra Magic Hours and Special late night parties are covered by start and stop times.

Walking / Disney's Monorail

Shades of Green is located within walking distance of Disney's Polynesian Village Resort. It's about a ten to fifteen minute walk. From there you can take the monorail to the Magic Kingdom, the Transportation and Ticket Center (to transfer to the EPCOT monorail, or visit other Magic Kingdom Resorts.

Shady Shuttle

The Shady Shuttle will run you to the edge of Shades' property, about half way to the Polynesian for the walk to the monorail station.

Paid Transportation

Renting a Car

All the national chains rent cars at the Orlando International Airport. Be sure to check for military rates or use other discounts for which you might be eligible such as USAA or using points from one of your loyalty programs.

On Walt Disney World property you can rent from Alamo Rent-A-Car or National Car Rental at the Car Care Center located near the Magic Kingdom. Alamo also has a desk at Shades of Green.

Complimentary shuttle service from select Walt Disney World Resort hotels to the Disney Car Care Center can be arranged by calling (407) 824-3470 ext. 1.

Taxis at Walt Disney World

A taxi fare between the furthest points on Disney World property should rarely exceed $20 plus tip.

When using taxis on Disney property, use only the ones colored yellow that have meters! They have various names on the side (Yellow Cab, Checker, City or Safety), but are all operated by Mears Transport, which has an official relationship with Disney.

Your resort concierge can call a cab for you or you can call yourself at (407) 699-9999.

Uber

Ubering around property is very convenient and often the cheapest paid method of getting around. Typical Uber-x prices from Shades of Green are:

- Magic Kingdom $2.00

- Epcot $10.50
- Hollywood Studios $10.50
- Animal Kingdom $10.85
- Disney Springs $11.50

Minnie Vans

In 2017 Disney World began offering a new "uber like" service called Mini Vans. These are a fleet of polka dotted (they look like Minnie's dress) SUVs and cargo vans (with the ability to carry scooters). For 20 dollars they will take you anywhere on property. They can seat up to six giests, and car seats are on board at no additional fee.

The Minnie Vans are a test program (to see if guests will go for it). There have been other transportation test programs in recent months, which have been cancelled due to lack of use. But the Minnie Vans seem to be expanding.

Minnie vans service an ever growing list of resorts i.e. they are stationed there and are also stationed at the parks. Though they will come to pick you up anywhere if you call 407-828-3500. The vans can also be requested via the Lyft app. Minnie Vans must be activated in your Lyft app by going to your resort front desk or the My Disney Experience app.

Minnie Vans operate from 6:30 am to 12:30 am and only operate on property.

Note: Being a test program this service could be cancelled but at this point it is expanding past the initial beginning test.

How can I get to Universal Studios or Sea World?

In order to get to Universal Studios Orlando, Disney Resort Guests will need to arrange for either a taxi, limo, rental car, or Uber. Taxis and limos can be anywhere from $80 to $120 round trip. Those who rent a car will also have to pay for parking at Universal, which is $20 per day.

See the Airport Transportation section a few pages back for info on military discounts on round trip limo service and a deal on Uber. Typical Uber prices are about $20 one-way to Universal Orlando, $17.50 one-way to SeaWorld Orlando, and $30 one-way to Legoland Florida.

There is an Alamo Rent a Car kiosk just off the Shades of Green lobby where you could rent a car for the day or more if you have other excursions planned.

There is a shuttle bus available at Shades. You need to make a reservation 24 hours in advance with the Shades of Green Ticket Sales Office. The round trip cost is $ 10.00 per adult (12+) and $ 5.00 per child (4-11), under age 4 is free. There is only one run each way per day so you need to stick to their times. The shuttle departs Shades at 8:15 am, it leaves Universal at 6:30 pm and SeaWorld at 6:45.

Stroller Rentals

Disney Strollers

Disney strollers are made from rigid plastic and they don't recline. They do offer a canopy for sun protection and seat belts. *Note: these plastic strollers really heat up in the afternoon Florida sun!*

There is a pouch on the back to hold items, but no cup holders. These strollers can only be used within the parks! This means that at the end of a long day, you will be stuck carrying your children back to the car, tram, bus, or monorail.

A Stroller rented from Disney is expensive at $15.00 per day to rent a "single" stroller and $31.00 per day to rent a "double" stroller. If you're going to need a stroller for more than one day you can rent them at the "multi-day" rate of $13.00 per day for a "single" and $27.00 per day for a "double."

Disney strollers are only for use in the theme park they are not available at water parks or at the resorts, which means you have to carry your child to and from the park and everywhere else on vacation, or they'll have to walk. *Note infants and children under age 2 don't do well in Disney strollers, they just aren't designed for them.*

One plus is that rentals are good all day at multiple parks. When visiting more than one park in a single day, after the first rental simply present your rental receipt at another park to obtain a replacement.

The Solution

There are many companies in the Orlando area that rent modern, clean, well-maintained strollers for the length of your vacation. These companies will deliver the stroller to your resort and pick it up when you are finished with it for much less than Disney charges, plus you'll have it 24/7.

A 10% Military Discount is available for readers of this book from Amusement Park Rentals on stroller rentals. Just go to militarydisneytips.com/blog/stroller/ and use the **10MILITARY** discount code.

Scooter Rentals

Disney World rents scooters (ECVs) and wheelchairs in the theme parks and at Disney Springs. The issues with these rentals are the same as above for strollers, they are expensive and are only for use in the theme park. Also they only have a limited quantity of these and they may not be reserved.

Scooter rental fees are $50 per day with an additional $20 deposit in the theme parks and a $100 deposit at Disney Springs.

Rentals are good all day at multiple parks. When visiting more than one park in a single day, after the first rental simply present your rental receipt at another park to obtain a replacement.

The Solution

There are many companies in the Orlando area that rent clean, well maintained scooters for the length of your vacation. These companies will deliver the scooter to your resort and pick it up when you are finished with it for much less than Disney charges, plus you'll have it 24/7.

A 10% Military Discount is available for readers of this book from Amusement Park Rentals on scooter rentals. Just go to **militarydisneytips.com/blog/scooter/** and use the **10MILITARY** discount code.

Wrap Up

There are so many options for getting to and around Walt Disney World finding the right option for your family should be no problem.

Ready for More?

That's it for getting around for most of us, but some of our brethren need just a little more assistance. Next we will cover Disney Disability Information.

12. Walt Disney World Disability Information

What's This Chapter About?

Many of our brethren are dealing with visible and or invisible reminders of their service to our nation. This chapter outlines Disney's efforts to make these individuals' vacation as smooth as possible.

As part of the rollout of the new FastPass Plus system, Disney recently completely overhauled its system for accommodating guests with disabilities.

Here is how the system works and what those with special needs can expect.

Before you arrive

Disney has extensive information for guests with disabilities available on their official website. This should be your first stop when seeking information because it comes directly from the source and does change over time.

Parking for Guests with Disabilities

Designated parking areas are available throughout Walt Disney World Resort for Guests with disabilities. A valid disability-parking permit is required.

Theme Park Parking

Guests with the ability to walk short distances and step onto courtesy trams should park in the main parking lots of Magic Kingdom park, Epcot, Disney's Hollywood Studios and Disney's Animal Kingdom theme park. Courtesy trams will then transport Guests to each theme park's Entrance Complex.

Parking for Guests with mobility disabilities—including those traveling with personal wheelchairs, electric scooters or other mobility devices—is available adjacent to the Entrance Complex at each of the theme parks. Please be aware that courtesy trams do not serve these locations.

For further directions on parking options, Guests should inquire at the Parking Toll Booths.

At the Theme Parks

You should get a copy of the *Guide for Guests with Disabilities* for each theme/water park that you'll be visiting during your vacation. This is a brochure, which provides a detailed overview of services and facilities available for guests with disabilities at each location.

You can pick up a copy at all Guest Relations locations within all 4 Disney Theme Parks, 2 Disney Water Parks, your Disney Resort front desk and concierge areas, and at Disney wheelchair rental locations.

This guide provides a detailed overview of the services and facilities available for guests with disabilities, including information about:

•Parking

•Companion restroom locations

•Accessible drinking fountain locations

- Auxiliary aids

- Telephone assistance

- Transportation facilities

- Specific attraction entrance and boarding procedures, as some attractions allow guests to remain in a wheelchair and some are transfer-accessible.

Guests with specific disability concerns can visit Guest Relations locations at any of the Disney Theme or Water Parks for additional information and assistance.

Each theme park has a First Aid Station where you can store medications and spare oxygen tanks, or drop by in order to receive any needed assistance.

Trained Service Animals

It is important to note that Disney cast members are not permitted to take control of service animals. Guests with service animals should follow the same attraction entrance guidelines as those guests who use wheelchairs.

Each Theme Park allows guests to use backstage locations for service animal relief areas. Please consult your *Guide for Guests with Disabilities*, for specific information.

The Disability Access Service Card

Walt Disney World guests may obtain a Disability Access Service Card (DAS) from Guest Relations located at the front of each of the four theme parks. Guest Relations Cast Members will discuss your individual needs with you. Based upon your specific needs DAS or other accommodations may be provided.

The Disability Access Service Card is intended for guests whose disability prevents them from waiting in a conventional queue environment. This service allows guests to schedule a return time that is comparable to the current queue wait for the given attraction. Once a return time is issued, guests are free to enjoy other theme park offerings such as meeting a character, grabbing a bite to eat, enjoying entertainment or even visiting another attraction until their listed return time. Return times are valid at any time after the listed time, there is no return window.

A Guest whose disability is based on the necessity to use a wheelchair or scooter does not need a DAS. Depending on the attraction, Guests utilizing a wheelchair or scooter will either wait in the standard queue or receive a return time at the attraction comparable to the current wait time.

Guests may only have one active return time. As soon as an outstanding attraction return time is redeemed, guests may receive a new return time for the same or different attraction.

Another member of your travel party can obtain a return time. However, the Guest in possession of DAS must board the attraction with his/her party.

This service can be used in addition to Disney's FastPass Plus service.

The official guide to the Disability Access Service Card is available for download in PDF format. If you plan to request this accommodation, I highly recommend that you review the file thoroughly.

Unlike FastPass+ reservations, procurement of the DAS is not available prior to your arrival at the theme park. Requests for the DAS accommodation are made in person at the theme park Guest Relations locations.

Types of Accommodations Available

Visual and Hearing Challenges

Disney offers many accommodations for guests with visual and hearing challenges

Some examples of these accommodations include:

- Assistive Listening systems
- Reflective Captioning
- Sign Language interpretation
- Text Typewriter telephones
- Handheld Captioning
- Video Captioning
- Audio Description devices
- Braille guidebooks
- Digital audio tour

Cognitive or Sensory Disabilities

Guests with cognitive or sensory disabilities, which make it difficult for the guest to wait in the traditional queue are offered an alternate waiting environment via the DAS card.

Disney has created *A Recourse for Guests with Cognitive Disabilities including Autism Spectrum Disorder* which is available as pdf download. Some of the information in this guide is applicable to guests with Anxiety Disorders, PTSD, as well as sensory challenges, so even if the need is unrelated to Autism, it is worth a review.

Mobility or Endurance Issues

Guests with mobility or endurance issues are offered the accommodation of wheelchair or ECV (scooter) rental if they do not already have their own assistive device and are offered the alternate entrance accommodation.

Guests are encouraged to utilize either of these accommodations in addition to the FastPass+ reservation system.

Wheelchairs and Electric Conveyance Vehicles

Wheelchairs and Electric Conveyance Vehicles (ECVs or "scooters") are available for rent from Disney on a daily basis in all the theme parks. Quantities are limited and they are available on a first-come-first-serve basis. Guests are permitted to bring their own mobility assistive devices.

Scooters and wheel chairs rented from Disney come at a Disney price and are only for use in the park they were rented in. There are many Orlando based companies that rent at a cheaper daily rate, which you can obtain for your entire vacation. These companies will deliver your rental right to your resort prior to your arrival and pick it up after your departure.

Guests using wheelchairs or ECVs are provided the accommodation of alternate entrance. It should be noted that, due to safety regulations concerning the number of mobility-impaired guests that may utilize an attraction at one time, the wait for a particular attraction may actually be longer when using this accommodation. Options for boarding procedures are posted at the entrance to each attraction and may vary.

Scooter Rentals

Disney World rents scooters and wheelchairs in the theme parks and at Disney Springs. These rentals are expensive and are only for use in the theme park. Also they only have a limited quantity of these and they may not be reserved.

Scooter rental fees are $50 per day with an additional $20 deposit in the theme parks and a $100 deposit at Disney Springs.

Rentals are good all day at multiple parks. When visiting more than one park in a single day, after the first rental simply present your rental receipt at another park to obtain a replacement.

The Solution

There are many companies in the Orlando area that rent clean, well maintained scooters for the length of your vacation. These companies will deliver the scooter to your resort and pick it up when you are finished with it for much less than Disney charges, plus you'll have it 24/7.

A 10% Military Discount is available for readers of this book from Amusement Park Rentals on scooter rentals. Just go to **militarydisneytips.com/blog/scooter/** and use the **10MILITARY** discount code.

Physical Access

Most attractions, restaurants, shops and shows are accessible to all guests. In some cases, however, guests may need the assistance of a member of their party to fully utilize these areas. Also, at some attractions guests using wheelchairs may need to transfer from their wheelchairs onto an attraction vehicle. Disney Cast Members are not permitted to physically lift guests from wheelchairs. Disney recommends that guests who need assistance plan to visit with someone who can physically assist them, when necessary.

Prosthetic Devices

A Prosthesis Information Sheet is available at Guest Services. It will detail the restrictions in place for attractions for different types of prosthesis. These restrictions are different for each theme park. Cast Members operating attractions reserve the right to determine guest safety on an individual basis. The deciding factor appears to be whether or not the guest is able to be adequately restrained (on thrill rides) or is able to properly brace him-or herself, with or without the prosthesis.

Multiple Disabilities

If the guest has both a cognitive and a mobility disability, the guest should request both accommodations.

Multiple Guests with Disabilities

If there is more than one guest in a travel party with the need for accommodation with a Disability Access Service Card, it is highly recommended that each guest obtain his or her own card. This allows the guests to "split up" if needed and still make use of the accommodations.

Wrap Up

It is important for you to know that the American's With Disabilities Act prohibits Disney from requesting "proof" of disability or even a specific diagnosis. You are, of course, free to divulge your diagnosis if you so choose.

Disney Cast Members are discouraged from accepting "doctor's notes" that could support the guest's request for accommodation. This is to avoid the perception that Disney is requiring proof, which would be against Federal Law.

Please be aware that Cast Members are not health care providers and most likely will not have a clear understanding of your needs if you simply provide them with a medical diagnosis. Therefore, it is important that the guest or the guest's representative be able to clearly articulate the need.

While the DAS card is most commonly requested for use by guests with cognitive, sensory, or mental health challenges, there are other invisible medical challenges for which a guest may find the card useful. Again, it all depends upon the individual need. Some examples are:

•Medical conditions that may result in a rapid change in blood sugar, necessitating immediate treatment

•Medical conditions that may result in seizures, necessitating immediate treatment

•Medical conditions that make it difficult for a guest to wait in a traditional queue, yet preclude the guest from utilizing a wheelchair or ECV

If you require additional information about Services for guests with disabilities at the Disney Resorts, please call the numbers below!

Resources

Disability information for specific resorts - Walt Disney World Resort Special Reservations 407-939-7807 (voice) or 407-939-7670 (TTY)

Guide for Guests with Disabilities: WDWformilitary.com/guide

A Recourse for Guests with Cognitive Disabilities including Autism Spectrum Disorder: WDWformilitary.com/resource

If the two links above no longer work you can find the info here:

WDWformilitary.com/services

For information on Military Discounted Scooter Rentals: WDWformilitary.com/scooter

Ready for More?

In the next chapter I'm going to cover some tips, ideas, and guidelines for you, based upon my experiences touring Disney World since 1971.

13. Tips for Your Walt Disney World Vacation

What's This Chapter About?

My family and I have over 47 years of experience touring Disney's theme parks. This chapter contains some of our best tips to help you enjoy your vacation.

We've seen all the good and all of the "not so good" during our time in the parks which I'll share with you here.

This chapter also contains some "theme park etiquette." Things we've experienced that you should or shouldn't do. While mostly unintentional, these things can detract from your and other's theme park enjoyment.

The Basics

Activating Your Disney Armed Forces Salute Tickets – Most likely the day that you arrive at Walt Disney World will not be a theme park day. Depending on your travel method you could be arriving any time between late morning and evening. Why not save yourself a little time the next morning when you want to get to the park as soon as you can by activating your tickets ahead of time?

Your Disney Armed Forces Salute tickets may be activated at all of theme park main entrances as well as the Transportation and Ticket Center, Epcot's International Gateway, both water parks, and the Disney Springs Guest Relations. You can fit a stop by one of these locations into a pleasant afternoon or evening.

Here are some Ideas:

- Take a trip to Disney Springs for a meal, shopping, or entertainment and activate your tickets at their Guest Relations location
- Take a tour of the resorts around the Magic Kingdom monorail loop. Have a meal and or cocktails and stop by the Magic Kingdom Guest Relations windows to activate your tickets
- From the BoardWalk Resort Area take a stroll or boat ride to Epcot's International Gateway or the Disney Hollywood Studios main entrance to activate your tickets

Note your whole party must be present for activation of the Disney Armed Forces Salute tickets.

Arrival and Departure Day Activities - Most likely you've spent most of your arrival day getting to Walt Disney World. You might feel that using a whole day of theme park tickets for just a few hours would be a waste. Or at the end of your trip you've used up your park tickets during your stay and will be leaving for home in the afternoon. Here are some free or low cost things you can do to pass an evening or morning at Disney World.

1. Chill out at your Resort Pool - Having just spent all day getting to Walt Disney World or getting ready for a full day going home can drain you. Perhaps you'd just like to spend some time relaxing at your own hotel. Take a dip in the pool or a soak in the hot tub.

2. Have a great meal - You've got to eat anyway so have a meal at one of Disney's great restaurants. Stop by one of the resorts, explore Disney Springs, or the BoardWalk.

3. Go to Disney Springs - Explore the Shops and wonderful dining options located there. Or stop by World of Disney for souvenir shopping. The Lego Imagination Center has a 3,000-square-foot outdoor play area filled with thousands of LEGO blocks. Visit the Ghirardelli Soda Fountain & Chocolate Shop and enjoy a sundae, they offer a 20% military discount.

4. Rent a boat - Most of Disney's Moderate, Deluxe and Disney Vacation Club resorts have a marina where you can rent various types of watercraft. You can rent a kayak, canoe, pedal boat, two-person sailboat, pontoon boat, or high-speed 2-person boat.

5. Visit Disney's BoardWalk - The BoardWalk is a fabulous entertainment area with lots of dining and entertainment options located out the back door of the BoardWalk Resort. You can park at the BoardWalk Resort if you are driving; just tell the Security Host at the gate you're there to walk on the BoardWalk. There are several restaurants along the BoardWalk and in the evening roaming street performers (jugglers, comedians, fire-eaters, jazz ensembles, etc.). Located within walking distance are the Yacht and Beach Club Resorts as well as the Swan and Dolphin Resorts, which offer even more dining options. There is a bridge near the Swan and Dolphin that offers a decent view over the trees of the Illuminations show at EPCOT.

6. Fort Wilderness campfire program - Sing around the campfire and watch a free Disney movie. It's open to everyone. Held every evening, at about 7:00 PM in fall and winter and about 8:00 PM in spring and summer, near the Meadow Trading Post. The program starts with a sing-a-long and marshmallow roast. You can bring your own food or buy it from the Chuck Wagon, which sells s'more kits, pizza and hot dogs. Chip and Dale meet the guests and sign autographs. Then a Disney movie is shown on a large outdoor screen. There is some seating on bleachers and benches, or you can lay out a blanket. No reservations necessary.

7. Enjoy your Disney Resort's nighttime activities. Most Disney resorts now offer at least free outdoor movies and in some instances fire pit activities like s'mores.

8. Take a tour of the Disney Resorts - The resorts are so beautiful, especially at Christmas. We love to check them out and see which one we'd like to stay at next. While touring you could have a drink in one of their lounges or grab a snack. Be sure to be on the lookout for Hidden Mickeys.

9. Tour Disney World's Monorail/Magic Kingdom Resorts (the Contemporary, Polynesian, or Grand Floridian). Park at one of the resorts, just tell the Security Host at the parking lot entrance that you're there to have a drink in their lounge. You can then ride the monorail between the resorts.

Here are some ideas for these resorts:

- Contemporary - The fourth floor houses a cocktail lounge as well as dining and shopping options. The California Grill is located on the 15th floor and has superb views of the Magic Kingdom. If you time it right you can have dinner and watch the Wishes fireworks over dessert. Watch from your table or go onto the observation deck. The sound track from Wishes is piped in to enhance the show. Reservations are highly suggested! If you'd just like to see the fireworks you need to get there early, just tell the host at the fourth floor podium that you'd like to have a drink in the California Grill bar. There is a maximum capacity so if they've reached it you won't be able to go up. If they do fill up, another viewing option is the fourth floor observation deck located facing the Magic Kingdom. After the Wishes Fireworks are over walk out back to the marina to see the Electrical Water Pageant on Bay Lake.
- Polynesian - The Lobby area and second floor above house the lounges, dining, and gift offerings. Or have a drink at the pool bar and watch Wishes and Electrical Water Pageant from the sandy beach.
- Grand Floridian - The Lobby area and second floor above house the lounges, dining, and gift offerings. Watch Wishes and Electrical Water Pageant from the sandy beach or marina.

10. Visit Wilderness Lodge and explore the fabulous lobby. Catch the shuttle boat at the Contemporary or Magic Kingdom. The Wilderness Lodge's huge fireplace which extends many stories up through the open central lobby area has been constructed to simulate the strata of the

Grand Canyon. You can go to each floor to see and read about that particular level. Each level looks just like what you'd see in the real Grand Canyon. There are also display cases on each floor with geologic items to see.

11. View the animals at the Animal Kingdom Lodge - During the day or at night with night vision goggles.

12. Play a round of Mini Golf - There are two mini golf courses: Fantasia Gardens, near Disney's Hollywood Studios, and Winter Summerland, near Blizzard Beach Water Park. Military Discounted Tickets are available at Shades of Green.

Mid-Day Breaks – during the busiest periods of the year, such as summer, Disney World's parks are open for very long periods of time each day. For example the Magic Kingdom can open at 8 am and close at 1 to 3 am. In the summer heat, staying through from opening to late at night is a recipe for disaster, sure to bring on the dreaded Disney melt down for most kids.

You can see it happen every day in the parks during the few hours after noon. Tired kids in sensory overload begin crying, screaming, falling down or just refusing to move and their tired, exasperated parents are just trying to contain the situation.

There is the famous quote "I paid a lot of money to come to Disney, you're going to have fun 'darn' it!"

A sure way to avoid this is the mid-day break. It's not just for the kids though. Central Florida is HOT and HUMID in the summer months. By noon it is possible to not have a single dry spot on your clothing!

Those who use the mid-day break will spend the morning in a park till about lunchtime. You can eat in the park or elsewhere after you leave. But the key is to get out! Temperatures will reach their peak about 2 or 3 pm. That's the time you want to be taking a nap in your air conditioned room or a having a dip in your resort's pool, not pounding the pavement in the theme park!

Having a resort that is convenient to get to (on property) makes this much easier.

Once you get back to your resort you can grab some lunch if you haven't already, get your sweaty clothes off, have a nap (whether just the kids or everyone) and then head to the pool.

Later, about 5 or 6 pm, with dry clothes and feeling refreshed you can head back to the same park, or a different one if you have a hopper ticket, having missed the daily summer afternoon rain shower and enjoy the evening as long as you'd like.

Dry clothes, socks, and maybe even shoes do a lot to improve your mood!

I highly recommend this! We did it when our kids were younger during family vacations and my wife and I still do it now that it is just the two of us.

Sunscreen – I have lived in Florida and even though I was "adapted" every Disney World theme park day would start with an application of sunscreen before leaving my room. Even in the winter my face gets a coat. You are going to be in the sun 10 to 12 hours a day, don't risk a burn in the strong Florida sun, especially early in your vacation!

Don't wear clothing that exposes skin that rarely sees the sun! Dress normally.

Fitness Preparation – You may have just scored an excellent on your military fitness test, but that in no way assures you're in prefect shape for the 10 to 14 hour days of being mostly on your feet at a Disney park.

In the months prior to your vacation add in lots of walking (several, hour long plus walks a week), strengthening your core, and keeping your back and legs loose with stretching or yoga. Long days of walking many miles in the parks and lots of standing can wear on your lower half!

Shoes – I've seen all kinds of footwear at Disney! Everything from flip-flops to huge wedge heels or stilettos. Just don't!

Because of the amount of time you will be spending on your feet you want good, broken in, comfortable, supportive shoes. Get a new pair of running, walking, or cross-fit shoes about a month before your trip. You do not want to be breaking them in at WDW! The newer gel or memory foam models are especially good.

Device Charging – an issue of modern life, that no one would have ever thought of, even when Disney World's most recent theme park was built, is that the majority of theme park guests might one day need access to an electrical outlet to charge anything.

Disney World had taken some small steps in trying to address this issue.

In the Magic Kingdom during the expansion and renovation of Fantasyland, a nice shady device charging area was added into "Old Fantasyland" near where the new bathrooms were added between the Small World/Peter Pan Area and Liberty Square. This area has limited seats, tables, and plugs.

In 2017 the FuelRod company began installing vending machines that sell charged or exchange used backup batteries. These USB charging devices attach to your phone and transfer their charge to the phone.

Once used up you can recharge the FuelRod yourself from an electrical outlet or exchange it for free at one of the many FuelRod machines. Machines are located all over WDW property (parks, resorts, and DIsney Springs).

Personal Security, Safety, Severe Weather, Shelter in Place

Personal Security is a topic that should be near and dear to a military member/family's heart. Especially in today's world we should never let our guard down.

As you are enjoying your vacation it's easy to be totally focused in the moment and you should be. This is your time to de-stress. I just encourage you to keep a small bit of your attention on what's going on around you, just as you do when interacting with and in your local community.

The big threats are focused on our centers of government and worldwide trade, but Disney is a huge collection of people all in a small area. Just stay aware of your surroundings.

Rest assured that Disney has procedures and plans in place to deal with almost anything.

As you tour the parks you'll encounter local law enforcement officers and local/Disney K-9 units at all the park entrances and uniformed Disney Security within the parks. But what you won't see are the many undercover Disney Security members that are roaming the parks for your protection.

Disney has procedures whether reactive or preventative for dealing with and keeping their guests safe from many unlikely scenarios. Whether a criminal/terror situation or severe weather, Disney has shelter in place and evacuation plans. Some of these were put into play on September 11, 2001.

Disney parks have had 100% bag checks for many years, but in 2016 instituted a partial "random" screening by metal detector of a percentage of park guests. This then morphed into a 100% screening of guests at all entrances.

Theme Park Etiquette

This section discusses things that you should think about as you tour the Disney parks. I've been visiting the parks since 1971 and have experienced everything possible! Below are some things to do or avoid.

Being in a Disney park for the first time is a new, unfamiliar experience and you will most likely be in sensory overload while trying to find your way around. But there are multiple thousands of people all around you trying to enjoy their day as well. Study ahead of time so that you are familiar with layouts and what you want to do before you get there.

Stopping – Do not come to a dead stop while walking around Disney World, whether to look at a park guide map, talk to someone in your party, fiddle with or load a stroller, scold a child, or show off the latest WWF move, especially if you are in an entrance or exit way, a narrow walkway, or just after exiting a store or restaurant (into the active walkway). There WILL be someone right behind you and someone behind them (often double or triple digits worth of people) who will be affected! Instead look around you and find an out of the way place to step off to prior to stopping.

Walking – Do not walk with your whole party abreast! Try to keep it to pairs. All people walk at different speeds and there will be people trying to get around you. Four to six plus people slowly walking abreast will create a huge traffic jam.

Walking – Always look where you are walking, never stare to the side or behind you while moving forward. Always walk forward not to the side or backwards.

Running – DON'T

Bag Check – Have all closed areas on your bag(s) open and ready for inspection prior to your turn! Those without bags can walk right through the non-bag check entrance and wait on the other side of the bag check area for the person with the bag, this makes the lines shorter.

Cutting – Young kids have small bladders, it's a fact. Make sure you visit the bathroom prior to getting in line. Don't send one person to get in line while the rest of the party visits the restroom. But if the need arises for a little one while in line it is understandable and acceptable (I think) to send one parent off with the child and then rejoin the party after if you are comfortable with that.

Your whole party should wait in line! It is not fair to others to have one or two wait in line for the whole party while the rest shop, eat, or do anything else and then join the ones who have been waiting as they near the ride boarding area.

Ordering in Quick Service Restaurants – All of Disney World's Quick Service Restaurants have large overhead menus often with pictures and recently have begun handing out handheld menus to look over while you wait in line. Decide what you'd like to order prior to getting into the line to order, so that you will be ready to tell the cast member what you want when it is your turn. Do not keep both the cast member and those behind you waiting while you are deciding what to order when you are at the register.

Tables in Quick Service Restaurants – This particular item is a highly contested one, with firm proponents on each side. But these are my thoughts, which I humbly think are correct...

Imagine, ordering food for your family of four at a Disney park fast food location, after being served your party carries the 2 or 3 trays of food and drinks into the dining area to enjoy your meal and every single table is occupied. Not Fun! What is even worse though is that half of the tables are being saved by one person from a party that is still in line waiting to order their food!

If every party would get their food and then get their table the process would be smooth and due to the natural timing, tables would always be opening up as guests with their food were looking for one.

In fact Universal Studios Orlando for a time posted signs in their fast food restaurants asking their guests to do just this. They requested that you not occupy a table until you have your food.

Disney World has recently taken small steps in this direction. During High volume periods they will have cast members enforcing a "you must already have your food to get a table" rule.

Also when you finish your food get up and move on. No long conversations over soda refills or coffee.

Smoking - If you are a smoker, please only smoke in the designated areas. This includes e-cigs.

Strollers and Scooters – Please try to be considerate of the ankles of those around you. There are times and locations where quarters are very tight. Move slowly, don't try to zig-zag around or pass people. Keeping it slow and straight might take you a little longer to get where you are going, but everyone else around you will get there in one piece too.

Running with a Stroller – DON'T

Parade/Show Viewing – Many families arrive well in advance of the scheduled times for parades, shows, and fireworks presentations. They do so to ensure prime viewing locations. If you decline to spend the time waiting for prime real estate do not arrive late and push your children in front of, or crowd those who put in the time for that spot, so that your kids can see better.

On the other hand if you do have a prime spot, do not put your kids on your shoulders and block the view of those behind you.

Attraction/Show Seating – When seating the guests for the next showing/performance, a Disney cast member will be asking on the PA system that you select a row then, "Move all the way to the end of a row (or three-quarters of the way when the show isn't going to be full), and fill up every available seat." This is so that everyone coming into the seating area can get a seat without having to climb over those who plopped down in the middle of a row so that they could have the best view. If you don't want to sit on the far end, then don't be the first person to rush into a row. Hold back and let an appropriate number of people go into the row ahead of you so that you can sit in the middle of the row.

Cell Phones – On silent in Attractions. No bright screens illuminating all around and behind you in dark shows!

Flash Photography – Don't do it on dark rides or shows!

Well that's about it.

The above are just a collection of tips and pet peeves from my years in the parks. Being as mindful of those around you as possible will make not only your vacation, but everyone else's vacations go just a little bit smoother.

But also be mindful that there are those who haven't read all of this great advice and might not be up to speed!

So when you are moving forward in a line or mass of people at a reasonable speed and the family of four ahead of you stops dead in their tracks to look at their guide map (or do some WWF moves, yes this did happen to me), just shrug it off and continue enjoying the Happiest Place on Earth!

Ready for More?

Sadly it is time for us to begin wrapping this up. Next we'll do just that.

14. Wrapping It All Up

Walt Disney World holds a special place in my heart. I hope it does, or will in yours too!

My family has so many great memories and experiences that were made there at many different stages of our lives. I write this as a retired E-9 who often enjoys going to WDW with just my wife, there are so many adult oriented things that we love to do there as a couple. But in year's past we've gone with our children, when they were adults, teens, tweens, and young to very young kids. In the fairly near future we will have trips with our new grand baby. There has always been a plethora of things to do and see for each stage of our family's life.

There is a WDW experience for every budget. Going now or recently, as I did before I retired is certainly at a different price point than how we did it as a young E-5's family staying at Shades of Green for our first ever multi-night WDW vacation. That's the beauty of Walt Disney World; with all the various options you can have a fantastic vacation no matter your pay grade!

I want to touch again, as I did in the introduction on what an immersive experience Disney World can be. Disney is very good at what it does in this respect and it is a win-win. I firmly believe that Walt Disney World is one of the best, if not the best place on earth for military families to take time out from their hectic stressful lives, that the majority of the US population does not understand, to de-stress and just be together in a place where nothing else matters. For a time to just be together, experiencing new and wonderful things.

My thanks go out to the Walt Disney Company for their firm support of the military community that has been at an all-time high these last nine years with the Disney Armed Forces Salute and the Heroes Work Here military hiring program. It has been a pleasure and my honor to work with my Disney contacts over the years, providing input from the military perspective and being able to get some positive changes instituted.

And I'm thankful for you, the reader! Thankful for your service to our nation and also for the understanding and sacrifice of all the military spouses and children! It truly is a greater calling. Thanks so much for the purchase of this book, I hope that it was truly useful to you!

Be sure to check out my website, MilitaryDisneyTips.com, there you will find plenty more information and all of the new and newsworthy things that affect our community.

Also if you wouldn't mind, please drop by Amazon by using the following link to leave a review for this book. Your review helps the book gain visibility, so that others can find it on Amazon and helps them in making their decision to purchase this book. It does not matter if you purchased the book on Amazon or not, all reviews are accepted.

Review here: wdwformilitary.com/review

Thanks and See ya real soon,

Steve Bell
Washington Township, Ohio, April 2018

Other Books by Steve:

The Essential Guide to Shades of Green: shadesofgreenguide.com

Disneyland for Military Families: disneylandformilitary.com

About the Author

Steve Bell is widely recognized as THE Military Disney Discount Expert. With the knowledge gained in 47 years of touring Walt Disney World and three years working on the front lines in the Magic Kingdom, he has spent 23 years helping fellow military members plan for and save on their WDW vacations.

Steve is the founder of the hugely popular MilitaryDisneyTips.com website. He recently retired from the Air Force after 31 years of service, with tours as a Career Enlisted Aviator with over 7000 hours heavy jet time, a Civil Search and Rescue Subject Matter Expert, and an aircraft mechanic.

Besides sharing Disney information with the military community, Steve continuously advocates on behalf of his brethren with Disney to correct poor military discount policy and expand discounts where possible.

My thanks go to my family. Without their assistance and love, everything would not have been possible!

Through the many years of military life it takes a great family to support the military member. I was supported by the finest!

Freedom isn't free and we all paid our dues. Thanks for everything Tracy, Will, & Heather!

Made in the USA
Lexington, KY
29 May 2018